W9-ADT-344

IN THE

MIND'S EYE

ENHANCING HUMAN PERFORMANCE

Daniel Druckman and Robert A. Bjork, *Editors*

Committee on Techniques for the Enhancement
of Human Performance

Commission on Behavioral and Social Sciences and Education

National Research Council

LIBRARY
COLBY-SAWYER COLLEGE
NEW LONDON, NH 03257

NATIONAL ACADEMY PRESS
Washington, D.C.   1991

BF
481
.I5
1991
c.1

NATIONAL ACADEMY PRESS • 2101 Constitution Avenue, N.W. • Washington, D.C. 20418

NOTICE: The project that is the subject of this report was approved by the Governing Board of the National Research Council, whose members are drawn from the councils of the National Academy of Sciences, the National Academy of Engineering, and the Institute of Medicine. The members of the committee responsible for the report were chosen for their special competences and with regard for appropriate balance.

This report has been reviewed by a group other than the authors according to procedures approved by a Report Review Committee consisting of members of the National Academy of Sciences, the National Academy of Engineering, and the Institute of Medicine.

Support for the project that is the subject of this report was provided by the Army Research Institute.

Library of Congress Cataloging-in-Publication Data

In the mind's eye : enhancing human performance / Daniel Druckman and
    Robert A. Bjork, editors.
        p.   cm.
      "Committee on Techniques for the Enhancement of Human Performance,
    Commission on Behavioral and Social Sciences and Education, National
    Research Council."
      Includes bibliographical references and index.
      ISBN 0-309-04398-0 (cloth); ISBN 0-309-04747-1 (paper)
      1. Performance—Psychological aspects. I. Druckman, Daniel,
    1939- . II. Bjork, Robert A. III. National Research Council
    (U.S.). Committee on Techniques for the Enhancement of Human
    Performance.
    BF481.I5 1991
    158—dc20   91-23941
                                             CIP

24009820

Copyright © 1991 by the National Academy of Sciences

No part of this book may be reproduced by any mechanical, photographic, or electronic procedure, or in the form of a phonographic recording, nor may it be stored in a retrieval system, transmitted, or otherwise copied for public or private use, wihout written permission from the publisher except for the purpose of official use by the United States government.

Printed in the United States of America

First Printing, September 1991
Second Printing, June 1992

COMMITTEE ON TECHNIQUES FOR THE ENHANCEMENT OF HUMAN PERFORMANCE

ROBERT A. BJORK (*Chair*), Department of Psychology, University of California, Los Angeles

MICHELENE T. H. CHI, Learning Research and Development Center, University of Pittsburgh

ROBERT W. CHRISTINA, Department of Physical Therapy and Exericise Science, State University of New York, Buffalo

JAMES H. DAVIS, Department of Psychology, University of Illinois

GERALD C. DAVISON, Department of Psychology, University of Southern California

ERIC EICH, Department of Psychology, University of British Columbia

RAY HYMAN, Department of Psychology, University of Oregon

DANIEL LANDERS, Department of Physical Education, Arizona State University

FRANCIS J. PIROZZOLO, Department of Neurology, Baylor College of Medicine

LYMAN W. PORTER, Graduate School of Management, University of California, Irvine

JEROME E. SINGER, Department of Medical Psychology, Uniformed Services University of the Health Sciences

RICHARD F. THOMPSON, Department of Psychology and Neurosciences Program, University of Southern California

DANIEL DRUCKMAN, *Study Director*
DONNA REIFSNIDER, *Senior Project Assistant*

The National Academy of Sciences is a private, nonprofit, self-perpetuating society of distinguished scholars engaged in scientific and engineering research, dedicated to the furtherance of science and technology and to their use for the general welfare. Upon the authority of the charter granted to it by the Congress in 1863, the Academy has a mandate that requires it to advise the federal government on scientific and technical matters. Dr. Frank Press is president of the National Academy of Sciences.

The National Academy of Engineering was established in 1964, under the charter of the National Academy of Sciences, as a parallel organization of outstanding engineers. It is autonomous in its administration and in the selection of its members, sharing with the National Academy of Sciences the responsibility for advising the federal government. The National Academy of Engineering also sponsors engineering programs aimed at meeting national needs, encourages education and research, and recognizes the superior achievements of engineers. Dr. Robert M. White is president of the National Academy of Engineering.

The Institute of Medicine was established in 1970 by the National Academy of Sciences to secure the services of eminent members of appropriate professions in the examination of policy matters pertaining to the health of the public. The Institute acts under the responsibility given to the National Academy of Sciences by its congressional charter to be an adviser to the federal government and, upon its own initiative, to identify issues of medical care, research, and education. Dr. Samuel O. Thier is president of the Institute of Medicine

The National Research Council was organized by the National Academy of Sciences in 1916 to associate the broad community of science and technology with the Academy's purposes of furthering knowledge and advising the federal government. Functioning in accordance with general policies determined by the Academy, the Council has become the principal operating agency of both the National Academy of Sciences and the National Academy of Engineering in providing services to the government, the public, and the scientific and engineering communities. The Council is administered jointly by both Academies and the Institute of Medicine. Dr. Frank Press and Dr. Robert M. White are chairman and vice chairman, respectively, of the National Research Council.

Contents

Preface

This is the second report of the Committee on Techniques for the Enhancement of Human Performance. The committee's first report, *Enhancing Human Performance: Issues, Theories and Techniques*, was published by the National Academy Press in 1988. That report was the product of a process that began in 1984 when the Army Research Institute (ARI) asked the National Academy of Sciences/National Research Council to form a committee to assess the promise of some "new age" techniques designed to enhance human performance. Those techniques, developed largely outside the academic research establishment, offered the potential to accelerate learning, improve motor skills, alter mental states, reduce stress, increase social influence, foster group cohesion, and—in the parapsychological domain—produce remote viewing and psychokinetic control of electronic devices. In response to ARI's request, a committee of 14 experts, selected for their expertise in relevant basic-science areas, was appointed under the auspices of the Commission on Behavioral and Social Sciences and Education (CBASSE) within the National Research Council and began its work.

The reaction to the release of *Enhancing Human Performance* was considerable, at both the public and professional levels. A press conference was well attended, and the subsequent media coverage of the committee's recommendations was extensive; reviews of the book appeared in a number of magazines and professional journals. In general, reaction to the report was very favorable (see, e.g., the thorough review by Philip Morrison in *Scientific American* [1988]). The committee was not without its critics, however. Advocates of certain techniques that were not viewed favorably accused the committee of being biased or closed minded, and others found certain of the committee's (relatively few) positive recommendations to be less than tough minded. (For a summary of reactions to the committee's first report, see J.A. Swets and R.A. Bjork [1990]: Enhancing human performance: an evaluation of "new age" techniques considered by the U.S. Army. *Psychological Science* 1(2):85-96.)

The committee's second agenda emerged in part as a consequence of its first report. It became apparent that certain techniques that had not been on the committee's initial agenda deserved attention, such as using a model of the expert as a guide to training, and that other topics deserved more thorough analysis, such as meditation and other methods of altering mental states. Other techniques for committee study were suggested by virtue of their popular attention, particularly subliminal self-help audio tapes, self-assessment techniques to aid career development, and sports-psychology techniques to sustain performance under pressure. Still other topics resulted from meetings with Army staff, who encouraged the committee to explore possible innovations in training based on academic research, particularly with respect to long-term retention of critical skills and transfer of those skills to altered contexts; and who provided information on career development in the Army, on the special problems of maintaining high performance in high-stress/high-risk settings, and on the problems of detecting—and avoiding the detection of—deception. The final topics for the new agenda, managing pain and enhancing team performance, were added after committee discussions at the beginning of its second phase. With its mission fully in place, the committee embarked on the same mixture of activities that characterized its first phase; the committee's activities are discussed in Chapter 1 and detailed in Appendix A.

Looking back on a committee process that was efficient, productive, and stimulating, it is now my pleasure as committee chair to acknowledge contributors to that process. Various people within the Army were more than helpful. Dr. Edgar M. Johnson, director of the Army Research Institute, has been a steady source of support, encouragement, and wise advice during the entire life of the committee. Our project monitors from the Army Research Institute, Dr. Michael Drillings and Dr. Judith Orasanu, provided able administrative and technical advice, and Major John H. Hagman of the Uniformed Health Services University, Department of Military Medicine, was a valuable source of information and advice in our work.

To General Maxwell Thurman (ret.), whose enthusiasm and vision played a major role in initiating our work, the committee owes a special debt. In his commitment to research—and to the belief that each of us should be all that we can be—he has been a continuing source of inspiration and support. His constructive reactions to the first report, his many ideas for follow-on ARI projects, and his ability to convey the training and performance needs of the Army did much to shape the agenda and orientation of the committee's second phase. Similarly, General John Crosby (ret.), who assisted General Thurman and the committee since its inception, has also been a valuable friend of the committee.

Other key people in the Army made it possible for the committee to complete various projects and site visits. Dr. Owen Jacobs of the Army Research Institute provided invaluable advice and information relevant to career programs in the Army, and Dr. Herbert Barber at the Army War College helped the committee administer a career-instrument survey and provided advice. General Stanley Hyman arranged for a subcommittee to visit Fort Belvoir in order to discuss the Army's concerns surrounding the issue of deception, and Major Robert Roland of the Special Operations Command made special arrangements for committee members who went to Fort Bragg to talk with Army leaders about group performance and training. The committee also profited from the Army representatives who spoke at our meetings (see Appendix A).

Several individuals outside the Army were also critical in the committee's activities. Vic Braden, founder and director of the Vic Braden Tennis College, opened his training facilities to the committee and provided an instructive overview of his teaching methods in tennis and other sports. Raymond Mulligan, Curriculum Development Coordinator at the L.F. Sillin Nuclear Training Center in Connecticut, arranged for members of several subcommittees to see the special training and performance needs of operators and other personnel in nuclear power environments.

The authors of the committee's commissioned papers, Laura Darke, Manuel London, David Shannahoff-Khalsa, and Paul Thayer, deserve special appreciation for their good work. We also wish to thank the panel of scientists who reviewed our report on behalf of the Research Council; it profited greatly from their criticisms and suggestions. Our report also profited from the gifted editorial hand of Eugenia Grohman, CBASSE Associate Director for Reports; we appreciate her understanding of the issues and her ability to make technical writing readable. We also appreciate Elaine McGarraugh's thorough and organized job of proofing and copy editing the entire manuscript. And we are grateful to Donna Reifsnider, the committee's administrative assistant, who cheerfully handled innumerable details across all stages of the committee process.

For John Swets, a treasured friend, I want to add a word of personal thanks. As chair of the committee's first phase, he served as an expert, if impossible, model. Throughout the committee's second phase he remained a constant source—when asked—of good advice and honest opinions.

To Dan Druckman, our study director, I want to express my profound respect and gratitude. We took full advantage of his talents as a writer and editor, as a scholar of unusual breadth, and as a manager; it was his tenacity and planning that must be credited with keeping the committee mostly on track and on time. Finally, I want to express my personal debt to the committee members themselves—for their cooperation, their wisdom, and their good humor.

ROBERT A. BJORK, *Chair*
Committee on Techniques for the
Enhancement of Human Performance

IN THE
MIND'S EYE

PART I

Overview

THE TWO CHAPTERS IN THIS PART PROVIDE the background for the committee's study and a summary of its key findings and conclusions. Chapter 1 describes the history of the project, summarizes the conclusions of the committee's first report, describes tasks for the second phase of work, and presents overviews of each of the chapters in this book.

The committee's key findings and conclusions are summarized in Chapter 2. Three types of conclusions are presented: those that summarize implications from completed research, those that call for needed research, and those that have practical implications for organizational contexts. The committee's detailed conclusions on each topic are presented in the final sections of each chapter.

1

Background

THE COMMITTEE'S FIRST PHASE

Six years ago the Army Research Institute (ARI) asked the National Research Council (NRC) to assess a field of popular techniques designed to enhance human performance. As a class, these techniques were considered extraordinary: they were developed outside of mainstream research in the behavioral sciences and were accompanied by strong claims for high effectiveness. The "new age" techniques, many of which grew out of the human potential movement of the 1960s, were getting much attention in the popular press and being widely touted and sold to government and industry training programs. The Army's interest in assessing these techniques was propelled by its desire for large and quick enhancements of human performance, by any means available, and by substantial advocacy that fields such as parapsychology offered substantial potential for waging exceptionally advanced warfare.

In consultation with ARI, the NRC committee selected for evaluation a number of unconventional techniques that had been proposed to the Army to speed up the process of bringing unskilled and sometimes undereducated recruits to the level needed for an increasingly technical military force. Specifically, the Army was interested in accelerated learning, improved motor skills, altered mental states, stress reduction, interpersonal influence, group cohesion, and certain parapsychological processes. In addition to evaluating the claims of these techniques, the committee examined two other general questions: What are the appropriate criteria for evaluating claims for such techniques in the future?

What research is needed to advance understanding of performance enhancement in areas related to those techniques?

In its report, *Enhancing Human Performance: Issues, Theories, and Techniques* (Druckman and Swets, 1988), the committee presented conclusions for several areas of performance: whether more basic or applied research is warranted; whether Army training programs could benefit from new findings and procedures; and what, in particular, might be worth monitoring for possible breakthroughs. Finding that the claims made for many of the techniques did not withstand scientific scrutiny, the committee warned against substituting personal experience and marketplace popularity for research evidence.

The committee's work produced specific answers to questions regarding how to improve performance. On the positive side, the committee found scientific evidence for: the possibility of priming future learning by presenting material during certain stages of sleep; improving learning by integrating certain instructional elements; improving skilled motor performance through various combinations of mental and physical practice; reducing stress by providing information that increases a person's sense of control; and maximizing group performance by taking advantage of organizational cultures to transmit values. On the negative side, the committee found: a lack of supporting evidence for such techniques as visual training exercises, hemispheric synchronization, and neurolinguistic programming; a lack of scientific justification for the parapsychological phenomena reviewed; some potentially negative effects for group cohesion; and ambiguous evidence for the effectiveness of the learning package known as suggestive accelerative learning and teaching techniques. (See also Swets and Bjork [1990] for a summary of the committee's findings.)

The favorable reports received from various field units encouraged the Army to follow many of the committee's recommendations, including support for field experiments on mental practice conducted at Fort Knox and Redstone Arsenal; a renewed interest in stress-reduction procedures, including meditation; a reduced interest in programs designed to train officers to use neurolinguistic programming and hemispheric synchronization; and a decision to discourage applications of parapsychological techniques. The Army also decided to ask the committee to continue work in the area of enhancing human performance.

THE COMMITTEE'S SECOND PHASE

The committee's mandate for a second phase consisted of following up some recommendations made in the first report, in particular, to address broad theoretical principles underlying training programs. A consideration of training issues is driven by practical needs: as the largest training institution in the world, the Army faces increasing demands for technical skills needed to perform sophisticated combat and noncombat missions. Related to these demands are issues of long-term career development: career planning must now take into account the cultivation and perpetuation of skills needed to perform complex tasks. A variety of factors are relevant, including basic psychological knowledge, skills acquisition and maintenance, expert modeling, optimizing performance under special conditions, performing under pressure, and team performance. These are some of the topics that formed the agenda for the committee's second phase of work.

In this phase, the committee turned from an evaluation of some popular techniques claimed to enhance human performance to a consideration of more basic issues of performance. These issues can be divided broadly into three parts: training and career development, altering mental states for improved performance, and performing, at both the individual and team level. Work on these issues was implemented through a subcommittee structure (see Appendix A).

Training issues were considered as three topics: problems of training for long-term retention of skills; modeling of expertise on complex skills; and developing careers over the long term. Four topics were included in the study of altering mental states: an evaluation of subliminal self-help audio cassette tapes in terms of what is known about subliminal learning; a review of the literature on the effects of meditation; a survey of what is known about the psychological aspects of managing pain; and an examination of issues concerned with deceiving and detecting deception in both laboratory and field settings. The problem of deception was included in part because of its relevance to practical issues of military security and in part because of its relevance to the topic of altering mental states for performance, which in turn relates to performing. Under the third set of issues, two topics were considered: techniques that facilitate preparing to perform, drawing on a large literature from the expanding field of sports psychology; and team performance, including a review of what is known about group problem solving and interactive decision making and a consideration of that basic knowledge in the context of real-world problems faced by such large organizations as the military.

The topics grew out of a framework for depicting processes and strategies for enhancing human performance. Arranged in one order, the topics reflect a sequence of stages from training strategies (stage 1), to preparation to perform strategies (stage 2), to actual performance (stage 3), to the postperformance retention of skills (stage 4). Arranged in another way, the topics reflect a focus on either emotional (mental states), cognitive (modeling), or motor (performance) skills. Cutting across these schemes are issues of context and levels of analysis. With regard to context, we considered implications of training programs for career development. With regard to levels of analysis, we asked whether training strategies that work for individuals also work for groups: if not, why not? What are appropriate strategies for enhancing group performance?

The committee's approach to evaluation issues was presented in its first report (Druckman and Swets, 1988). One of the two key evaluation issues concerns basic research in terms of plausibility of inferences and causation. The second issue concerns field tests: Does a program work in field settings? Is it cost effective? The philosophy of evaluation discussed in that volume also guided the committee's work in this phase of its activities.

A large variety of information contributed to the committee's work; the committee benefited from the advice of experts who either prepared commissioned papers or hosted site visits at their laboratories or training facilities (see Appendix A). Papers prepared by Manuel London on career development, by Paul Thayer on self-assessment techniques, by David Shannahoff-Khalsa on meditation, and by Laura Darke on pain management complemented the published literature on those topics and provided useful conceptual frameworks not found elsewhere. Visits to Fort Bragg, Fort Belvoir, West Point, the U.S. Olympic Committee, Vic Braden's tennis college, and the Sillin Nuclear Training Center in Connecticut alerted the committee to real-world training issues and the way that actual programs to enhance performance are developed. An experiment on mental practice conducted at the Redstone Arsenal in Alabama provided an opportunity to confront the problems of doing experiments in field settings, as well as further insight into the issue of generality of laboratory results. And a survey of Army War College students contributed to the committee's analysis of career development. Our findings from all of these activities, in addition to reviews of the most recent available research and the state of the art, are presented in this report.

THE REPORT

This section gives readers an overview of the report, summarizing the key themes for each chapter. The next chapter presents the committee's key findings and conclusions. Though addressing the Army's concerns in particular, the conclusions have a broad relevance to training and performance in educational and industrial contexts as well, and they add to the research literature on enhancing human performance.

Training

Optimizing Long-Term Retention

Skills and knowledge gained in instructional programs are often exercised much later, even as long as a year or more following training. Thus, the committee examined training procedures that may be optimal for long-term posttraining effectiveness. Learning procedures are often evaluated by how rapidly they bring the learner to some criterion level of performance. There is now abundant research suggesting that procedures that might appear optimal if measured by short-term performance may be less than optimal if performances are measured weeks, months, or years after training. In this chapter the committee examines training procedures for enhancing the long-term retention of expertise, of nonexpert cognitive skills and knowledge, and of motor skills.

Modeling Expertise

The potential of modeling experts for enhancing performance was suggested by the committee's prior review of neurolinguistic programming (NLP), by recent research findings, and by developments in sports training. In its otherwise pessimistic evaluation of NLP, the committee found promise in the importance that NLP attributes to decoding an expert's behavior as a guide to training a beginner. Research on the nature of expertise has flourished in recent years and may provide a foundation for training programs. In this chapter the committee addresses issues related to understanding the knowledge that experts possess and how this knowledge is organized. This discussion draws on a large body of contemporary research on the concept of expertise. Other issues concern the nature of feedback in the context of apprenticeship learning and guided participation as well as issues concerned with transfer of training and generalization from a few training examples. The latter issue has special relevance to the many Army training programs where a skill is learned in one context and must be performed in another setting.

Developing Careers

Two broad issues on careers are addressed by the committee: long-term career development in the military and the value of self-assessment techniques in career counseling. An attempt is made in this chapter to develop a broad perspective on career development. The perspective reflects insights from recent literature on managerial development and performance in organizations and is a basis for a framework or model of careers that can be used to guide planning for an officer's progression through the ranks. A class of techniques designed to improve performance through increased self-insight is widely used in public and private organizations, including the Army. Although they have considerable appeal to both trainers and trainees, they have been subject to little rigorous research. In this chapter the committee surveys the use of these techniques in the Army, reports the results of a pilot evaluation of the impact on respondents, and conducts an appraisal of the most popular instrument of this genre, the Myers-Briggs Type Indicator.

Altering Mental States

Subliminal Self-Help

A large market for subliminal audiotapes suggests that many people believe that they contribute to self-improvement. Although many manufacturers claim that their tapes can alter attitudes, enhance confidence, and reduce anxieties, they do not provide references to studies demonstrating such effects. Despite the lack of supporting scientific evidence for particular methods, however, psychological research leaves little doubt that subliminal learning does occur. In its first report, the committee recommended taking a second look at phenomena associated with learning during sleep or without conscious awareness. A renewed interest by researchers in subliminal learning is due to recent results showing that some measures of memory seem sensitive to types of learning without awareness. These research developments, together with the marketplace popularity of various self-help techniques, led the committee to examine these phenomena further. Two issues in particular are highlighted in this chapter: the difference between subjectively perceptible and objectively detectable stimuli and reasons for an apparent improvement in performance in the absence of detectable subliminal suggestions. Although there are implications for these issues from the basic research literature on the history and current status of subliminal perception, no attempt is made to review that large literature.

Meditation

During its first phase the committee recommended investigations of methods designed to alter mental states to ascertain whether they might suggest any practical applications. Results obtained from a number of studies suggest that altered states of consciousness may affect a variety of physiological processes related to performance. Altered states can occur through the use of such methods as meditation and related relaxation therapies as well as through nonpharmacological ways of coping with physical pain. Of particular relevance to the military is the use of psychological methods to help people endure extremely stressful situations. This chapter considers what is known about effects of meditation and discusses the problem of application of meditation techniques in diverse situations. In this chapter the committee considers such issues as the role of meditation in reducing stress and hypertension, methodological problems in studies designed to evaluate effects on arousal (e.g, whether the effects are due uniquely to the meditation technique), and explanations of such well-known feats of endurance as "pit burials." The chapter includes a summary of a critique of an earlier report (prepared by Brener and Connally [1986] for the Army Research Institute) that reviewed much of the scientific literature on meditation.

Managing Pain

A topic of considerable importance to the military is the way people cope with pain. A large literature on the psychology of pain and pain management provides some insights into coping skills. This chapter focuses on both defining the various types of pain and considering some treatments that have received attention in research on acute and chronic pain; it describes four dimensions of pain management and summarizes the seven psychological factors that influence the experience of pain. Among the treatments for acute pain that have been evaluated are providing sensory and procedural information to patients about surgery, relaxation training, training in coping skills, stress inoculation training, biofeedback, and hypnosis. With regard to chronic pain, the emphasis is on controlling pain behaviors: for example, one approach uses operant conditioning techniques to reward reduced reliance on medications and health care services.

Hiding and Detecting Deception

Problems of hiding and detecting deception were construed by the committee to be part of the more general topic of physical manifestations of mental and emotional states. Focusing primarily on nonverbal manifestations, this chapter reviews experimental literature on cues to lying and on problems in detecting deception. A number of nonverbal behaviors have been found to indicate deception as practiced by laboratory subjects; particularly revealing are cues "leaked" by individuals who are highly motivated to succeed in perpetrating a deception. This chapter considers many aspects of nonverbal behavior and the experimental findings with subjects—both amateurs and experts—who try to detect deception.

A Broad Concept of Deception

A key question is whether the laboratory results on nonverbal indicators of deception can be generalized to other real-world situations and to populations other than those who are usually the subjects of laboratory experiments. This chapter considers broad issues of definition with a view toward developing a conceptual framework that provides a basis for studying deception at several levels of analysis. A number of taxonomic formulations of deception are reviewed with special attention paid to differences among cultures and subpopulations in the perpetration and detection of deception. The broadened perspective taken in this chapter allows for consideration of forms of deception other than lying and the practice of deception by organizations or governments as well as by individuals.

Performing

Optimizing Individual Performance

After one has been trained—that is, after one has acquired the necessary skills for a given task—there are issues related to performing effectively when it matters. Research in sports psychology suggests that such preparation strategies as mental rehearsal and automating preperformance motor routines may prime or stabilize the cognitive motor programs that underlie skilled performance. The committee's previous review of experimental studies on mental practice confirmed the effectiveness of the technique; less is known about the effectiveness of the technique in applied settings, which is one focus of this chapter. A variety of other techniques that have received attention in the academic sports psychology literature are also discussed. Some of these techniques may help to induce or maintain bodily states that are correlated with high performance. A small number of studies on these strategies have been completed to date and, along with site visits to West Point and the U.S. Olympic Training facilities, form the basis for the committee's conclusions.

Enhancing Team Performance

In this chapter the committee addresses questions of similarities and differences between individual and group performance. Two questions are of particular interest: What is an optimal mix of training time spent in developing individual skills and group practice? What modifications are needed for studies of undifferentiated groups to be applied to training of stratified and multifunctional groups? From a practical standpoint, these issues are important because of the variety of Army squads and units whose tasks pose complex training requirements. From a research perspective, these issues call attention to literatures in social psychology and human factors on group versus individual performance and raise questions concerning the applicability of laboratory results to field settings. Although a number of efforts have been made to engineer improvements in group performance—such as brainstorming procedures, Delphi technique, and nominal group technique—surprisingly little evaluation research has been done to determine their effectiveness. Moreover, long-term training of teams has rarely been studied. In this chapter the committee discusses the problems of limited research, difficulties of doing group research in university settings, and the particular contextual considerations for team training in the military. The military is uniquely suited for research on group problems both with respect to the pool of available subjects for such studies and the realistic conditions under which group performance can be observed.

REFERENCES

Brener, J., and S.R. Connally
   1986   Meditation: Rationales, Experimental Effects, and Methodological Issues. Paper prepared for the U.S. Army Research Institute for the Behavioral and Social Sciences, European Division. Department of Psychology, University of Hull, London, England.
Druckman, D., and J. Swets, eds.
   1988   *Enhancing Human Performance: Issues, Theories, and Techniques*. Committee on Techniques for the Enhancement of Human Performance, Commission on Behavioral and Social Sciences and Education, National Research Council. Washington, D.C.: National Academy Press.
Swets, J.A., and R.A. Bjork
   1990   Enhancing human performance: an evaluation of "new age" techniques considered by the U.S. Army. *Psychological Science* 1(2):85-96.

2

Findings and Conclusions

In this chapter we present key findings and conclusions for each of the topics investigated. Each conclusion derives from a review and evaluation of literature on that topic. Together, the various lines of research covered in this report reveal the complexity of the problems involved in enhancing human performance. At the same time, the research also clearly indicates approaches that can improve training and guide the preperformance preparation of teams and individuals. The research also helps illuminate special performance issues, such as changing one's mental states, detecting deception, and developing the careers of individuals in large organizations.

Most of the committee's conclusions are summaries derived directly from research findings; others however, are suggestions for research where we need to know more or are recommendations for actions based on what we do know.

TRAINING

Optimizing Long-Term Retention and Transfer

Training procedures are typically evaluated, explicitly or implicitly, by how rapidly they bring the learner to some criterion level of performance. Performance during training, however, is often a poor index of the learner's level of learning and understanding. Training programs should be evaluated not by performance during training but, rather, by the extent to which those programs support the learner's long-term post-training performance in real-world contexts.

Measuring Learning and Performance Two important dimensions of posttraining performance are the ability to resist forgetting and interference over periods of disuse of a given skill and the ability to generalize training to contexts and tasks that differ in their surface characteristics from the training contexts or tasks. Depending on the relative priorities given to those two dimensions of posttraining performance, the optimal package of training components will differ somewhat. One general principle, however, is that tests of a learner's progress during training should, as much as possible, measure performance as it will be measured on the posttraining task(s) in the posttraining setting(s).

Retention Given posttraining tasks and conditions that are identical or similar to the training tasks and conditions, posttraining performance is enhanced as the level of original learning is increased. That level can be increased by putting greater demands on the learner—making the criterion of mastery more difficult, for example, or requiring supplementary (postmastery) practice after the criterion has been reached. Introducing variations in the conditions and sequencing of practice, the immediate consequence of which is to degrade performance, may be a particularly promising way to increase the level of original learning, and, hence, posttraining retention.

Skills that demand little attention or effort to perform are regarded as automatic; the more automatic a given skill, the higher the likelihood that the skill can be retained over nonuse periods without refresher training. Certain types of procedural tasks, however, tend to be easily forgotten, especially when their components have a low degree of internal organization or cohesiveness. The rate of forgetting of procedural tasks is a function of the number of steps needed to perform the task, and the steps most likely to be forgotten are those not cued by the equipment, environment, or preceding steps.

Several instructional strategies to enhance the retention and transfer of procedural tasks can be identified: distributing rather than massing practice time; relating the knowledge to be learned to the relevant knowledge learners already have in memory; teaching techniques (e.g., mnemonics) that learners can use to provide their own elaborations; having the training regimen require repeated use of the knowledge to be learned; and providing for and encouraging the use and elaboration of acquired knowledge and skill during nonuse periods. In general, a learner should be an active participant, not a passive observer, during the training process.

However well designed the initial training, refresher training may still be needed during prolonged posttraining periods of disuse in order to maintain a given level of knowledge and skill. Refresher training can, however, become less frequent over time, and the training needs of retrainees are also different in kind from those of new trainees; relatively efficient, cost-effective techniques can be used to maintain a given level of original learning in retrainees.

Transfer of Training In general, the similarity of goals and cognitive processing between training and transfer tasks is a critical factor in enhancing transfer. The learner, therefore, should be challenged by means of manipulation of practice variables, such as feedback, contextual (or intratask) interference, and number and variability of examples. These manipulations, which may impair performance in the short term, not only help the learner to process the learning task more deeply, but suggest appropriate processes for transfer, particularly to related but distinct posttraining tasks.

Modeling Expertise

As an instructional method, the modeling of complex cognitive skills poses special problems. The observable behavior of an expert reveals little of the expert's underlying cognitive processes. By observing an expert, a student can learn a set of executable actions that are linked to a corresponding set of specific conditions. But such learning does not typically result in the ability to generalize beyond those specific conditions or to understand the principles behind the actions.

It is widely recognized that instruction should proceed by integrating new knowledge with old knowledge, but eliciting and representing the knowledge of the tutor and the student are difficult problems. However, improved methods of eliciting knowledge from experts and characterizing the present state of a learner may make a promising training approach for modeling expertise, especially in contexts in which a computer can be used as an interactive tool. New learning techniques that involve active participation by a learner, such as self-explanations, self-questioning, and self-monitoring, are promising avenues for further research and may even be candidates for experimental programs at this time.

The use of computers to deliver instruction, as well as to diagnose student progress, is an important technological advance in and out of the classroom. To be maximally effective, however, a training program must include a sophisticated model of the student, which permits a match between the computer's "understanding" and the student's understanding. Such a match makes possible the tailoring of the individualized branching, diagnosis, and correction of misconceptions by each student.

Developing Careers

Career Planning Despite the widespread popularity of many career counseling techniques, which include self-assessment instruments, the decisions to use them are rarely based on research results attesting to their effectiveness. The committee recommends that such decisions be made within the context of a planned, systematic, and organization-wide approach to career development, for the Army as well as any other large, complex organization. In addition to such career planning, evaluations should be made of the cost-effectiveness of alternative career intervention activities with regard to the timing of the intervention and the methods used by the intervenors.

The Myers-Briggs Type Indicator   At this time there is not sufficient, well-designed research to justify the use of the Myers-Briggs Type Indicator (MBTI) in career counseling programs. Much of the current evidence is based on inadequate methodologies. Better evaluation studies, conducted according to rigorous methodological standards, are recommended. One type of evaluation would compare "successful" and "unsuccessful" careers over the long term. Positive results obtained from these studies, if replicated with different samples, could justify use of this instrument in career counseling programs. Other self-assessment instruments currently in use or contemplated for use in counseling programs should also be subjected to the same rigorous evaluation.

Research on the effects of guided discussion, such as the discussions held on feedback from the MBTI or other self-assessment instruments, is recommended. Such research should distinguish between subjective reactions to the experience and observed effects on subsequent actions and career performance.

ALTERING MENTAL STATES

Subliminal Self-Help

The committee's review of the available research literature leads to our conclusion that, at this time, there is neither theoretical foundation nor experimental evidence to support claims that subliminal self-help tapes enhance human performance. Several key considerations underlie this conclusion.

Although recent research suggests that stimuli perceived in the absence of conscious awareness may have short-term effects on the performance of relatively simple tasks under controlled laboratory conditions (such as color naming or lexical decision), this research cannot be construed as evidence that long-term changes in complex actions, cognitions, or emotions—such as smoking, self-confidence, or depression—can be effected through exposure to subliminal suggestions under such varied real-life circumstances as reading, relaxing, or even sleeping.

Some experiments have found that some commercially available self-help audiotapes contain masked messages that are both subjectively imperceptible and objectively undetectable; as such, these tapes do not meet the minimum stimulus condition for demonstrating subliminal perception. Although some self-help audiotapes now available on the marketplace may satisfy this minimum condition, the responsibility for identifying those products should rest, at least initially, with their proponents. If detectable messages are found, controlled studies of their effects could be undertaken.

Several sociopsychological phenomena, including effort justification and expectancy or placebo effects, may contribute to an erroneous judgment that self-help products are effective, even in the absence of any actual improvements in emotion, appearance, attitude, or any other physical or psychological quality.

Meditation

In scientifically controlled studies, meditation does not reduce arousal any more than does simply resting quietly. In many studies, the combined use of various relaxation-training techniques precludes attributing positive effects to meditation by itself. Lifestyle changes to reduce conflict are also apparently instrumental, a sensible enough conclusion and one that is consistent with the growing recognition that successful interventions must usually be multifaceted.

The philosophical context for most meditation practices is important. It may be that meditation and relaxation—including perhaps relaxation achieved with certain forms of biofeedback—effect cognitive change, such as an enhanced sense of self-efficacy and a belief that one can control his or her stress reactions.

A particular challenge to those who advocate meditation is whether benefits generalize to everyday situations or to conditions of special challenge. Does the person take time out during the day to meditate, or is there some more enduring, systemic reduction in arousal level that does not require conscious attention to practice? Perhaps changes are brought about by the person's lowered reactivity to challenge, and these positive social-environmental shifts present the individual with a less stressful environment. We do not believe that data exist to answer this question.

The highly publicized feats of some yogis who can remain buried for many hours without suffocating are probably due to confidence in their ability to slow their respiration rate, as well as faith that they can survive the ordeal if only they do not panic. Consistent with findings from the committee's earlier report, perceived control and predictability serve to reduce anxiety.

The assertion that the proper application of Kundalini Yoga can help develop "the soldier-saint" in whom is instilled the desire and superhuman ability to excel in the art of war is not supported by scientific evidence.

Managing Pain

Research on pain control suggests that people can be taught non-pharmacological ways to cope with physical pain. Central to the current understanding of pain is the role of cognitive factors. A person's understanding of the physiological events that underlie pain can have a profound effect on whether he or she actually experiences pain.

Procedures known to be useful for reducing stress—such as relaxation, providing information about what to expect, and enhancing a person's sense of control—also reduce pain because stress increases a person's experience of pain. Distraction is also an effective strategy for coping with pain. And suggestions given under hypnosis can help people cope with pain, for example, imagining that an affected limb is not really a part of them. Chronic pain is best managed by identifying and controlling psychological perpetuating factors. In most cases this would involve combining pure behavior-learning approaches with other cognitive-behavioral and relaxation interventions.

Hiding and Detecting Deception

A number of nonverbal behaviors have been found to be associated with deception. Particularly revealing are body movements and tone of voice changes, although a number of other behaviors have also been shown to be indicators of deception in certain situations. Nonverbal behaviors reflect feelings or emotions more directly than they reflect specific intentions to deceive. Emotions—psychological states—can be considered as intervening variables, relating to observed behaviors and to inferred intentions.

Motivated liars are easier to detect than nonmotivated liars. When emotionality is high, as in the case of tasks with high stakes associated with outcomes, nonverbal behaviors can be especially revealing. The revealing behaviors are likely to be those in the liar's unattended channels, which are "leaked" as a result of behavioral inhibition or rigidity.

Detectors, both amateurs and experts, are generally inaccurate despite high levels of confidence in their judgments. Neither feedback nor enhanced suspiciousness seems to improve accuracy. However, training detectors and providing them with a plan for processing information about relevant cues does seem to increase accuracy of detection.

Techniques developed for laboratory research are useful in studying deception. They provide a structured and systematic approach to analysis germane to detecting deception in a variety of situations. The techniques are especially useful to an analyst who has access to videotaped interactions or who can interact with a subject over long periods of time. The videotaped exchanges can be replayed for details easily overlooked in the course of an ongoing conversation. They can also be used to train individuals to code nonverbal behavior for leakage clues.

A Broad Concept of Deception

Detection of deception depends on leaked cues, which in turn depend on the psychological state of the deceiver, that is, whether it reflects guilt. Detection of deception would be improved if one could anticipate the sorts of scenarios that constitute social transgression or a guilt-producing state for individuals. Although some components of emotional expression may be universal, many other expressions are influenced by culture and context. Research on the folk psychology of deception and on the prototypical structure of lying provide examples of methods for assessing perceptions of socially unacceptable deceptions within cultural groups. With suitable refinements, these methods can be used to discover those scenarios and deceptive acts that might induce leakage for particular cultures and individuals.

PERFORMING

Optimizing Individual Performance

A large literature in sports psychology reports progress in identifying the psychological and physiological conditions for improved performance on a wide variety of tasks. Numerous experiments provide some basis for distinguishing between effective and ineffective preperformance interventions.

Mental Health and Athletic Success   The mental health model has produced inconsistent results in differentiating successful and less successful athletes in terms of individual mood scales. However, measures of global mood have been effective in distinguishing when athletes are experiencing a psychologically unhealthy, overtrained state.

Physical Versus Mental Practice   If the goal is to maximize performance in the shortest amount of time, physical practice is superior to mental practice. However, if nonphysical practice time is available or if a person cannot physically practice, then the small effects due to mental practice can be useful for facilitating performance and for better retention.

Cognitive-Behavioral Interventions The effects of cognitive-behavioral interventions—such as relaxation, imagery, mental preparation strategies, skill modeling, and direct attempts to alter cognition—are small to moderate. They will be enhanced if the treatments emphasize: multiple components (e.g., relaxation, modeling, imagery, cognitive restructuring); direct administration by an investigator or therapist (rather than a tape); many sessions; people who have concentration problems; and tasks that can be objectively scored.

Preperformance Preparation In skills for which the environmental conditions are constant (e.g., archery), an individually designed preperformance routine with multiple components (i.e, preparation rituals) has been shown to facilitate performance. In sports that involve aiming (e.g., rifle shooting), better performers have a greater cardiac deceleration within 3-5 seconds of executing a motor response, and better performances are associated with a moderate increase above baseline in alpha activity in the left hemisphere of the brain with little or no change in the right hemisphere. However, too great an increase in left hemisphere alpha is associated with worse shots. Such electrophysiological patterns as heart rate deceleration and EEG asymmetries, which are related to performance, can be used during the preparatory period (3-5 seconds before response execution) to assist in determining the efficacy of preperformance routines.

Exercise and Stress Evidence shows that aerobic exercise results in quicker recovery from psychosocial stressors than the absence of such exercise.

Neuroscience and Peak Performance Further understanding of the bases for performance is likely to come from ongoing research in neuroscience and on "peak performance." Recent neuroscientific studies using imaging techniques have shown that even simple motor processes have complex neurophysiological correlates. Research on high performance behavior has made progress in identifying the affective, attentional, and cognitive states associated with such behavior.

Enhancing Team Performance

Many problems and issues in team performance are potentially answerable by research, but research on group structure and function, once a mainstay in social psychology, is not now a major focus of the work. Moreover, most of these studies are of unstratified groups, making them less relevant for real-world problems involving stratified groups and command structures.

Research on group problem solving indicates that teams perform at suboptimal levels. While a number of techniques (e.g., the Delphi technique, nominal group technique) have been used to improve the group process and outcomes, few of these interventions have been evaluated systematically.

The research on group processes has focused in recent years on decision making with an emphasis on jury-like studies. Some of this is directly relevant to group training, but it leaves unaddressed many of the group performance questions.

The strategy of studying real groups in actual working conditions has contributed to the understanding of the groups studied, but the findings have proven difficult to generalize.

Some of the difficulties of experimentation on group performance are logistic. It is difficult to find a suitable number of comparable groups that remain stable over time to compare the effects of experimental differences on their training and performance. Large numbers of comparable groups do exist in the Army and other military services, and they provide the possible experimental subjects and conditions for effective study of team training, decision making, and performance. Since the military recruits young people who are comparable to the entering U.S. labor force, the results of such group studies may also have applicability to industrial and commercial settings.

PART II

Training

THIS PART CONSIDERS A NUMBER OF ISSUES related to training for optimizing performance over the short and long term. Chapter 3 addresses basic issues of learning from the standpoint of skill acquisition, retention, and transfer, with an emphasis on the durability and flexibility of posttraining performance. Chapter 4 addresses the learning strategy of modeling expert performance. These issues benefit from active research traditions that have resulted in large literatures from which conclusions can be drawn. Much of the relevant research is summarized in these chapters.

A somewhat different approach is taken in Chapter 5, in which training is considered in relation to the development of careers over the long term. These issues benefit from recent work done on performance in organizations: that literature is used as a basis for the framework proposed as a guide for research and development activities in the Army and related organizations.

The usefulness of any training program depends on whether the skills acquired can be used in other settings and long after the training experience. The many variables that influence retention and transfer of skills are discussed in Chapter 3. With regard to retention, considerations include the original level of learning, task organization, and the time since training. With regard to transfer, key issues are the similarities between training and transfer tasks and conditions and how knowledge is used in the training and transfer situations.

A new topic receiving attention by learning psychologists is the modeling of expert performance. The committee's decision to consider this topic resulted from its earlier work on modeling in the areas of motor skills and influence strategies. The treatment of modeling in Chapter 4 deals primarily with complex cognitive skills. It is apparent that the kinds of direct modeling or imitation approaches that may work for acquiring relatively simple skills are not relevant for more complex performances. The discussion in this chapter calls attention to such considerations as the nature of experts' knowledge, ways to effectively extract that knowledge, and ways to impart it to the learner.

As noted, the last chapter in this part deals with career development. In this chapter we propose a systematic approach to issues of career development, and we evaluate widely used self-assessment instruments believed to contribute to enhanced performance. The approach consists of a set of propositions, based on research findings, that can be implemented in current programs. The evaluation focuses primarily on the popular Myers-Briggs Type Indicator (MBTI).

3

Optimizing Long-Term Retention and Transfer

This chapter considers training conditions that do or do not facilitate posttraining performance. We focus on two aspects of posttraining performance: its durability (long-term retention), that is, the extent to which a training program yields a level of learning that supports performance after long periods of disuse; and its flexibility (transfer), that is, the extent to which a training program prepares a learner to perform under real-world conditions that may differ from those present during training. Our primary concerns are the training of adults rather than children and the training of cognitive-motor procedural skills, such as programming a computer, repairing a mechanical or electronic device, hitting a serve in tennis, parachuting out of an airplane, or receiving and transmitting Morse Code, rather than on classroom learning.

Focusing on the training of adults and on procedural tasks helps to limit the scope of this chapter, but covering all aspects of training so defined in one chapter is still prohibitive; a broader view is provided in the recent book by Farr (1987). Among the issues we do not address are individual differences among learners, instructor variables, such as motivating trainees and improving instructor-trainee rapport, and technological innovations, such as computer-based instruction and the use of simulators; those issues are addressed in recent reviews by Montague (1988) and Walberg (1990), as well as in Farr (1987). We also do not focus on how the individual components of complex tasks should be integrated. (Chapter 4 takes a broader view of complex cognitive tasks and includes a discussion of some of the ways computers can assist training.) Even with our mission defined more narrowly, the relevant literature deriving from basic and applied research in education, psychology, cognitive science, physical education, and sports psychology is enormous: thus, the references we cite should be viewed as representative, not exhaustive.

Procedural knowledge is now commonly distinguished from declarative knowledge (Winograd, 1975). Declarative knowledge is knowledge of facts or static information (e.g., in what year did Babe Ruth hit 60 home runs?), and it, in turn, is typically subdivided into episodic and semantic knowledge: episodic knowledge is context dependent, such as knowing what you ate for lunch today; semantic knowledge is independent of context, such as knowing what Europeans typically eat for breakfast (see e.g., Tulving, 1985).

Procedural knowledge is knowing how to execute the procedures necessary to perform a given task. Procedural knowledge underlies cognitive and motor skills (many of them automated), such as how to change a flat tire on a car, use a typewriter by touch, operate a computer, disassemble and reassemble a rifle, ride a bicycle, or play a game. Skills are acquired mainly by doing or practice and are not learned quickly. Retention of skills, or the lack thereof, is typically measured by the extent to which they can be performed, rather than by the extent to which they can be "recalled" per se. In fact, at high levels of skill, in which many of the procedural components of a skill become automatic, people become unable to describe in any detail what procedures they are carrying out in what order. A person may have to resort to consciously observing his or her own behavior, for example, to tell a friend how to ski or operate a standard-transmission automobile.

It seems obvious that the major goal of any training program is to prepare trainees to perform effectively on a posttraining task in a real-world setting; achieving that goal, however, is complicated by several factors. First, what is observed by those responsible for training programs is, typically, the performances of trainees during the training process itself. Such performance is a highly imperfect index of the kind of learning, comprehension, or understanding that will sustain performance of the skill or knowledge over periods of disuse. Someone who meets high standards of performance at the end of training may fail to perform adequately some months later. Acquisition of a given skill during training also does not provide evidence that the learner will be able to perform in contexts that differ from the training context or on altered versions of the training task that may arise in real-world settings. The term "context" includes the task, practice conditions, and cognitive processing used by a trainee.

The crux of the problem is that learning and performance are not the same. As we indicate at several points in this chapter, procedures that enhance performance during training may or may not enhance long-term retention and transfer to altered contexts; conversely, procedures that introduce difficulties for the learner and impair performance during training may foster durable and flexible posttraining skills (for some examples, see Schmidt and Bjork, 1992). In short, the goal is to have training programs that optimize learning—some relatively permanent change in the capacity for responding—but what is observed during training is performance localized in a given place and time. At a later time, in another place, the learner may perform quite differently and that performance is often at an inadequate level. The performance observed during training may be mediated by rote memory or cues specific to the training procedure rather than being indicative of any substantial learning or understanding.

This problem is aggravated in training settings in which those who are responsible for training do not see the posttraining performance of the individuals they have trained. In such a setting, the instructor's judgment as to the efficacy of different training procedures may be governed entirely by the tacit assumption that what yields high performance during training will yield high retention and transfer after training. In any organization in which the people responsible for the maintenance of critical skills and knowledge (refresher training, retraining, and so forth) are not the same people who are responsible for initial training—the military is such an organization—this inferential problem is going to be particularly troublesome.

LONG-TERM RETENTION

When one assesses posttraining performance on some task, the time interval from the end of training to the performance "test" can be varied, the task can be the same or an altered version of the training task, and the situational context can be similar to or different from the training context. Thus, someone trained to repair a certain type of pump in a nuclear power plant might attempt the first such actual repair many weeks or months after being trained, the pump may differ in certain respects from those encountered in training, and the repair may need to be executed under conditions of heat or other pressure that was not present during training. It is common to speak of retention when performance on the actual training task is assessed under posttraining conditions that are essentially the same as the training conditions. The term transfer is used when the posttraining task or setting differs from the training task or setting. For convenience, and to be compatible with the literature, we tend to follow that usage, but it is important to emphasize that retention so defined is a special case of transfer. That is, since the posttraining context will never match exactly the training context—if for no other reason than that the physical, emotional, and mental state of the learner will not be exactly the same—a test of retention can be viewed as a test of the transfer of training to contexts that appear to match the training context.

In attempting to make our review compatible with the literature, in which the learning-performance distinction is often blurred or forgotten by researchers, we often need to speak of the level of "learning" achieved during training when level of performance would be the more correct expression. Terms such as "original learning" and "overlearning" are too common for us to avoid. In the next section particularly, when we discuss retention and transfer as a function of the level of original learning, we have tried to restrict our coverage to research situations in which it can be generally assumed that the performance levels measured as evidence of differing levels of learning do, indeed, denote just that. In later sections we deal with training situations in which performance during training is a poor measure of the level of learning achieved.

Original Learning

There is considerable agreement that the long-term retention of a task can be improved by increasing the level of original learning or mastery (e.g., Annett, 1979; Farr, 1987; Gardlin and Sitterley, 1972; Hagman and Rose, 1983; Hurlock and Montague, 1982; Naylor and Briggs, 1961; Schendel et al., 1978; Prophet, 1976). Indeed, the level of original learning for a task is the best single predictor of long-term retention for any given retention interval. Thus, any variable that can help trainees achieve a higher level of original learning or mastery of a task is capable of enhancing its retention (Hurlock and Montague, 1982).

Most often, the training variable manipulated is the amount of practice on a task. Typically, this manipulation is accomplished by making the criterion of mastery more difficult to achieve so that more practice is needed to achieve the criterion. The additional practice needed to achieve the more difficult criterion produces a higher level of original learning, which enhances retention. For example, suppose a basketball coach is training young, novice players to shoot free throws (foul shots). He or she decides that all of the players should be able to make 25 out of 50 shots attempted by the end of 8 weeks of training, which is a reasonable criterion of mastery. But the coach could also make the criterion of mastery more difficult to achieve, requiring that the players be able to make 35 out of 50 shots, or, alternatively, that the players be able to make 25 out of 50 shots under more difficult conditions (after wind sprints, with simulated crowd noise, at alternate baskets, and so forth).

In either case, more practice would be needed to achieve the more difficult criterion, but the additional practice would produce a higher level of original learning, which, in turn, should lead to greater retention.

Setting the Criterion of Mastery

Determining the appropriate level of original learning of a task that trainees must acquire in order to ensure the desired level of retention is not easy. How the level is selected—that is, how it is defined and assessed in terms of when the criterion of mastery is satisfactorily achieved— is quite arbitrary. Typically, the level is measured in terms of trials or time taken or number of errors committed until the criterion of mastery has been achieved. In most of the studies the committee reviewed, the criterion has been set either at a minimal mastery level, such as the first errorless performance trial, or at somewhat more than minimal level: for example, the three successive errorless trials required by Rigg and Gray (1981) in their research on U.S. Army enlisted personnel learning a procedural task. More recently, Jones (1985) suggested another way to determine when the level of original learning is satisfactorily achieved. He recommended that in addition to selecting some arbitrary criterion of mastery, the acquisition curve be used to determine when performance has stabilized at or above the criterion level. When the slope of the acquisition curve has begun to level off above the criterion level, learning would be considered complete.

Automaticity

The level of original learning can also be assessed in terms of the degree of automaticity of performance by using a dual-task paradigm, in which a secondary task is given to trainees to sample their spare cognitive capacity while they are learning the primary task (Shiffrin and Schneider, 1977; Schneider and Shiffrin, 1977; Schneider et al., 1984). An acceptable degree of automaticity and, hence, level of original learning, is the point at which neither the primary nor secondary task causes a performance decrement on the other. Although the dual-task paradigm is an acceptable method of assessing automaticity, it is not without its problems (see, e.g., Fendrich et al., 1988; Jonides et al., 1985). Theoretically, skills that require only a minimum of attention and cognitive capacity to perform are either completely or partly automatic, whereas skills that require cognitive resources and effort involve controlled processes. Schneider et al. (1984) define an automatic process as one that does not make use of general cognitive resources. In other words, capacity reductions do not influence automatic processing. Moreover, an automatic process is not subject to conscious control and, thus, can be executed in response to relevant external stimuli to which little attention is paid.

Whether or not a skill is classified as automatic or controlled depends largely on the level of original learning. Many skills require controlled processes early in learning, but the processes become automatic with extensive practice and especially so if that practice contains a high degree of consistency. Practice consistency means that a trainee makes the same response each time a certain stimulus or class of stimuli is presented. The assumed explanation for this phenomena is that retention of a skill depends heavily on the extent to which a skill is automatic: that is, it can be performed without conscious awareness. The more automatic the skill, the greater the chance that the skill will be retained over nonuse periods without refresher training or rehearsal. It is important to note, however, that the automated parts of a skill that are acquired through practice (e.g., speed in soldering a joint) are expected to deteriorate during nonuse periods, while the automated parts of a skill that are less dependent on practice (e.g., encoding of temporal or spatial information) are not. Thus, for designing a skill maintenance program, more emphasis should be placed on the automated parts of the skill that are acquired through practice.

Overlearning

Regardless of the criterion of mastery selected for original learning, one way to enhance retention is to provide supplementary practice on a task after the criterion is achieved. In the previous basketball example, for instance, the coach could have the players continue to practice free-throw shooting even though they have achieved the criterion of making 35 out of 50 shots. This method may be interpreted as postmastery learning and is usually referred to in the literature as overlearning. Level of overlearning is usually expressed as simply the number of practice trials that trainees perform after the criterion of mastery has been achieved, or it is expressed in percentage terms—50 percent overlearning, for example, means that trainees receive half again the number of trials that they took to achieve the mastery criterion. The arbitrary nature of mastery and overlearning criteria can make it difficult to do certain comparisons across studies. A trial that is part of mastery for one study can be part of overlearning for another study. It depends on how one defines *when* original learning is complete, how one *quantifies* the level of original learning or mastery, and how one *defines* the level of overlearning.

Those complications notwithstanding, it is clear that retention is better for overlearned tasks (e.g., Loftus, 1985; Schendel and Hagman,

1982; Slamecka and McElree, 1983). For enhancing retention, when to introduce the supplementary trials does not appear to be a critical factor; the level of overlearning is far more important than the time at which the supplementary trials are introduced (Schendel and Hagman, 1982). The literature also reveals, however, that providing overlearning trials reaches a point of diminishing returns (e.g., Bell, 1950; McGeoch and Irion, 1952; Melnick, 1971). In other words, increasing the number of overlearning trials may not produce proportionate increases in retention. Thus, although 100 percent overlearning may result in better retention than 50 percent, the additional gain that occurs may not be worth the additional time and practice.

Task Cohesion and Organization

In the literature on task retention, a given task is often classified as a discrete motor task, a continuous motor task, a procedural task, or a verbal task. Discrete tasks are characterized by a clearly defined beginning and end, such as responding to a signal by pressing a lever or saying a word. Continuous motor tasks require responding to information presented continuously—such as driving a car, which is a familiar example of a tracking task. Procedural tasks consist of a particular sequence of operations executed in the same way each time that the task is performed, such as disassembling and reassembling a rifle. Verbal tasks involve materials ranging from letters to nonsense syllables to words to meaningful prose, such as doing a crossword puzzle.

Considerable attention has been devoted in training to procedural tasks, probably because they are so easily forgotten and are common in almost all work situations. Such tasks may vary on several dimensions, such as the number of steps they contain, the degree to which performing one step cues another, the freedom to vary from a fixed sequence, the extent of planning required to execute the task, and the number of decision points. Shields et al. (1979) found that the rate of forgetting for a procedural task is predominantly a function of the number of steps needed to perform the task. Moreover, they found that what tended to be forgotten most were the steps not cued by equipment or by the preceding steps.

Consistent with such an argument, there is consensus in the literature that continuous motor tasks are better remembered than discrete or procedural tasks mainly because the former have a higher degree of inherent organization. Prophet (1976) proposed that the poor retention exhibited for certain procedural tasks—such as instrument flying—was due primarily to a low degree of internal organization or cohesiveness. Thus, regardless of the type of task, it appears that it is the degree of organization or cohesiveness of the task that is a principal determinant of the level of original learning that is achieved and the amount that is retained in the long term (e.g., Hagman and Rose, 1983; Hurlock and Montague, 1982; Prophet, 1976; Schendel et al., 1978).

Enhancing Retention

Distribution of Practice

We have focused thus far on amount of practice during training, and have assumed that the level of performance achieved during training is a reasonable index of the level of learning achieved. For a fixed amount of practice, however, learning (as measured by a later retention test) depends on the temporal distribution of practice, and the nature of that dependency illustrates that performance during training is an unreliable indicator of learning. In general, massing of practice on some component of the to-be-learned task produces better performance in the short term (e.g., during training) but much poorer performance in the long term than does spacing of practice. In some cases, massed practice yields long-term recall performance less than one-half the level that results from spaced practice, and two massed practices are often not appreciably better than a single study trial (see, e.g., Glenberg, 1979; Glenberg and Lehmann, 1980; Melton, 1970; and Rothkopf and Coke, 1966).

The so-called spacing effect—that practice sessions spaced in time are superior to massed practices in terms of long-term retention—is one of the most reliable phenomena in human experimental psychology. The effect is robust and appears to hold for verbal materials of all types and for motor skills (for reviews, see Crowder, 1976; Dempster, 1990; Lee and Genovese, 1988). A recent indication of how durable the advantages of spacing may be across truly long posttraining intervals was reported by Bahrick and Phelps (1987). They tested subjects' recall of English-Spanish word pairs 8 years after the original training phase. During the training phase, successive practice sessions were separated by 30 days, 1 day, or 0 days. The level of retention was highest for the 30-day spacing of study sessions, next highest for the 1-day spacing, and lowest for the 0-day spacing, with performance for those in the 30-day condition more than twice that for those in the 0-day condition.

Given the benefits of spaced practice and the fact that those benefits have been known to researchers since the beginning of controlled research on human memory (Ebbinghaus, 1913), one would expect that spaced repetition would be a major component of modern programs of training and instruction. The fact that this not seem to be the case is something of a puzzle (see Bjork, 1979; Dempster, 1990). Part of the solution to that puzzle, of course, may be a point we have already stressed: during the training process itself, spaced practice may appear inferior to massed practice.

Another factor in the apparent neglect of scientific findings on distribution of practice by those responsible for the design of training programs is time pressure: massed sessions take less total time than do spaced sessions. A study by Baddeley and Longman (1978), carried out for the British Post Office, illustrates the point. Given a new sorting system, which required postal workers to enter postcodes into a sorting machine using a standard typewriter keyboard, a large number of postal workers needed to be taught to type in a relatively short period of time. Baddeley and Longman examined four different training schedules, ranging from 1 hour of practice per day (spaced) to 4 hours of practice per day (massed). In terms of the learning curve—a plot of mean keystrokes per minute as a function of hours of practice—spaced practice was far more efficient than massed practice. To reach any given level of performance, however, it took the 1-hour-per-day group many more days than it took the 4-hours-per-day group, and the authors report that the former group was the least satisfied because the members felt they were falling behind the groups that were getting more practice per day. Thus, spaced practice produced much more efficient learning as a function of time on task, but took more days, which could certainly be a negative factor from a management standpoint.

Fostering Understanding

Just as the organization or cohesiveness of the components of a task makes it easier to learn and remember, so too does the organizing influence of understanding (Horton and Mills, 1984; Wertheim, 1985; Wetzel et al., 1983). In a story, independent or vaguely related occurrences are similar to steps of a procedural task that are not logically arranged and, hence, do not signal each other. When relevant organizing information is provided before reading a fragmented story, this information supplies a coherent structure within which to interpret more effectively the exact meaning of the story (Owens et al., 1979). Moreover, when this structure is also compatible with a trainee's general knowledge of the world, recall is enhanced (Morris et al., 1979).

There is considerable evidence suggesting that long-term retention of procedural tasks that are based on complex rules or principles can be enhanced by augmenting instruction with explanations or information designed to increase a learner's understanding of the to-be-learned tasks (Gentner, 1980, 1982; Smith and Goodman, 1984; Tourangeau and Sternberg,

1982; Kieras, 1981; Sturges et al., 1981). Although researchers differ to some extent on how they define explanations, it seems useful to categorize them as linear, structural, and functional (Stevens and Steinberg, 1981; Smith and Goodman, 1984). Linear explanations tell a trainee what to do—that is, what steps to follow and in what order. Structural explanations clarify how or why different task components belong together. Functional explanations inform the trainee about the cause-and-effect relationships among task components. In general, linear and structural explanations are used for static tasks, such as assembling a piece of equipment; functional explanations are used for dynamic tasks, such as operating a piece of equipment. In an examination of some of the literature dealing with the long-term retention of conceptual information and procedures inherent in expository prose as a function of structural explanations, Konoske and Ellis (1985:13) conclude that effective structural explanations "should include spatial and component-part information . . . as well as . . . goal statements. In addition, structural information should be communicated using text, schematics, graphs and illustrations, whenever possible."

In another study, Kieras and Boviar (1984) provided subjects in an experimental group with a "mental model" functional explanation of a new device that they were required to learn to operate: a mental model is an internal conceptual structure that corresponds to some aspect of the world (see, e.g., Gentner and Stevens, 1983). The subjects in the control group were not provided with any explanation; they had to learn the procedures solely by memorizing them. The researchers found that the functional model was more effective for enhancing retention one week after original learning than was learning by rote. They explained the superiority of the functional model by claiming that it was more pertinent to the operation of the device and could be used to cue operational procedures that might not otherwise have been retained. This finding and explanation supports Farr's (1987) position that the long-term retention of procedural knowledge and skills can be greatly enhanced if trainees understand why tasks must be performed in a particular order and way; the relationship of the parts to the whole task; and how new task information is related to what is already known. Farr (1987:78) claims:

Understanding enables the trainee to (a) furnish himself with cues to help retrieval; (b) recognize the relationship of externally provided or system-provided cues to the sought-for-memory; and/or (c) rebuild or regenerate what was apparently forgotten by capitalizing on the conceptual/ideational scaffolding supplied by the understanding. Understanding also provides organizational coherence, thereby chunking and integrating the information into fewer knowledge-representation/retrieval structures, and decreasing the memory burden.

Qualitative explanations, whether direct or analogical, can enhance retention by functioning as an instructional strategy to help a learner establish a meaningful relationship between new information and what is already known and understood. Evidence supporting this approach is provided by Mayer (1975), who used linear and structural explanations on a computer to enhance the learning and retention of software programming. There is considerable evidence to suggest that qualitative explanations help a learner develop models for making new knowledge fit more meaningfully into his or her existing knowledge structures by relating the new knowledge or skill to what has been previously learned and understood. The resulting effect is that the learning and retention of principle- and rule-based complex tasks are enhanced (Gentner, 1980, 1982; Kieras, 1981; Sturges et al., 1981; Tourangeau and Sternberg, 1982).

In summary, qualitative explanations that promote understanding of a to-be-learned task are effective for enhancing retention, presumably because they enable a trainee to reach a higher level of original learning. (The role of such explanations is discussed further in the next chapter as an important part of training techniques that use the expert as a model to guide the trainee.)

Involving the Learner

An important generalization that emerges from several domains of basic and applied research is that long-term retention is enhanced when a learner is an active participant rather than a passive observer during the training process. The inefficiency of humans as passive receivers of information reflects a fundamental property of human memory: a person does not behave like a simple recording apparatus. The storage of new information is a matter of actively interpreting that new information is terms of what is already known, and the reliable retrieval of information from memory requires practicing the retrieval process. Several kinds of research support this generalization.

Cooperative Learning, Peer Teaching, and Related Techniques   In the field of education there is abundant evidence that participation by students accomplishes more learning than presentations by instructors. Cooperative learning procedures—in which small groups of students work together on a common problem or project—have been shown to enhance later performance (see, e.g., Johnson et al., 1981; Slavin, 1983) as do peer teaching, proctoring, and coaching programs, in which students participate in the teaching process on a one-on-one or group level (see, e.g., Goldschmid and Goldschmid, 1976; Kulik et al., 1980).   In

LIBRARY
COLBY-SAWYER COLLEGE
NEW LONDON, NH 03257

fact, the performance of both the givers and receivers of such student instruction appears to profit from the interaction, and the attitudes of students about the instructional process become more positive as well. In sum, cooperative learning techniques, peer-teaching techniques, and all other such programs in which students take an active role in their own learning lead to improved performance (see, e.g., Rothkopf, 1981).

Practice on Procedural Tasks   Overall, it is probably an understatement to say that most training programs involve too much in the way of talking, presenting, and demonstrating on the part of a trainer and too little in the way of answering, producing, and practicing on the part of the trainee. Especially in the case of procedural tasks, listening and watching are ineffective compared with doing—although, of course, doing requires some initial level of learning. For example, watching someone demonstrate how to use an oxygen mask or inflatable lifevest or how to give cardiopulmonary resuscitation is not good preparation for executing those tasks when they are needed. Procedural skills must be practiced and exercised (see, e.g., Schneider, 1985). With increasing complexity of a task, a large amount of practice may be necessary to meet criterion levels of skill, and, initially, components of the task may need to be practiced separately.

The Effects of Generation   The "generation effect" (Slamecka and Graf, 1978) refers to the fact that verbal information generated by subjects (learners) in response to cues presented by an experimenter is better remembered at a later time than is information presented for study. Generation effects have been demonstrated with many types of verbal materials and with a variety of initial cuing procedures. It has also been shown (e.g., Wittrock and Carter, 1975) that subjects who generate their own organization of verbal materials (such as a hierarchical grouping of related words) remember those materials better at a later time than do subjects who are simply given such an organization. In general, there is much to be said for the "Socratic method" of instruction, in which the instructor's goal is to get the learner to produce answers and solutions.

Tests as Learning Events   Related to the effects of generation is the finding that the act of retrieving information presented earlier facilitates later retrieval of that information (see, e.g., Bjork, 1975; Landauer and Bjork, 1978; Rea and Modigliani, 1985). That is, an act of recall is itself a potent learning event—more potent, in general, than is an opportunity to study the information in question. From the standpoint of long-term retention, tests appear to play the important role of reducing the forgetting that would otherwise take place. Landauer and Ainslie (1975), for example, found that in a college-style technical course, performance on a repeated final examination 1 year later was greatly facilitated by an intervening test with that exam at 6 months. The group with the 6-month test showed virtually no memory loss across the year (from the end-of-course final exam to the repeated final exam 1 year later), and they performed at a much higher level on the 1-year test than did the group with no intervening test.

Another virtue of tests is that they appear to trigger subsequent study opportunities (e.g., Izawa, 1970). That is, more learning appears to take place on the basis of information presented after a test of a learner's memory for that information than takes place without such a test. One interpretation of such results is that tests provide feedback to the learner—clarifying to some extent what has been learned and what remains to be learned—which puts the learner in a better position to take advantage of subsequent information.

The advantage of tests embedded in the training process may grow as the posttraining retention interval gets longer. In contrasting the effects of prior study and test trials, Hogan and Kintsch (1971) found that study trials were superior to test trials in terms of performance at the end of the experimental session, but that test trials were superior to study trials on a test of recall 48 hours later. Once again, then, a condition that may appear to produce better performance during training (in this instance, study trials) may not be optimal in terms of long-term retention.

Refresher Training

Since the focus of this chapter is on original training and what can be done therein to enhance long-term retention and transfer, a thorough discussion of an important related matter—the kinds of posttraining interventions that are useful in maintaining performance at a high level over time—is beyond its scope. In this section, however, we do want to make clear that in many cases posttraining refresher programs are necessary, whatever the program of initial training.

As a retention interval (i.e., nonuse period) increases, the absolute amount of forgetting increases at a negatively accelerated rate (Annett, 1979; Gardlin and Sitterley, 1972; Hagman and Rose, 1983; Hurlock and Montague, 1982; Naylor and Briggs, 1961; Prophet, 1976; Schendel et al., 1978). Refresher learning, practice, or rehearsal is typically needed during such nonuse periods to maintain a given level of knowledge or skill. An important practical consideration, however, is whether a relearning program is even feasible. If it is not, as in emergency situations in which the originally learned knowledge or skill must be at a high enough level to ensure errorless performance in the first real-world execution, then a more intensive refresher program is recommended.

Being able to predict how much forgetting is likely to occur over any given posttraining retention interval is important for determining the refresher training, practice, or rehearsal conditions needed for maintaining performance at an acceptable level. Two approaches to predicting such forgetting have been proposed. An algorithm used by Rigg and Gray (1981; also, Rigg, 1983), which is based on mathematical learning theory, uses performance data from a trainee's initial learning trial to predict the likely rate of forgetting. The approach seems promising, but the empirical tests of the algorithm are too sketchy at present for evaluating it. The algorithm developed by Rose et al. (1984, 1985) for procedural tasks is based on the internal organization or cohesiveness of a given task. This technique, referred to as user's decision aid, estimates how often refresher training should be given to a unit of soldiers to maintain proficiency at a particular level. Although this aid is a promising algorithmic technique for dealing with procedural-task forgetting during nonuse periods, it is obviously more desirable to protect against such forgetting in the first place, if possible, by implementing conditions in training that lead to a high level of original learning and enhanced retention.

The spacing of refresher training, practice, or rehearsal has been found to be important for maintaining any given level of achieved knowledge or skill over nonuse periods. Bahrick (1979) recommends that the spacing be at intervals approximately equal to the expected nonuse interval separating successive occasions when that knowledge or skill needs to be exercised. A related idea is that novices in a given field should get rehearsals of a given skill at about the same intervals that professionals in the field tend to need to exercise that skill.

An important practical point on refresher training is that the practice or rehearsal needs of retrainees appear to be different from those of new trainees. Relatively efficient, cost-effective techniques can be used to maintain a given level of original learning or mastery during nonuse periods for retrainees. One such technique is to substitute covert (imaginary) practice and symbolic rehearsal for the conditions that were used in original training (Annett, 1979; Naylor and Briggs, 1961). Research by Landauer and Bjork (1978) and Bjork (1988) suggests that it may even be optimal to expand the successive intervals between practice sessions. Another technique is to reduce the fidelity of simulation during refresher training, practice, or rehearsal because it does not have to be as high as in original training (Naylor and Briggs, 1961). A third technique is to employ selected part-task training or conceptual simulation instead of the complete original training conditions (Hutchins et al., 1985; Stevens and Steinberg, 1981; Young, 1983). Lastly, brief or partial cuing conditions can also be used as an effective technique: for example, procedural skills can often be rapidly remembered by reminder information, written or oral.

TRANSFER OF TRAINING

As just noted, training performance (i.e., level of original learning) may or may not be an effective predictor of posttraining performance when the training and posttraining contexts are the same or quite similar. When the training and posttraining contexts differ, however, many of the most effective procedures for facilitating the kind of learning that supports transfer apparently impair performance during training. In this section we first discuss the role of level of original learning and perceived similarity between tasks as general factors in the transfer of training; we then discuss some specific procedures during training that enhance transfer to different posttraining contexts.

General Factors in Transfer

Level of Original Learning

The level of original learning is not only a major determinant of retention, it is also a major determinant of transfer. Positive transfer increases with the level of original learning as long as structurally similar responses are required in the training and transfer tasks. The greater the similarity between the tasks, in terms of both stimulus and response requirements, the greater the positive transfer between them (e.g., Ellis, 1965; Osgood, 1949; Schmidt and Young, 1987).

One might expect, for example, some positive transfer between a tennis serve and an overhand volleyball serve because of the similarities in stimuli (a tossed ball) and response requirements (an overhand throwing motion). However, when a new response is paired with a previously learned stimulus, negative transfer may initially occur (Siipola, 1941). An example of negative transfer occurred in the evolution of the butterfly stroke in swimming (described by Fischman et al., 1982). Before the 1960s, the butterfly stroke was swum using a breaststroke kick. The introduction of the dolphin kick produced some negative transfer among butterfly swimmers, probably because of the pairing of this new kick with the traditional armstroke. When there is little or no association between the stimulus-response requirements of two tasks, no transfer is expected: one would not, for example, expect significant transfer effects between the movement patterns of golf and bowling.

It seems important to know the specific relationships between level of original learning, task similarity, and positive transfer, but we found no recent studies that examined the transfer of cognitive or motor tasks as a function of the amount of learning. Several studies of complex problem solving, however, suggest that performance improves with practice of the rules defining the task (e.g., Anzai and Simon, 1979; Kotovsky et al., 1985).

When negative transfer is expected from a training task to a posttraining task—that is, when structurally dissimilar responses are required in the training and transfer tasks—the effects of level of original learning are more complicated. Research on animal learning and on human verbal learning (Mandler, 1968) found that as the level of original learning increases, transfer becomes increasingly negative but that transfer becomes positive at high levels of original learning. Mandler proposed that negative transfer due to response competition increases monotonically to an asymptote as training is extended and the level of original learning increases. Extended training, however, also produces a type of generalized learning that is consistent with the transfer task as well as the training task. Such generalized learning has positive influences that eventually become stronger than the negative influence of response competition. Such an interpretation is consistent with the "learning to learn" idea—that is, learning general problem-solving strategies that are suitable for both training and transfer tasks.

Perceived Similarity Between Tasks

It has been known for some time that, in general, the basis for transfer from a training task to a transfer task are the common components shared by both tasks (Thorndike, 1903). The greater the number of components common to the training and transfer tasks, the greater their similarity, which should lead to greater positive transfer. Gick and Holyoak (1987) propose that *any* salient similarity between training and posttraining tasks will influence a trainee's perceived similarity between the tasks, which in turn will trigger retrieval of the trainee's mental representation of the training situation during the transfer task. The greater the perceived similarity between the training and posttraining tasks, the more likely it is that a trainee will attempt to transfer what was learned during training to the posttraining task. If transfer is attempted, then the direction of transfer—whether it is positive or negative—will be determined by the similarity between the training and posttraining tasks in terms of features that are causally relevant to the goals of the tasks or to the responses required in the posttraining task.

The features of a given task may be either structural or surface characteristics (Holyoak, 1985). Structural characteristics are causally related to goal attainment; surface characteristics have no such relationship. In the absence of structural similarity, perceived similarity could be based on surface features that may produce negative transfer. It is important to understand that perceived similarity is not simply a function of the objective properties of the two situations. Perceived similarity is also a function of other factors, such as the knowledge or expertise of the individual (Chi et al., 1981) and the context of the two situations (Tversky and Gati, 1978).

It has also been hypothesized that similarity of goals and processing between training and transfer tasks may enhance perceived similarity between those tasks, which will then prompt reminding and transfer even in the absence of explicit instructions or hints to apply the pertinent relevant knowledge (Gick and Holyoak, 1987). In an interesting two-phase experiment, Weisberg et al. (1978) found that the absence of shared goals does not aid memory. In the first phase, subjects were asked to learn a list of paired associates, one of which was the pair box-candle. In the second phase, the subjects were asked to solve Duncker's box-candle problem, which is to figure out a way to attach a candle to a wall using only the materials provided (which include a candle and a box of tacks). The solution involves emptying the box of tacks, using one tack to mount the empty box on the wall, and using melted wax to affix the candle to the top of the box. Weisberg et al. (1978) found that the prior paired-associate learning task did not aid the subsequent problem-solving task. Thus, it is the goal of the task itself, not the particular parts of the problem, that prompts past experience. What is important is the similarity of processing between training and transfer tasks. The chance of obtaining positive transfer is more likely when performers process the training and transfer tasks in a similar way so that compatible responses in both tasks are produced (Bransford and Franks, 1976; Bransford et al., 1979; Lung and Dominowski, 1985; Morris et al., 1977).

In summary, whether or not transfer occurs from training to posttraining is a function of perceived similarity between the two contexts. Perceived similarity of the two tasks is a function of any salient shared component and of a number of other factors, such as expertise and context. To a great extent, an individual's expertise on the subject determines whether the similarities observed are surface features or structural features. Whether actual transfer is positive or negative depends on the actual amount of structural similarity. Transfer is positive when the training and transfer responses are highly similar, that is, when they contain many shared structural components and few distinctive components. Thus, the *amount* of transfer obtained between situations is a function of the perceived similarity; the *direction* of transfer is a function of the objective structural similarity. The greater the perceived similarity of the situations, the greater the amount of transfer. No transfer takes place when two situations are perceived as unrelated, regardless of the degree of response similarity. If a learner does not perceive the similarity between training and posttraining contexts, the level of performance achieved in training clearly will not predict posttraining performance.

Enhancing Transfer

Some of the most promising methods of training for transfer to altered contexts create difficulties for a learner during training. Some of the most promising of those methods involve creating certain types of interference, introducing variability, and reducing the frequency of external feedback.

Providing Contextual Interference During Training

Research on contextual interference shows that learning that requires more cognitive processing is related to better retention and transfer. Contextual interference involves changes in the training context, including changes in the task, practice conditions, and the processing used by trainees. Contending with such changes demands cognitive processing that can, in turn, enhance the level of original learning. These changes have been referred to as "contextual variety," which Battig (1979) believes is closely related conceptually to "transfer appropriate processing" (Bransford et al., 1979). Battig also considers contextual variety to be a way of overcoming the boundaries in memory performance imposed by encoding specificity—in which there is a need to reinstate the original encoding context during a test—to improve performance (Tulving and Thomson, 1973).

One example of contextual interference is provided in a study conducted by Shea and Morgan (1979). They studied the learning of three similar procedural motor tasks that required adult subjects to knock down a series of barriers (with their hands) in a designated order as fast as possible without making any errors. Each of the tasks consisted of a separate pattern of barrier contacts for each trial of training. The three tasks were practiced in two ways, "blocked" and "random": blocked practice involved performing 18 trials of one task before performing 18 trials of each of the other two tasks; random practice involved a random ordering of the three tasks over the 54 total trials. Following training, subjects transferred to either blocked or random conditions with a 10-minute and a 10-day interval. The major finding was that random practice produced poorer performance than blocked practice in training, but it produced superior performance in the posttraining context. This finding has been supported by other studies of adult learners (see Magill and Hall, 1990, for a review).

Another example, using a laboratory task, involved learning certain finger movements; the interference was having or not having the trainees also learn to articulate nonsense terms (e.g., XENF) to match the finger movements. The result was more proficient transfer performance on a different version of the finger task for those who learned the nonsense terms (Battig, 1956, 1966). This finding could be interpreted as showing that the contextual interference between word pronunciations and finger movements generated enhanced transfer. In other words, intratask interference in training produces greater intertask transfer.

Battig (1972, 1979) and others (for reviews, see, e.g., Fendrich et al., 1988; Magill and Hall, 1990; Shea and Zimny, 1983) have confirmed this effect and demonstrated that having to overcome high contextual interference during training produces poor performance in training but enhanced retention and transfer, for both cognitive and motor tasks. Whether or not contextual interference occurs is largely contingent on the degree to which the posttraining task is the same as the one used in original learning. This result follows directly from the "encoding specificity principle" (Tulving and Thomson, 1973) and from the findings of classical intertask transfer research—that an appreciable change from the original learning or encoding situations usually results in decrements in retention or transfer (Battig, 1979).

Battig (1979) explains this effect by proposing that multiple and variable processing strategies have to be used to overcome high contextual interference in order to encode the knowledge or skill being learned. Theoretically, training or practicing under a condition of high contextual interference produces more elaborate and distinctive processing, which enhances retention. Presumably, elaborations during processing produce memory structures for the knowledge or skills learned that are richer and more discriminable and thus lead to easier retrieval. The extent to which positive transfer is enhanced is believed to be a function of the degree to which the contextual interference induces processing strategies that are appropriate for learning other tasks (Morris et al., 1977; Bransford et al., 1979). Since contextual variety should lead to more elaborate and distinctive encoding, it is likely to offer stronger resistance to the typically negative effects that are found when posttraining tasks are changed. In other words, encoding specificity is more likely to be overcome if the original encodings occurred under high contextual variety. Conversely, similar task contexts should induce processing consisting mainly of the development of discriminative and organizational change suited to the specific task demands. Thus, item similarity in original learning of a task should produce better retention or transfer when the task is the same in posttraining as it was in original training. In summary, incorporating contextual variety in training introduces functional interference that makes learning less context dependent and involves trainees in processing activity that in turn produces enhanced retrieval from memory and the ability to adapt their performance to different contexts.

Several studies involving retention and comprehension of verbal materials bear an interesting relationship to the idea of contextual interference. Mannes and Kintsch (1987) had subjects study a brief technical article (on industrial uses of microbes) after studying either an outline that was consistent with the organizational structure of the article or one that was inconsistent (but contained the same information). On tests of verbatim knowledge (e.g., verbatim recall of statements from the article or true-false judgments of whether a given statement did or did not appear in the article), the consistent outline produced better performance, but on tests that required drawing inferences or proposing (or ranking) possible solutions to potential problems, the inconsistent outline produced better performance. The consistent outline apparently resulted in a simpler, more coherent representation in memory, which served to guide verbatim recall and recognition, but did not support processes of generalization and inference. The inconsistent outline, in forcing subjects to resolve organizational discrepancies, apparently resulted in a more embellished, abstracted representation in memory, a representation that contained fewer literal details from the article but that permitted more of the kind of extrapolation that underlies generalization and inference.

Smith et al. (1978) demonstrate that simply varying the environmental context across study sessions on a list of words improves later recall in a novel setting. Smith and Rothkopf (1984) show that such environmental variation can enhance retention of instructional content as well: they manipulated whether four successive 2-hour lectures in a miniature statistics course were given in the same location or in four different locations. They found that recall of key concepts a week after the course was better for students in the varied-context condition. They also found—consistent with the advantages of distributed practice and for both the same-context or varied-context conditions—that presenting the four lectures on four successive days resulted in better recall than presenting all the lectures on one day.

It is of interest to note that training under high contextual interference enhances task retention and transfer in a fashion analogous to supplementary practice: that is, it increases the level of original learning or overlearning. This retention and transfer outcome suggests that training under high contextual interference may be conceptualized as being functionally equivalent to training with additional practice (Farr, 1987). It also suggests that the level of overlearning is being indirectly manipulated by varying the level of contextual interference during training, and so could be viewed as similar to directly manipulating the level of overlearning by varying the amount of supplementary practice.

It can also be argued that even direct manipulations enhance retention and transfer to some extent as a result of the quality of processing during original learning and overlearning. Typically, the enhancement of retention that results from giving supplementary practice to increase the level of overlearning is attributed to the strengthening of connections due directly to the additional trials. However, Mandler (1968) argues against this interpretation because he believes that a retrievable trace is primarily the product of organization—that mere acts of rehearsal or repetition associated with additional practice do not by themselves produce a retrievable trace. Rehearsal or repetition simply allows a learner to establish initial categories and place items into them or to reorganize the categories. Of course, rehearsal or repetition may also provide a learner with the opportunity for more elaborate, deeper processing of information, as Battig (1979) originally proposed. Mandler's position is clearly too extreme in that certain types of stimulus-driven learning take place as a product of mere exposure and repetition, without intentionality on the part of the learner (see Roediger, 1990, for a review of such phenomena); in terms of subsequent purposeful recall of information, however, it seems safe to say that the quality of processing is clearly more important than the duration of processing. The large body of work carried out within the "levels of processing" framework (Craik and Lockhart, 1972) supports this generalization, and that work also supports the generalization that it is the nature of initial processing, not the subject's intent to learn or remember, by itself, that determines later recall performance.

Increasing Variability and Variety in Training

In this section we examine some transfer studies in which performers learned by examples without being given a rule for or a definition of a category. In two of these studies (Gick and Holyoak, 1983; Homa and Cultice, 1984) positive transfer of knowledge was found to increase with the number of examples provided during training for a category-learning task. Theoretically, increases in the number of examples in training should increase the chance of learning the most appropriate rules for transfer on the basis of the features that are structurally associated with category membership. However, optimal positive transfer depends on the representativeness or variability of the examples provided with respect to the category (Anderson et al., 1979). High variability of examples in training generally facilitates transfer; low variability increases the chance that trainees will undertake the transfer task without rules for classifying examples that they have never encountered before (Fried and Holyoak, 1984). Although high variability of examples in training tends to enhance transfer if learning is successful, it may impair learning at the outset, especially if the examples are few in number (Peterson et al., 1973).

When a large variety of examples are given during training, the order in which they are presented may affect learning (Nitsch, 1977). Moreover, the optimal order of examples may depend on performers' approach to the learning task. Using a classification task, Elio and Anderson (1984) found that transfer was better when examples with low-variability were presented first, but only when learners were instructed not to look for a deterministic rule for category membership (i.e., an implicit learning strategy). Examples with high variability examples were best presented first if learners were instructed to look for a rule defining category membership. In general, it is important to realize that instructions given to learners can influence the processing strategies they use during training, which in turn can affect both learning and transfer (Brooks, 1978; McAndrews and Moskovitch, 1985; Medin and Smith, 1981; Sweller et al., 1982).

The findings discussed thus far are based on transfer studies in which subjects learned by examples without being provided with a rule for or definition of a category. When an abstract rule or definition of a category for the task is given to subjects, the inclusion of examples with such abstract training facilitates transfer (Cheng et al., 1986; Gick and Holyoak, 1983; Nitsch, 1977). There is some evidence, however, that in certain situations only a minimal number of examples need to be provided (Fong et al., 1986). It appears that including an abstract rule with examples in training is particularly useful when the training and transfer items are superficially dissimilar (Gick and Holyoak, 1983) or when it is difficult to determine the rule from the examples alone (Cheng et al., 1986; Fong et al., 1986).

In the motor domain, much of the recent research on variability of practice has been conducted within Schmidt's (1975, 1982) schema theory of discrete motor skill learning (discussed above). This theory proposes that practice produces abstract rules that control classes of movement responses, with each class being represented by a generalized motor program. For example, kicking motions such as those involved in kicking a soccer ball are assumed to be generated by a generalized motor program. Kicking a soccer ball a certain distance at a given speed is produced by specifying parameters (e.g., overall duration or force of the response) for the generalized program. Parameters are selected on the basis of schemata or rules, developed from past experience with the program: these schemata specify the association between the environmental outcomes of the kicking movements and the values of the parameters selected. When an individual wants to kick a certain distance, his or her schema specifies the parameter for the generalized motor program for kicking, and the program is executed with this parameter value. Thus, the movements needed to generate each individual kick do not have to be stored or represented, and the soccer player can produce novel kicking movements that have not been used before. An important prediction of this theory is that increased variability of practice pertinent to the generalized program would impair performance in training, but would yield enhanced performance in posttraining on a transfer test to a novel task within the same response class. Many studies have investigated this prediction, and although the evidence is not entirely consistent, there is a reasonable amount of support for it (e.g., Catalano and Kleiner, 1984; Margolis and Christina, 1981; for a review, see Shapiro and Schmidt, 1982).

Recently, however, Schmidt and Young (1987) have interpreted the variability of practice effects found in previous studies in terms of blocked or random practice, that is, in terms of contextual interference. They suggest that the variability-of-practice effects may be nothing more than random-practice effects. Certain results, however, obtained by Wulf and Schmidt (1988) with adults and by Pigott and Shapiro (1984) and Wrisberg and Mead (1983) with children, seem difficult to interpret in terms of contextual interference effects.

In summary, training manipulations that involve number, variability, and order of examples for category-learning tasks and variability of practice for motor-learning tasks may impair training performance, but they appear to increase learning so that posttraining performance is enhanced. This is yet another line of evidence that indicates that the level of performance achieved in training is not a good predictor of learning and posttraining performance in transfer.

Reducing Feedback

Feedback is an integral part of most training programs. It can be defined as information resulting from an action, and it can be intrinsic or augmented. Intrinsic feedback is the information people receive as a natural consequence of their actions and takes two forms: proprioceptive feedback is the sensing of muscle, joint, or tendon activity, as in the feeling from executing a golf swing; visual feedback comes from the outcome of an activity, as in the flight path of a golf ball. Augmented feedback, which is the focus of this section, is information performers would not ordinarily receive as a result of their actions. It is provided by a source external to the performers, such as an instructor, mirror, or videotape system. Augmented feedback can be verbal, as when an instructor explains how to correct an error, or it can be nonverbal, as when an instructor demonstrates how to make a correction or shows a videotape replay of an individual's performance. Typically, augmented feedback comparing the performance outcome with some goal outcome is referred to as knowledge of results; augmented feedback that characterizes the movement pattern itself is referred to as knowledge of performance. (For other descriptions of different types of feedback, see e.g., Schmidt, 1988:423-426).

It has been known for some time that augmented feedback has a substantial effect on learning and performance during training (e.g., Thorndike, 1927). The focus here is on the influences that feedback has on retention and transfer during training. Much of the recent relevant research has been carried out in the motor domain (for reviews, see Newell, in press; Salmoni et al., 1984; Schmidt, in press). That research has challenged a commonly accepted generalization about augmented feedback that emerged from an abundance of prior research (see Bilodeau, 1966, 1969). That generalization is that any increase in feedback in training—in its immediacy, accuracy, or frequency—will improve learning and performance. Over the years, that generalization served as a basis for incorporating augmented feedback in the design of training programs and simulators. However, evidence from some recent studies in the motor domain (e.g., Schmidt et al., 1989; Winstein, 1988; Winstein and Schmidt, 1990) and several earlier studies in the verbal domain (e.g., Landauer and Bjork, 1978; Krumboltz and Weisman, 1962) raise questions about the validity of the generalization.

Generally, these studies manipulated augmented feedback in training by giving it less frequently, such as on every fifth trial instead of every trial; or by giving it on every early trial but gradually eliminating it on later trials; or by giving it in summary form over a set of trials. Essentially, these studies reveal that training with augmented feedback that is given less frequently or in summary form produces poorer performance in training than feedback administered after every trial, but it produces better posttraining performance in retention and transfer. These results can be interpreted as indicating that frequent augmented feedback during training functions primarily to guide behavior toward the criterion (i.e., training) performance but that it also may create a dependency in which the feedback is relied on to guide behavior, and the learning needed to produce proficient posttraining performance in retention or transfer either does not occur or occurs only at a weak level. This dependency on frequent augmented feedback could be the result of the trainees' not using information-processing strategies that would ordinarily be used to learn the task in training if feedback were available less often. Without having adequately learned the task, the trainees are at a disadvantage for retention or transfer when there is no (or less) feedback.

In summary, augmented feedback has traditionally been structured to bring about rapid acquisition of a task so that some criterion level of performance in training is achieved as quickly as possible. But the evidence now suggests that some of the commonly accepted ways in which augmented feedback has been manipulated to facilitate training performance are less than optimal for enhancing learning and posttraining performance. The evidence in this section (see also Schmidt and Bjork, 1992) indicates that the kind of feedback manipulations that enhance learning and posttraining performance actually decreases the rate at which performance improves during training.

The common denominator of the training procedures reviewed above is that they teach processes that can be called on by a posttraining task at a later time, particularly if the posttraining task and setting differ from the training task and setting. That is, such procedures induce "transfer-appropriate processing" (Morris et al., 1977). In responding to the "difficulties" introduced by contextual interference, variability in the conditions of practice, reduced feedback, and so forth, the learner is taught to carry out processes that result in a more elaborated mental representation of the task—a representation that can, to some extent, be used in a different context. The learner is better prepared, so to speak, not only to perceive the similarities between the training task and the different versions of that task in posttraining contexts, but also better equipped to perform by having achieved the more generalized declarative and procedural knowledge demanded by that category of task.

CONCLUSIONS AND IMPLICATIONS FOR TRAINING

Measuring Learning and Performance The effectiveness of a training program should be measured not by the speed of acquisition of a task during training or by the level of performance reached at the end of training, but, rather, by a learner's performance in the posttraining tasks and real-world settings that are the target of training.

Two important dimensions of posttraining performance are the ability to resist forgetting and interference over periods of disuse of a given skill and the ability to generalize training to contexts and tasks that differ in their surface characteristics from the training contexts or tasks. Depending on the relative priorities given to those two dimensions of posttraining performance, the optimal package of training components will differ somewhat. One general principle, however, is that tests of a learner's progress during training should, as much as possible, measure performance as it will be measured on the posttraining task(s) in the posttraining setting(s).

Retention Given posttraining tasks and conditions that are identical or similar to the training tasks and conditions, posttraining performance is enhanced as the level of original learning is increased. That level can be increased by putting greater demands on the learner—making the criterion of mastery more difficult, for example, or requiring supplementary (postmastery) practice after the criterion has been reached. Introducing variations in the conditions and sequencing of practice, the immediate consequence of which is to degrade performance, may be a particularly promising way to increase the level of original learning, and, hence, posttraining retention.

Skills that demand little attention or effort to perform are regarded as automatic; the more automatic a given skill, the higher the likelihood that the skill can be retained over nonuse periods without refresher training. Certain types of procedural tasks, however, tend to be easily forgotten, especially when their components have a low degree of internal organization or cohesiveness. The rate of forgetting of procedural tasks is a function of the number of steps needed to perform the task, and the steps most likely to be forgotten are those not cued by the equipment, environment, or preceding steps.

Several instructional strategies to enhance the retention and transfer of procedural tasks can be derived from the research on learning: relating the knowledge to be learned to the relevant knowledge learners already have in memory; teaching techniques (e.g., mnemonics) that learners can use to provide their own elaborations; having the training regimen require repeated use of the knowledge to be learned; and providing for and encouraging the use and elaboration of acquired knowledge and skill during nonuse periods. In general, a learner should be an active participant, not a passive observer, during the training process.

However well designed the initial training, refresher training may still be needed during posttraining periods of disuse in order to maintain a given level of knowledge and skill; refresher training can become less frequent over time. The training needs of retrainees are different from those of new trainees; relatively efficient, cost-effective techniques can be used to maintain a given level of original learning in retrainees.

Transfer of Training   In general, the similarity of goals and cognitive processing between training and transfer tasks is a critical factor in enhancing transfer.   A learner, therefore, should be challenged by means of manipulation of practice variables, such as feedback, contextual interference, and number and variability of examples.   These manipulations, which may impair training performance, not only help the learner to process the learning task more deeply, but also suggest appropriate processes for transfer, particularly to related but distinct posttraining tasks.

REFERENCES

Anderson, J.R., P.J. Kline, and C.M. Beasley
   1979   A general learning theory and its application to schema abstraction. In G.H. Bower, ed., *The Psychology of Learning and Motivation*, Vol. 13. New York: Academic Press.

Annett, J.
   1979   Memory for skill. In M.M. Gruneberg and P.E. Morris, eds., *Applied Problems in Memory*. London: Academic Press.

Anzai, Y., and H.A. Simon
   1979   The theory of learning by doing. *Psychological Review* 86:124-140.

Baddeley, A.H., and D.J.A. Longman
   1978   The influence of length and frequency on training sessions on the rate of learning to type. *Ergonomics* 21:627-635.

Bahrick, H.P.
   1979   Maintenance of knowledge: questions about memory we forgot to ask. *Journal of Experimental Psychology, General* 108:296-308.
   1987   Retention of Spanish vocabulary over 8 years. *Journal of Experimental Psychology: Learning, Memory, and Cognition* 13:344-349.

Battig, W.F.
   1956   Transfer from verbal pretraining to motor performance as a function of motor task complexity. *Journal of Experimental Psychology* 51:371-378.
   1966   Facilitation and interference. In E.A. Bilodeau, ed., *Acquisition of Skill*. New York: Academic Press.
   1972   Intratask interferences as a source of facilitation in transfer and retention. In R.F. Thompson and J.F. Voss, eds., *Topics in Learning and Performance*. New York: Academic Press.
   1979   The flexibility of human memory. In L.S. Cermark and F.I.M. Craik, eds., *Levels of Processing in Human Memory*. Hillsdale, N.J.: Erlbaum.

Bell, H.M.
   1950   Retention of pursuit rotor task after one year. *Journal of Experimental Psychology* 40:648-649.

Bilodeau, I.M.
   1966   Information feedback. In E.A. Bilodeau, ed., *Acquisition of Skill*. New York: Academic Press.
   1969   Information feedback. In E.A. Bilodeau, ed., *Principles of Skill Acquisition*. New York: Academic Press.

Bjork, R.A.
   1975   Retrieval as a memory modifier: an interpretation of negative recency and related

phenomena. In R.L. Solso, ed., *Information Processing and Cognition.* New York: Wiley.

1979   Information-processing analysis of college teaching. *Educational Psychologist* 14: 15-23.

1988   Retrieval practice and the maintenance of knowledge. Pp. 397-401 in M.M. Gruneberg, P.E. Morris, and R.N. Sykes, eds., *Practical Aspects of Memory II.* London: Wiley.

Bransford, J.D., and J.J. Franks

1976   Toward a framework for understanding learning. In G.H. Bower, ed., *The Psychology of Learning and Motivation,* Vol. 10. New York: Academic Press.

Bransford, J.D., J.J. Franks, C.D. Morris, and B.S. Stein

1979   Some general constraints on learning and memory research. In L.S. Cermack and F.I.M. Craik, eds., *Levels of Processing in Human Memory.* Hillsdale, N.J.: Erlbaum.

Brooks, L.

1978   Nonanalytic concept formation and memory for instances. In E. Rosch and B. Lloyd, eds., *Cognition and Categorization.* Hillsdale, N.J.: Erlbaum.

Catalano, J.R., and B.M. Kleiner

1984   Distant transfer and practice variability. *Perceptual and Motor Skills* 58:851-856.

Cheng, P.W., K.J. Holyoak, R.E. Nisbett, and L.M. Oliver

1986   Pragmatic versus syntactic approaches to training deductive reasoning. *Cognitive Psychology* 18:293-328.

Chi, M., P. Feltovich, and R. Glaser

1981   Categorization and representation of physics problems by experts and novices. *Cognitive Science* 5:121-152.

Craik, F.I.M., and R.S. Lockhart

1972   Levels of processing: a framework for memory research. *Journal of Verbal Learning and Verbal Behavior* 11:671-684.

Crowder, R.G.

1976   *Principles of Learning and Memory.* Hillsdale, N.J.: Erlbaum.

Dempster, F.N.

1990   The spacing effect: a case study in the failure to apply the results of psychological research. *American Psychologist* 43:627-634.

Ebbinghaus, H.

1913   *Memory* (H.A. Ruger and C.E. Bussenius, trans.). New York: Teachers College. (Original work published 1885; paperback ed., New York: Dover, 1964).

Elio, R., and J. Anderson

1984   The effects of information order and learning mode on schema abstraction. *Memory and Cognition* 7:397-417.

Ellis, H.C.

1965   *The Transfer of Learning.* New York: Macmillan.

Farr, M.J.

1987   *The Long-Term Retention of Knowledge and Skills: A Cognitive and Instructional Perspective.* New York: Springer-Verlag.

Fendrich, D.W., A.F. Healy, L. Meiskey, R.J. Crutcher, W. Little, and L.E. Bourne, Jr.

1988   Skill Maintenance: Literature Review and Theoretical Analysis. Technical report AFHRL-TP-87-73. Air Force Human Resources Laboratory, Brooks Air Force Base, Texas.

Fischman, M.G., R.W. Christina, and M.J. Vercruyssen

1982   Retention and transfer of motor skills: a review for the practitioner. *Quest* 33:181-194.

Fong, G.T., D.H. Krantz, and R.E. Nisbett

1986   The effects of statistical training on thinking about everyday problems. *Cognitive Psychology* 18:253-292.

Fried, L.S., and K.J. Holyoak
    1984 Induction of category distributions: a framework for classification learning. *Journal of Experimental Psychology: Learning, Memory, and Cognition* 10:234-257.

Gardlin, G.R., and T.E. Sitterly
    1972 Degradation of Learned Skills: A Review and Annotated Bibliography. Boeing Company, Seattle, Washington.

Gentner, D.
    1980 The Structure of Analogical Models in Science. Technical Report 4451. Bolt Beranek and Newman, Inc., Cambridge, Massachusetts.
    1982 Are scientific analogies metaphors? In D.S. Miall, ed., *Metaphor: Problems and Perspectives*. Brighton, England: Harvester Press, Ltd.

Gentner, D., and A.L. Stevens
    1983 *Mental Models*. Hillsdale, N.J.: Erlbaum.

Gick, M.L., and K.J. Holyoak
    1983 Schema induction and analogical transfer. *Cognitive Psychology* 15:1-38.
    1987 The cognitive basis of knowledge transfer. In S.M. Cormier and J.D. Hagman, eds., *Transfer of Learning: Contemporary Research and Applications*. San Diego, Calif.: Academic Press.

Glenberg, A.M.
    1979 Component-levels theory of the effects of spacing of repetitions on recall and recognition. *Memory and Cognition* 7:95-112.

Glenberg, A.M., and T.S. Lehmann
    1980 Spacing repetitions over 1 week. *Memory and Cognition* 8:528-538.

Goldschmid, B., and M.L. Goldschmid
    1976 Peer teaching in higher education: a review. *Higher Education* 5:9-33.

Hagman, J.D., and A.M. Rose
    1983 Retention of military skills: a review. *Human Factors* 25:199-213.

Hogan, R.M., and W. Kintsch
    1971 Differential effects of study and test trials on long-term recognition and recall. *Journal of Verbal Learning and Verbal Behavior* 10:562-567.

Holyoak, K.J.
    1985 The pragmatic of analogical transfer. In G.H. Bower, ed., *The Psychology of Learning and Motivation*, Vol. 19. New York: Academic Press.

Homa, D., and J. Cultice
    1984 Role of feedback, category size, and stimulus distortion on the acquisition and utilization of ill-defined categories. *Journal of Experimental Psychology: Learning, Memory, and Cognition* 10:83-94.

Horton, D.L., and C.B. Mills
    1984 Human learning and memory. *Annual Review of Psychology* 35:361-394.

Hurlock, R.E., and W.E. Montague
    1982 Skill Retention and Its Implications for Navy Tasks: An Analytic Review. NPRDC SR 82-21. Navy Personnel Research and Development Center, San Diego, Calif.

Hutchins, E.L., J.D. Hollan, and D.A. Norman
    1985 Direct Manipulation Interfaces. ICS Report 8503. University of California, La Jolla.

Izawa, C.
    1970 Optimal potentiating effects and forgetting-prevention effects of tests in paired-associate learning. *Journal of Experimental Psychology* 83:340-344.

Johnson, D.W., G. Maruyama, R. Johnson, and D. Nelson
    1981 Effects of cooperative, competitive, and individualistic goal structures on achievement: a meta analysis. *Psychological Bulletin* 89:47-62.

Jones, M.B.
    1985   Nonimposed Overpractice and Skill Retention. Technical report no. 86-55. Army
           Research Institute for the Behavioral and Social Sciences, Alexandria, Va.
Jonides, J., M. Naveh-Benjamin, and J. Palmer
    1985   Assessing automaticity. *Acta Psychological* 60:157-171.
Kieras, D.E.
    1981   Knowledge Representation in Cognitive Psychology. Technical report no. 7. Per-
           sonnel and Training Research Programs, Office of Naval Research, Arlington, Va.
Kieras, D.E., and S. Boviar
    1984   The role of mental model in learning to operate a device. *Cognitive Science* 8:255-
           273.
Konoske, P.J., and J.A. Ellis
    1985   Cognitive Factors in Learning and Retention of Procedural Tasks. Paper presented
           at the April meeting of the American Education Research Association, Chicago,
           Illinois.
Kotovsky, K., J.R. Hayes, and H.A. Simon
    1985   Why are some problems hard? Evidence from Tower of Hanoi. *Cognitive Psychol-
           ogy* 17:248-294.
Krumboltz, J.D., and R.G. Weisman
    1962   The effect of intermittent confirmation in programmed instruction. *Journal of Edu-
           cational Psychology* 53:250-253.
Kulik, J.A., C.C. Kulik, and P.A. Cohen
    1980   Effectiveness of computer-based college teaching: a meta-analysis of findings. *Re-
           view of Educational Research* 50:525-544.
Landauer, T.K., and K.I. Ainslie
    1975   Exams and use as preservatives of course-acquired knowledge. *The Journal of
           Educational Research* 69(3):99-105.
Landauer, T.K., and R.A. Bjork
    1978   Optimum rehearsal patterns and name learning. In M.M. Gruneberg, P.E. Morris,
           and R.N. Sykes, eds., *Practical Aspects of Memory*. London: Academic Press.
Lee, T.D., and E.D. Genovese
    1988   Distribution of practice in motor skill acquisition: learning and performance effects
           reconsidered. *Research Quarterly for Exercise and Sport* 59:277-287.
Loftus, G.R.
    1985   Evaluating forgetting curves. *Journal of Experimental Psychology: Learning, Memory,
           and Cognition* 11:397-406.
Lung, C.T., and R. Dominowski
    1985   Effects of strategy instructions and practice on nine-dot problem solving. *Journal of
           Experimental Psychology: Learning, Memory, and Cognition* 11:804-811.
Magill, R.A., and K.G. Hall
    1990   A review of the contextual interference effect in motor skill acquisition. *Human
           Movement Science* 9:241-289.
Mandler, G.
    1968   Association and organization: facts, fancies, and theories. In T.R. Dixon and D.L.
           Horton, eds., *Verbal Behavior and General Behavior Theory*. Englewood Cliffs,
           N.J.: Prentice-Hall.
Mannes, S.M., and W. Kintsch
    1987   Knowledge organization and text organization. *Cognition and Instruction* 4:91-
           115.
Margolis, J., and R.W. Christina
    1981   A test of Schmidt's schema theory of discrete motor skill learning. *Research Quar-
           terly for Exercise and Sport* 52:474-483.

Mayer, R.E.
1975 Different problem-solving competencies established in learning computer programming with and without meaningful models. *Journal of Educational Psychology*
67:725-734.

McAndrews, M.P., and M. Moskovitch
1985 Rule-based and exemplar-based classification in artificial grammar learning. *Memory
and Cognition* 13:469-475.

McGeoch, J.A., and A.L. Irion
1952 *The Psychology of Human Learning*, 2nd ed. New York: Longman, Green, and
Company.

Medin, D.L., and E.E. Smith
1981 Strategies and classification learning. *Journal of Experimental Psychology: Human
Learning and Memory* 7:241-253.

Melnick, M.J.
1971 Effects of overlearning on the retention of a gross motor skill. *Research Quarterly*
42:60-69.

Melton, A.W.
1970 The situation with respect to the spacing of repetitions and memory. *Journal of
Verbal Learning and Verbal Behavior* 9:596-606.

Montague, W.E.
1988 What Works: Summary of Research Findings with Implications for Navy Instruction and Learning. Technical report NAVEDTRA 115-1. Office of the Chief of
Naval Education and Training, Pensacola, Florida.

Morris, C.D., J.D. Bransford, and J.J. Franks
1977 Levels of processing versus transfer appropriate processing. *Journal of Verbal
Learning and Verbal Behavior* 16:519-533.

Morris, C.D., B.S. Stein, and J.D. Bransford
1979 Prerequisites for the utilization of knowledge in recall of prose passages. *Journal of
Experimental Psychology: Human Learning and Memory* 5:253-261.

Naylor, J.C., and G.E. Briggs
1961 Long-Term Retention of Learned Skill: A Review of the Literature. ASD technical
report 61-390. Laboratory of Aviation Psychology, Ohio State University.

Newell, K.M.
In   Augmented information and the acquisition of skill. In R. Daugs and K. Bliscke,
press eds., *Motor Learning and Training*. Schorndorf, West Germany: Hoffman.

Nitsch, K.E.
1977 Structuring Decontextualized Forms of Knowledge. Unpublished doctoral dissertation. Vanderbilt University.

Osgood, C.E.
1949 The similarity paradox in human learning: a resolution. *Psychological Review*
56:132-143.

Owens, J., G.H. Bower, J.B. Black
1979 The "soap opera" effect in story recall. *Memory and Cognition* 7:185-191.

Peterson, M.J., R.B. Meagher, Jr., H. Chait, and S. Gillie
1973 The abstraction and generalization of dot patterns. *Cognitive Psychology* 4:378-
398.

Pigott, R.E., and D.C. Shapiro
1984 Motor schema: the structure of the variability session. *Research Quarterly for
Exercise and Sport* 55:41-45.

Prophet, W.W.
1976 Long-Term Retention of Flying Skills: A Review of the Literature. HumRRO final
report 76-35. Human Resources Research Organization, Alexandria, Va.

Rea, C.P., and V. Modigliani

1985 The effect of expanded versus massed practice on the retention of multiplication facts and spelling lists. *Human Learning* 4:11-18.

Rigg, K.E.

1983 Optimization of Skill Retention in the U.S. Army Through Initial Training and Analysis and Design. McFann-Gray and Associates, Monterey, Calif.

Rigg, E.E., and B.B. Gray

1981 Estimating Skill Training and Retention Functions Through Instructional Model Analysis. McFann-Gray and Associates, Monterey, Calif.

Roediger, H.L., III

1990 Implicit memory: retention without remembering. *American Psychologist* 45:1043-1056.

Rose, A.M., M.Y. Czarnolewski, F.E. Gragg, S.H. Austin, P. Ford, J. Doyle, and J.D. Hagman, Jr.

1984 Acquisition and Retention of Soldering Skills. Technical report no. 671. Army Research Institute for the Behavioral and Social Sciences, Alexandria, Va.

Rose, A.M., P.H. Radtke, H.H. Shettel, and J.D. Hagman

1985 User's Manual for Predicting Military Task Retention. Report no. AIR FR37800. American Institutes for Research, Washington, D.C.

Rothkopf, E.Z.

1981 A macroscopic model of instruction and purposeful learning. *Instructional Science* 10:105-122.

Rothkopf, E.Z., and E.V. Coke

1966 Variations in phrasing and repetition interval and the recall of sentence materials. *Journal of Verbal Learning and Verbal Behavior* 5:86-91.

Salmoni, A.W., R.A. Schmidt, and C.B. Walter

1984 Knowledge of results and motor learning: a review and critical reappraisal. *Psychological Bulletin* 95:355-386.

Schendel, J., J. Shields, and M. Katz

1978 Retention of Motor Skills: Review. Technical Paper 313. U.S. Army Research Institute for the Behavioral and Social Sciences, Alexandria, Va.

Schendel, J.D., and J.D. Hagman

1982 On sustaining procedural skills over a prolonged retention interval. *Journal of Applied Psychology* 67:605-610.

Schmidt, R.A.

1975 A schema theory of discrete motor skill learning. *Psychological Review* 82:225-260.

1982 The schema concept. Pp. 219-235 in J.A.S. Kelso, ed., *Human Motor Behavior: An Introduction.* Hillsdale, N.J.: Erlbaum.

1988 *Motor Control and Learning: A Behavioral Emphasis*, 2nd ed. Champaign, Ill.: Human Kinetics.

In Frequent augmented feedback can degrade learning: evidence and interpretations.
press In G.E. Stelmach and J. Requin, eds., *Tutorials in Motor Neuroscience.* Dordrecht, The Netherlands: Kluwer.

Schmidt, R.A., and R.A. Bjork

1992 New conceptualizations of practice: common principles in three research paradigms suggest important new concepts for practice. *Psychological Science* (June).

Schmidt, R.A., and D.E. Young

1987 Transfer of movement control in motor skill learning. In S.M. Cormier and J.D. Hagman, eds., *Transfer of Learning: Contemporary Research and Applications.* San Diego, Calif.: Academic Press.

Schmidt, R.A., D.E. Young, S. Swinnen, and D.C. Shapiro

1989 Summary knowledge of results for skill acquisition: support for the guidance hypothesis. *Journal of Experimental Psychology: Learning, Memory, and Cognition* 15:352-359.

Schneider, W.
1985 Training high-performance skills: fallacies and guidelines. *Human Factors* 27:285-300.

Schneider, W., and R.M. Shiffrin
1977 Controlled and automatic information processing: detection, search, and attention. *Psychological Review* 84:1-66.

Schneider, W., S.T. Dumais, and R.M. Shiffrin
1984 Automatic and control processing and attention. In R. Parasuraman and D.R. Davies, eds., *Varieties of Attention*. Orlando, Fla.: Academic Press.

Shapiro, D.C., and R.A. Schmidt
1982 The schema theory: recent evidence and developmental implications. In J.A.S. Kelso and J.E. Clark, eds., *The Development of Movement Control and Coordination*. New York: Wiley.

Shea, J.B., and R.L. Morgan
1979 Contextual interference effects on the acquisition, retention, and transfer of a motor skill. *Journal of Experimental Psychology: Human Learning and Memory* 5:179-187.

Shea, J.B., and S.T. Zimny
1983 Context effects in memory and learning movement information. In R.A. Magill, ed., *Memory and Control of Action*. Amsterdam, Holland: North-Holland.

Shields, J.L., S.L. Goldberg, and J.D. Dressel
1979 Retention of Basic Soldering Skills. Research report no. 1225. U.S. Army Research Institute for the Behavioral and Social Sciences, Alexandria, Va.

Shiffrin, R.M., and W. Schneider
1977 Controlled and automatic human information processing: perceptual learning, automatic attending, and a general theory. *Psychological Review* 84:127-190.

Siipola, E.M.
1941 The relation of transfer to similarity in habit-structure. *Journal of Experimental Psychology* 28:233-261.

Slamecka, M.J., and P. Graf
1978 The generation effect: delineation of a phenomenon. *Journal of Experimental Psychology: Human Learning and Memory* 4:592-604.

Slamecka, M.J., and B. McElree
1983 Normal forgetting of verbal lists as a function of their degree of learning. *Journal of Experimental Psychology: Learning, Memory, and Cognition* 9:384-397.

Slavin, R.E.
1983 *Cooperative Learning*. New York: Longman, Inc.

Smith, E., and L. Goodman
1984 Understanding instructions: the role of explanatory material. *Cognition and Instruction* 1:359-396.

Smith, S.M., and E.Z. Rothkopf
1984 Contextual enrichment and distribution of practice in the classroom. *Cognition and Instruction* 1(3):341-358.

Smith, S.M., A.X. Glenberg, and R.A. Bjork
1978 Environmental context and human memory. *Memory and Cognition* 6:342-353.

Stevens, A., and C. Steinberg
1981 Project Steamer: Taxonomy for Generating Explanations of How to Operate Complex Physical Devices. NPRDC Technical note 81-21. Navy Personnel Research and Development Center, San Diego, Calif.

Sturges, P., J. Ellis, and W. Wulfeck
1981 Effects of Performance-Oriented Text Upon Long-Term Retention of Factual Mate-

rial. NPRDC Technical report no. 81-22). Navy Personnel Research and Development Center, San Diego, Calif.

Sweller, J., R. Mawer, and W. Howe
1982   Consequences of history-cued and means-ends strategies in problem solving. *American Journal of Psychology* 95:455-483.

Thorndike, E.L.
1927   The law of effect. *American Journal of Psychology* 39:212-222.
1903   *Educational Psychology.* New York: Lemcke and Buechner.

Tourangeau, R., and R. Sternberg
1982   Understanding and appreciating metaphors. *Cognition* 11:203-244.

Tulving, E., and D.M. Thomson
1973   Encoding specificity and retrieval processes in episodic memory. *Psychological Review* 80:352-373.

Tulving, T.
1985   How many memory systems are there? *American Psychologist* 40:385-398.

Tversky, A., and I. Gati
1978   Studies in similarity. In E. Rosch and B.B. Lloyd, eds., *Cognition and Categorization.* Hillsdale, N.J.: Erlbaum.

Walberg, H.J.
1990   Productive teaching and instruction: assessing the knowledge base. *Phi Delta Kappa* 71:470-478.

Weisberg, R., M. Di Camillo, and D. Phillips
1978   Transferring old associations to new situations: a non-automatic process. *Journal of Verbal Learning and Verbal Behavior* 17:219-228.

Wertheim, A.H.
1985   Some Remarks on the Retention of Learned Skills. Paper presented at NATO Conference on Transfer of Training, September-October, Brussels, Belgium.

Wetzel, S.K., P.J. Konoske, and W.E. Montague
1983   Estimating Skill Degradation for Aviation and Antisubmarine Warfare Operators (AWs): Loss of Skill and Knowledge Following Training. Technical report NPRDC SR-83-31. Navy Personnel Research and Development Center, San Diego, Calif.

Winograd, T.W.
1975   Frame representations and the declarative-procedural controversy. In D.G. Bobrow and A.M. Collins, eds., *Representation and Understanding: Studies in Cognitive Science.* New York: Academic Press.

Winstein, C.J.
1988   Relative Frequency of Information Feedback in Motor Performance and Learning. Unpublished doctoral dissertation, University of California, Los Angeles.

Winstein, C.J., and R.A. Schmidt
1990   Reduced frequency of knowledge of results enhances motor skill learning. *Journal of Experimental Psychology: Learning, Memory, and Cognition* 16:677-691.

Wittrock, M.C., and J.F. Carter
1975   Generative processing of hierarchically organized words. *American Journal of Psychology* 88:489-501.

Wrisberg, C.A., and B.J. Mead
1983   Developing coincident timing skill in children: a comparison in training methods. *Research Quarterly for Exercise and Sport* 54:67-74.

Wulf, G., and R.A. Schmidt
1988   Variability in practice: facilitation in retention and transfer through schema formation or context effects? *Journal of Motor Behavior* 20:133-149.

Young, R.M.
1983   Surrogates and mappings: two kinds of conceptual models for interactive devices. In D. Gentner and A. Stevens, eds., *Mental Models.* Hillsdale, N.J.: Erlbaum.

4

Modeling Expertise

Modeling an expert literally means watching and imitating what an expert does. For instance, in learning a motor task such as serving in tennis, it would mean a novice's observing how the tennis teacher throws her elbow back and how far she reaches behind her back with her racket. The observation itself may in fact be more accurate than the teacher's own analysis of how she actually serves. Conversely, in correcting the student's serve, the teacher can observe the outcome of the serve—where the ball landed—and conclude what might have been the postural cause and provide feedback accordingly. For "transparent" tasks such as motor tasks (playing tennis) or other physical skills (such as weaving), the connection between the purpose and process of an action taken and its outcome is direct, and correction is straightforward, although often difficult to achieve.

There are two obvious difficulties in using direct modeling for complex cognitive tasks. First, the rationale for the performance of the tasks is not only opaque to observers, but may also be implicit for the experts: they may not be able to describe their own thought processes or the rationale for them, even though they can perform the tasks. Second, in order to properly coach a novice, an expert may have to formulate an accurate mental model of the novice's understanding of the task (sometimes called the student model). But a novice's understanding of a task is not always obvious to the expert. These two key problems—which are woven throughout this chapter—suggest that there might be a limitation on the extent to which direct modeling of complex cognitive skills can be done.

For example, suppose that a trainee is asked to learn to diagnose a fault when the instrument panel shows three problems: warning light A is flashing (condition A), dial B is off (condition B), and the sound system is generating a warning tone (condition C). The expert arrives and on seeing the three conditions, takes the following three actions: checks the power supply (action X), swaps the board (action Y), and resets a gauge (action Z). By observing this sequence of actions, what can the trainee learn? The trainee could learn a set of individual local rules, such as: if condition A holds, then take action X; if condition B holds, take action Y, and so forth. In order to learn this simple sequence of conditional action rules, the trainee has to accomplish two processes. First, he or she must learn to identify what the precise condition is for each action. Was it the flashing light that mattered (condition A), or was it the yellow flashing light rather than a blue flashing light that mattered? Second, the trainee has to link the condition with the action. For example, dial B, saying "off," initiates resetting a gauge. Inducing these simple local rules are by no means trivial, but once learned, they can be quite powerful in troubleshooting a number of problems.

It may be, however, that the expert's actions were not meant to be interpreted as a sequence of local conditional rules, but that a conjunctive rule should have been learned: if the pattern of A, B, and C conditions occurs, then take actions X, Y, and Z. This means that if conditions A, B, and F occur, one would not take action X, action Y, and some alternative third action that is an appropriate action to condition F in isolation; instead, perhaps when the pattern of conditions A, B, and F, occurs, some totally different action should be taken. Alternatively, perhaps conditions A, B, and C lead the expert to realize that this is a special kind of fault Q, which normally can be solved by taking actions X, Y, and Z. If this is the case, then the trainee has to learn to identify what kind of conditions typically can be considered to be a type Q kind of fault so that the sequence of actions X, Y, and Z are appropriate. Direct modeling, in which a simple linking of actions to conditions is induced, typically results in nontransferable skills: the trainee has not understood and learned the reasons behind the actions, nor has the trainee accumulated the knowledge necessary to recognize the conditions which then generate the actions. (This simplistic example assumes that direct modeling is not accompanied by verbal explanations. The nature of effective explanations is itself an important and complex topic.)

In the first of this chapter's four sections, we consider direct modeling of complex cognitive skills. We focus on a body of contemporary research on cognitive apprenticeship. In the second section we review the ways in which experts excel, considering their possession of a greater knowledge base, the way that knowledge is organized, and processing strategies to solve problems. Since expertise is based on knowledge, which in turn generates the actions that experts take, we focus in the third section on the difficult process of extracting an expert's knowledge. The last section focuses on how knowledge extracted from experts can be imparted to novices.

COGNITIVE APPRENTICESHIP

There is one active body of research that promotes a technique for direct modeling of complex cognitive tasks, called cognitive apprenticeship (Collins et al., 1989). Cognitive apprenticeship borrows heavily from traditional apprenticeship, which is quite successful in teaching physical skills. Traditional apprenticeship involves three key components: observation, coaching, and practice. Observation means the apprentice participates as a spectator, observing a master or expert executing the target skill. Coaching refers to the guidance that the expert provides while the apprentice attempts to perform the task. Coaching physical skills involves two key features. First, the coaching or feedback is given in a continuous, on-line fashion. For example, as an apprentice in weaving is weaving the threads, the master might guide the apprentice's hands (Rogoff, 1986); it should be noted that the guidance provided in traditional apprenticeship is often physical demonstration, not verbal instruction. Second, the master provides conceptual "scaffolding," that is the support, in the form of reminders and help, necessary for the apprentice to perform an approximation of the composite task. The degree of scaffolding provided depends on the extent of help the apprentice needs. As the apprentice improves in his or her skill, the scaffolding can be "faded." The expert, therefore, must monitor the apprentice's "zone of proximal development" (Vygotsky, 1978), or "region of sensitivity to instruction" (Wood and Middleton, 1975). The zone of proximal development is the distance between the developmental levels at which children can perform a task alone and the level at which they can perform it with some assistance. Third, the apprentice practices with the master present. In this fashion, the apprentice begins by executing piecemeal aspects of the skill and yet enjoys the reward of the entire skill. The entire learning situation is embedded in practice or guided practice.

Cognitive apprenticeship consists of six key components: modeling, coaching, scaffolding (and fading), articulation, reflection, and exploration (Collins et al., 1989). The first three are provided mostly by the teacher (expert), and the last three are exercised by the learner (novice).

Modeling

Modeling cognitive tasks requires that the expert explain ("external-ize") as much of the process that underlies his or her actions as possible. For example, in solving a mathematics problem, the expert should talk out loud for the novice while coming up with the equation. This externalization is comparable to the think-aloud protocols that cognitive psychologists have been collecting as their data for analyzing the processes of problem solving (see Newell and Simon, 1972). Ideally, the train of thought should reveal all the knowledge that the expert is using, not only the factual and conceptual knowledge that is relevant to the substantive domain, but also such strategic knowledge as special heuristics for solving problems (such as "decomposing" the problem into subproblems or considering the problem as a "simplified or special case"); control strat-egies in making decisions, such as knowing which path to search; and learning strategies, such as scanning the table of contents before reading a book to get a general idea of what the book is about. The basic idea is to expose the complete thought processes of the expert, including searching the wrong paths, arriving at incorrect solutions, and so forth. Externalizing thought processes in this way should allow a novice to learn about heuristics that may be useful for solving problems.

There are two aspects to this procedure of externalizing one's thought processes. One aspect, which can be made known readily, is to make overt the solution trace that the expert is undertaking. That is, the expert simply articulates the operations he or she is carrying out as they are executed. The other aspect is more tacit and may not be exposed as readily: the expert explains the rationale for his or her selection of operations. The first aspect, exposing the "solution trace," tends to re-veal a strategy that the expert is following; the second aspect, exposing the rationale, may reveal the expert's knowledge structure. This proce-dure implies that modeling would be more effective in domains in which the use of a few strategies can promote learning and would be less effective in domains that require deep domain knowledge.

Schoenfeld's (1983) teaching of mathematics illustrates this distinc-tion. An excerpt of his protocol on finding the relationship between the roots of two polynomials with "reversed" coefficients shows the appli-cation of a special heuristic that he attempts to teach students to use. The heuristic is called "special cases," and the idea is to solve simpler cases, such as to find the roots of simpler quadratic equations rather than complex polynomials and to look for relations between the roots. If one fails to "see" any relationship among the roots, then the next step is to further reduce the polynomials to linear cases and solve for their roots. The expert thus reduces the complex polynomials to simpler equations:

first to quadratic, then to linear equations. The expert then observes a pattern in the solution of linear cases—that the roots are reciprocals of each other.

The key strategy that Schoenfeld wants to get across is to generate and test for a series of straightforward examples and then to see if some sort of pattern emerges. The processes of doing so are exposed to the student by having the expert talk out loud as he or she solves problems. Thus, basically, the expert is modeling the strategies of generate-and-test and is reducing the problem to simpler ones. What the expert is not modeling is the rationale for rejecting certain roots after testing or how to select a set of roots to consider in the first place. For example, the first pair of roots that Schoenfeld obtained from the quadratic equation were

$$\frac{-b \pm \sqrt{b^2 - 4ac}}{2a} \text{ and } \frac{-b \pm \sqrt{b^2 - 4ac}}{2c} .$$

He then dismisses these by saying, "I don't really see anything that I can push or that'll generalize." How did Schoenfeld know that these roots are uninteresting, without the potential for generalization? It is clear that by carefully grading the exercise problems for the students, they will have learned the strategy of reducing the problem to simple ones and of trying to look for patterns. However, no pattern can be detected unless a student has recognizable patterns already stored in memory. The point is that one can easily model the strategy that an expert is undertaking, but it is more difficult to model and expose the tacit knowledge that the expert might be using to carry out the strategy.

In sum, this kind of modeling (exposing the reasoning processes) is far superior to traditional instruction in which a student is simply given a solution (such as a worked-out example) and expected to induce the steps that were undertaken to arrive at the solution; however, some aspects of the rationale of an expert's reasoning processes may still remain tacit and not be easy for students to follow.

Coaching and Scaffolding

Coaching consists of observing students who are performing a task and offering hints, feedback, reminders, new tasks, or redirecting a student's attention to a salient feature—all with the goal of making the students' performance approximate the expert's performance as closely as possible. In traditional apprenticeship, coaching is fairly constant and continuous. From the protocol excerpt cited in Collins et al. (1989), the coaching provided by the teacher was predominantly in the form of prompts for students either to summarize, ask questions, make predictions, or clarify difficulties. Interspersed with prompts were feedback (such as remarks about the quality of the summary or definitions of terms) and modeling (used here more in the sense of imitation rather than exposing the reasoning process). As mentioned above, however, it is not clear how a teacher knows which prompts and guidelines to give—or what feedback to provide—unless the teacher has an accurate idea of the student's mental model.

Scaffolding refers to the support a teacher provides so that the student can succeed in performing the task. This support can be suggestions, hints, actual execution of parts of the task, or physical props such as providing cue cards (Scardamalia et al., 1984). Scaffolding thus involves cooperative execution by an expert and a student, in a way that allows the novice to take an increasingly larger burden for performing the task. In both scaffolding and coaching, the expert is required to monitor the student's progress and understanding. Such monitoring processes are demanding and complex, and they are not well understood by cognitive psychologists. It is not now clear which aspects of cognitive apprenticeship are more effective in promoting learning—modeling or scaffolding and coaching. It is likely that the advantage gained results from an interactive effect. An excellent example of a successful apprenticeship learning program is provided by Brown and Palincsar (1989), in which they used modeling, coaching, and scaffolding to teach students four strategic skills for reading comprehension: formulating questions about the text, summarizing, making predictions about what will come next in the text, and clarifying difficulties with the text. The students' acquisition and use of these skills improved their comprehension tremendously.

Articulation, Reflection, and Exploration

The purpose of modeling in cognitive apprenticeship is to encourage students to undertake three activities: articulation, reflection, and exploration. Articulation, defined broadly, involves any kind of overt constructive activity carried out by a student, such as explaining the reasoning in an example problem (Chi et al., 1989b), summarizing, predicting, clarifying and asking questions (Palincsar and Brown, 1984), posing problems (Sharples, 1980), editing or revising the text and formulating hypotheses (Collins and Stevens, 1983) or goals (Schuell, 1991). The cognitive outcome of these activities is the integration, synthesis, and linking of knowledge in memory.

Reflection refers to the process of evaluating one's own problem-solving processes and comparing them with another student's or the teacher's processes. Such comparison presumably leads to the perception of ambiguity, conflicts, and so forth, which will allow the student to modify his or her own problem-solving or decision-making processes. Reflection seems to involve complex processes: since it is known that confrontation by a teacher is not necessarily an effective means of instruction, it is not clear why self-perceived conflicts as obtained through reflection would be effective at promoting learning.

Exploration refers to the pursuing of new goals, formulating and testing new hypotheses, conducting experiments, and so forth. Although it may not be clear why each of these processes might work, the common characteristic of articulation, reflection, and exploration is the pursuit of activities that can foster an integration and synthesis of a student's newly acquired knowledge, so that additional knowledge can be inferred and constructed.

It is important to emphasize that in cognitive apprenticeship one cannot separate the role of the expert from the role of the learner. The expert's role entails modeling the target skill, preferably accompanying it with explanation of the rationales; modeling the use of learning and monitoring strategies; monitoring the student's progress and understanding; and providing feedback. How all this is accomplished in a social context is not yet understood. In fact, studies of tutoring show that experts in a tutoring situation often do not formulate ideas of students' mental models nor tailor feedback to the student's current level of understanding (Putnam, 1987). Hence, an important aspect of cognitive apprenticeship lies in the constructive activities in which the student or apprentice engages. We return to this point below.

HOW EXPERTS EXCEL

The cognitive science literature on expertise in the last two decades has concentrated primarily in demonstrating how experts excel in the domain for which they have expertise. The focus has been on three issues: how experts perform on laboratory tasks such as recall, recognition, problem solving, and decision making; how the knowledge of experts and novices differ; and how the strategies that experts and novices use to perform the tasks that they are given differ.

Measures in Laboratory Tasks

One way to try to assess the abilities of an expert is by means of standard laboratory tasks used by experimental psychologists, such as recall, recognition, comprehension, speed of performance, monitoring accuracies, automaticity, flexibility, and so forth. We illustrate the first four of these below.

One of the most widely used laboratory measures of expertise is recall. Experts such as chess masters can remember a far greater number of chess pieces from a chess board than can a beginning player. For example, if a chess board with pieces that define a midgame position is shown to both expert and novice chess players for 5 seconds, the expert player can reproduce the locations of about 25 chess pieces, while novices can reproduce only 5 or 6 pieces (Chase and Simon, 1973). This measure holds true for any game domain in which recall can be easily measured, such as the game of GO or bridge (Charness, 1979; Reitman, 1976)

Experts are also better than others at recognizing the important features of a stimulus, such as an X-ray, a diagram of an electronic circuit (Egan and Schwartz, 1979), or a topological map. Basically, they can detect whatever salient features or patterns exist in the stimulus (Lesgold et al., 1988) and can recognize during later trials which sets of stimuli have been presented earlier. Chase and Ericsson (1981) showed, for example, that a person who had managed to develop an outstanding memory span—the ability to give back over 100 digits presented at the rate of 1 digit per second—could also recognize which subsequences of digits were the ones that had been presented in a previous memory trial.

Not surprisingly, experts can also better comprehend passages in a domain for which they have expertise. Chiesi et al. (1979) have shown that experts can also understand event sequences much better than can nonexperts. In baseball, for example, such greater comprehension is demonstrated by the ability to generate action outcomes that could happen on the next play, given a specific game state. In addition, the actions that they generate are important to the game's goal structure.

Monitoring accuracy refers to how accurately experts can monitor or assess their own cognitive states, such as how well they have understood a passage, how accurately they can predict how much effort they need to spend studying, or what they think they can remember. Again, experts are far more accurate than novices in predicting and assessing their own state of comprehension. In a study looking at how good and poor problem solvers study physics examples taken from a textbook, Chi et al. (1989b) found that the good solvers were much more accurate at assessing whether they had understood a specific line in an example solution. Moreover, when experts do not understand something, they know more specifically what aspect of the example they do not understand, so that the questions they ask about an example are more specific and targeted. Poor solvers are much more inaccurate in their monitoring of their own comprehension; they almost always think they have understood the example. Likewise, skilled chess players are more accurate than less skilled players at predicting how many times they need to look at the chessboard before they will remember the locations of all the chess pieces (Chi, 1978).

An example from physics problem solving shows another dimension of students' knowledge. Because experts can "see" beyond the surface description of a problem, and "know" the solution procedure, they tend to solve a problem by the appropriate method, such as using the force law. A student, however, might solve a pulley problem the same way he or she solved a previous pulley problem, simply because they both involve pulleys, without realizing that these two problems may require two different solution methods.

In sum, experts excel on laboratory tasks in their domain of expertise (see also Chi et al., 1988; Hoffman, 1991). There are two ways to explain why they excel: in terms of their knowledge structures or in terms of the strategies and heuristics they use. Each of these is discussed below.

Organized Knowledge Structures

Experts are able to perform more efficiently than novices on the types of tasks summarized because they have more knowledge. However, it is not merely the presence of knowledge that is responsible for the demonstration of skilled performance; rather, it is how that knowledge is organized. More knowledge, if improperly organized, actually leads to a deterioration of performance (Anderson, 1974).

There are various ways to portray the organization of experts' knowledge, corresponding more or less to the kind of knowledge that is being used during task performance. This knowledge organization can be characterized by schemas (mostly for declarative knowledge), production rules (for procedural knowledge), and mental models (for both). Schemas and production rules allow an expert to use knowledge flexibly and efficiently, to represent problems in a deep way so as to access automatic processes, to recognize patterns and chunks, and so forth.

Schemas involve both conceptual and factual knowledge. Experts have many more concepts, as well as many more features associated with each concept, than do novices. More important, their concepts are interrelated in meaningful ways, as reflected in their category structures. Chi and Koeske (1983) have shown, for example, that for a given partial set of concepts that is available to both experts and novices, the experts' concepts are interrelated in meaningful ways that correspond to family types (in this research the subject domain is dinosaur knowledge); novices' concepts are not interrelated in meaningful categories. The existence and importance of meaningful patterns of associations have been known for quite some time in visual-perceptual domains, such as chess playing. Chase and Simon (1973) showed that chess masters "see" patterns of interrelated chess pieces on the chess board. It is these familiar patterns of pieces that enable them to select the best move because these familiar patterns are associated with optimal moves.

Experts know many more facts than do nonexperts. In a domain such as physics, it is obvious that students must learn many facts—such as "A point mass may be considered to be a body" in Newton's force law, or that g is the gravitational constant. In another example of knowing more facts, of taxi drivers' knowledge of routes, Chase (1983) found that expert drivers can generate a far greater number of secondary routes (lesser known streets) than novice drivers; furthermore, they can use this knowledge by generating short-cuts to reach a target destination when there is an impasse on the main routes.

Again, the organization of facts is what facilitates their efficient use and what distinguishes expertise. A commonly discussed representation for factual knowledge is the schema or mental model, which is a knowledge structure that captures the essential features of concepts, categories, situations, or events. Thus, one way that factual knowledge about a category or an event is made coherent is through the structure imposed by a schema. For example, a schema about the concept of dog would contain prototypical instances, as well as key features that are true of a generic dog. Each feature can be thought of as a dimension with a range of acceptable values. Similarly, a complete coherent mental model of a city permits expert cab drivers to take efficient secondary routes when they encounter road blocks on the primary routes.

Mental models are analogous to a "structured analog of the world" (Johnson-Laird, 1983:165). They represent not only the objects and properties comprising a system or event, but, more importantly, they represent the structural, functional, and causal relations among the components. Moreover, a mental model can be "run" so that it can capture the dynamic aspects of a system. In many ways, one can conceive of experts' superior skill as having more accurate mental models.

Procedural knowledge generally refers to how one performs a task. There are two kinds of procedural knowledge. Domain-specific procedural rules are specific how-to rules that have actions attached to the conditions of application in the domain. For instance, in the domain of electronic troubleshooting, seeing a flashing light might trigger a rule of checking the power switch or some other switch. Domain-specific procedural knowledge, as the name implies, is related to a specific domain and cannot be used in a different domain; expert chemists, for instance, cannot solve agriculture problems (Voss et al., 1983).

It is clear that experts possess a large quantity of procedural rules that enable them to perform a task automatically and efficiently, as soon as they "see" the conditions. It should be stressed that the conditions are visible for all to see, but only the experts realize the import or meaningfulness of what is seen. Experts can perform some tasks automatically because many of these procedural rules, over time and with repeated use, become combined into one larger rule. Thus, several rules would have all their conditions concatenated, and upon seeing the conditions, a sequence of actions is automatically taken. Procedural knowledge is generally represented by condition-action rules, and the entire set of rules is called a production system.

Metaknowledge is knowledge about what one knows, as well as one's ability to monitor one's own comprehension state. This kind of knowledge has been tapped by tasks such as asking people to judge the difficulty of a problem and to allocate time and resources efficiently, which necessitates being sensitive to their capabilities and limitations. For example, experts are much more accurate than novices at judging how difficult it is to solve a given physics problem (Chi et al., 1982); good students are better at allocating their time for studying; and good students also are better at knowing when they understand the material and when they do not (Chi et al., 1989b).

Strategies of Problem Solving and Reasoning

Besides having superior knowledge structures, experts are believed to excel in their use of general strategies. For instance, solving a problem by going backward from the unknown to the givens is usually called a means-ends strategy. With a means-end strategy, a person's entire trace of problem-solving actions is guided by a strategy for solution in which the problem solver starts by using the unknowns as the goals and then searches for equations that can satisfy the unknowns. This strategy can be used in many domains, whether physics, algebra, or taxi routes. Two other additional general strategies are described below.

Experts are often said to have complex general reasoning skills, such as analogical comparison or reasoning. Scientific discoveries are often made by using analogies, but it is easy to demonstrate that reasoning by analogy is a heuristic that is available to everyone, even young children. The difference between experts and novices lies in how one elicits a particular case as an analogical one. Experts tend to be superior at picking the right case for making the comparison. This ability, again, can be attributed to the richness of their knowledge base. For example, Chi et al. (1989a) have shown that for children aged 4-7, those who have expertise in the domain of dinosaurs reason in much the same way as those who are novices. The difference is that when expert children elicit analogical cases to help them understand the features of a novel dinosaur, the cases are drawn from other dinosaurs, in fact, dinosaurs from the same family; in contrast, novices use other animals as comparative cases from which to reason analogically. Similarly, Schauble et al. (1989) looked at how good and poor solvers predict the outcome of a simple circuit and found that the solvers' understanding of the circuit exhibited the use of analogies. Both the good and the poor solvers showed the same frequency of analogy usage. The success of the good solvers, however, seemed to depend on their ability to pick the right analogy, one that shows deep understanding of both the analogy and the target domain. Thus, it appears that the availability of general strategies per se is not the deciding factor in determining an expert's superior performance; rather, it is the application of a general strategy to a well-organized knowledge domain that is critical.

One type of a general "divide-and-conquer" strategy is simplification, or decomposition. The strategy involves breaking down a problem into its subparts, solving each subproblem, and, finally, putting all the subproblem solutions together. Jeffries et al. (1981) found that the way expert software designers solve a complex problem is by decomposing it into simpler problems for which they already know the solutions. Another variant of the divide-and-conquer strategy is "subgoaling," which is simply picking out an intermediate state on the solution path as the temporary goal. In effect, subgoaling also divides a problem into two or more subproblems, thus reducing the entire search space into a smaller one after the subgoal is reached.

One common interpretation of these results is that experts' performance is far superior to that of novices because they use these strategies. One could equally argue, however, that the use of these strategies is a manifestation of the content knowledge that the experts have, and that these general strategies are available to everyone, novices and experts alike. The strategies are not used efficiently by the novices because their inadequate knowledge base does not permit such use. Thus, adopting strategies alone is not adequate for guiding a novice's execution of a solution, even though the trace of an expert's execution of the solution reflects the use of such a strategy.

A domain-specific reasoning strategy could either be a specific procedural rule that an expert knows in a given domain (e.g., if light A flashes, push switch X) or the application of a general strategy to a specific piece of knowledge. For instance, when an expert radiologist reads an X-ray efficiently and correctly, it need not imply that he or she used a more sophisticated scanning strategy, but, rather, that the radiologist recognized one shaded area as malignant, which suggested that another area might also be malignant (Lesgold et al., 1988). That is, the scanning path was dictated by the knowledge of what related areas may be malignant. This declarative knowledge would lead an expert to scan the two targeted area consecutively. Similarly, chess masters scan the chessboard very efficiently, in that they focus on the key important pieces on the board, such as the locations of the queen, king, rook, etc. (Simon and Barenfeld, 1969). Although much research has been devoted to showing how efficiently experts use specific strategies, the committee concludes that such use of efficient strategies is often a manifestation of an underlying coherent and rich knowledge base. This conclusion suggests that direct instruction of general strategies for novices may not always be helpful.

When Do Experts Not Excel?

In general, experts excel only when they can use their rich domain knowledge. In the classic chess experiment referred to above, expert and beginner players were asked to recall chess pieces after having looked at a chessboard position for 5 seconds. The experts exhibited spectacular recall of chess pieces when these pieces were placed on the board according to meaningful game positions. When the position of the same pieces on a board were determined randomly, however, expert's recall levels dropped to the level of novices. Thus, the experts excelled only when the chess pieces formed meaningful configurations that corresponded to patterns that they had developed in memory over the course of years (Chase and Simon, 1973).

Psychological measures of expertise—such as amount of recall, time to complete a task, or efficiency in sorting and recognizing a variety of problems and patterns—all show that experts excel largely because the stimuli used for the tasks are familiar and prototypical so that the processing is fairly automatic. That is, the processing involves a recognition or match between stored memory representations and the external stimuli, as in the case of X-ray or circuit diagrams. However, when experts are presented with nonroutine cases (e.g., there are no stored representation of the problem or its solution), they use a deliberate reasoning heuristic, such as a means-ends strategy. Similarly, their speed and efficiency also deteriorate. Norman et al. (1989) found that expert dermatologists' recognition time for typical disease cases is faster and more accurate than that of novices. However, for atypical cases, experts' reaction time was actually slower than that of novices. Obviously, for nonroutine cases, experts cannot invoke automated perceptual skills that are derived from a rich knowledge base. In these atypical cases, they must resort to the step-by-step deliberation that novices generally have to undertake, relying on their general strategies rather than domain-specific procedural rules.

ELICITING KNOWLEDGE FROM EXPERTS

Because experts' knowledge is complex, multifaceted, and often tacit, the problem of eliciting what experts know is a nontrivial problem. Different techniques yield different forms of knowledge, some declarative and some procedural. In addition, because some knowledge is more easily verbalized than others, different techniques of knowledge elicitation may bias what is being elicited.

A variety of methods can be used to elicit experts' declarative knowledge. To elicit experts' knowledge of concepts, the interrelations among the concepts, and perhaps even the coherence of the concepts, a common technique is a concept-listing task (Cooke and McDonald, 1987). In such a task, the subject is simply asked to list all the concepts related to a topic. Some assessment of the organization can be gleaned from this simple task by examining the order of the listing, as well as the content of the concepts listed. For example, prototypical items of a category tend to be listed most frequently (Rosch et al., 1976). In order to elicit subjects' organization about a specific domain of knowledge (such as the form and content of schemata in memory), ordered recall and grouping are often used. The groups that subjects either indicate explicitly (such as the perceptually related pieces on the board of a GO game; Reitman, 1976), or indicate implicitly (by order of recall), reveal the frequency of associations and interrelations among concepts. These kinds of methods can reveal the tacit conceptual structures among concepts (Chi and Koeske, 1983). Yet another common method of eliciting experts' declarative knowledge is through interviews, question and answers, and explanations (Chi et al., 1989b) or asking for the basic approach (Chi et al., 1982). In the last method, experts and novices are simply asked to state their basic approach to solving a problem; their answers indicate the kinds and content of their schemata.

All these methods mentioned do not typically reveal the kind of procedural knowledge that is attached to conceptual knowledge. One method for eliciting procedural knowledge from experts or novices is simply to ask them to perform the task, such as troubleshooting, solving problems, or making decisions, and note the sequence of actions they take. The problem with this approach is that the solver's trace (or sequence of actions) does not tell us what knowledge generated the particular trace. Some computer simulation models that are sensitive to this issue try to design a model in which the trace can be derived from the knowledge. However, the knowledge that is modeled to generate the derivation of such a trace is never unique, so that many models can be constructed that generate the same trace. This outcome suggests that observing overt actions is too coarse a method to capture the underlying procedural knowledge. Nevertheless, overt behavior in the course of performing a task is more likely to provide knowledge of the procedures than experimental laboratory-type tasks. Hanisch et al. (1988) showed, for example, that when expert telephone system operators are asked to identify features of a telephone system, they tend to generate declarative knowledge. However, when they were asked to act in specified situations, their actions produced procedural knowledge.

Whatever the method of knowledge elicitation a great deal of effort can be expanded on the analyses of the data, especially those that are collected by interviews (structured or unstructured) and think-aloud protocols. Although it is generally true that different methods of elicitation tend to uncover different kinds of knowledge, with ingenuity one might be able to capture both declarative and procedural knowledge. Alternatively, one might be able to devise more comprehensive methods of eliciting knowledge from experts. Klein (1990) has a taxonomy of 10 types of knowledge that one could elicit from an expert: procedures; specific details; declarative knowledge; physical relations; interpersonal knowledge; perceptual-cognitive skills; perceptual-motor skills; goals; precedents (special cases or incidents); cultural knowledge. In order to elicit all these types of knowledge, he has adapted a method introduced by Flanagan (1954) that he calls the critical decision method. One of the two key features of this method is that it focuses on nonroutine cases, which is assumed to expose experts' knowledge more thoroughly than routine cases. The second key feature is that the critical decision interviews are accompanied by specific probes that should elicit knowledge corresponding more or less to each of the types listed above. So, for instance, in order to elicit the knowledge about goals, the subject may be asked directly, "What were your specific goals at this time?"

But even if all the knowledge an expert has can be thoroughly elicited, a major problem remains: how to represent that knowledge in a way that can be transmitted to a novice. For example, expert systems, which are computer programs that embody expert knowledge, typically represent the expert knowledge by rules. Such rule-based codings may not be adequate for representing cultural practice, interpersonal knowledge, or even perceptual knowledge. This is a substantial problem and the focus of much current research.

IMPARTING EXPERTS' KNOWLEDGE TO TRAINEES

Once we know how to elicit expert's knowledge, then we need to know how to teach this knowledge to novices. The goal is to instruct skills in a way to ensure transfer and learning with understanding. This section discusses three approaches: direct instruction, computer-aided support systems, and cognitive apprenticeship.

Direct Instruction

The most traditional way of instructing skills is through a formal classroom, using textbooks and teachers' lectures. We need not recount here the failures that have been encountered by this approach. The most serious problem is that knowledge learned in a training setting or classroom does not transfer to the criterion setting—the real world. The appropriate conditions under which such a skill needs to be accessed and executed are not attached to the actions during training. For instance, the first thing fire fighters are typically taught to do is search and rescue. However, they are not usually taught the conditions under which such a routine should be disregarded, such as when a fire is getting started, and there could be a good chance of extinguishing it (Klein, 1990). Skill instruction typically focuses on a set of executable actions, and the relation between the actions and the conditions are usually not specified in the classroom. If instruction takes place in the targeted context, however, actions can be associated with the proper conditions.

One approach to textbook learning in the classroom that may meet with more success is to focus attention on the worked-out solutions or examples in the textbook. Zhu and Simon (1987) have even shown a clear advantage if students are given only examples and problems to solve, as opposed to standard instruction with a textbook and instructor's presentations: a 3-year mathematics course can be reduced to 2 years. In laboratory studies, there is evidence showing that students prefer to rely on examples. Pirolli and Anderson (1985) found that novices rely heavily on analogies to examples in the early stages of learning: 18 of their 19 students used the example presented in the text as a template for solving their first programming problem. Futhermore, Chi et al. (1989b) further showed that not only are there quantitative differences in how frequently examples are used as a function of the students' skill at solving problems, but also that there is a qualitative difference in how examples are used. Successful solvers of physics problems used the examples about $2^{1}/_{2}$ times per problem solution; less successful solvers used the examples $6^{1}/_{2}$ times per problem solution. Successful solvers used the example only as a reference; less successful solvers reread virtually all of the example each time it was consulted, which suggests that they were searching aimlessly for a solution. Thus, beginning students rely on examples for learning to solve problems, even though there are differences among students in the extent of their reliance.

LeFevre and Dixon (1986) found that subjects actually prefer to use the example information and ignore the written instruction when learning a procedural task. One of the reasons that examples are so popular and useful, even though they are often inadequate in explaining the rationale behind each action taken in the solution, is that the examples contain many of the procedural actions that are not explicated in texts (Chi and VanLehn, 1991): the text usually presents concepts and principles; the examples contain the actions that are executed to solve the problem.

Although, in general, classroom instruction has not been very successful, there is room for improvement. As suggested above, two promising directions are to link the actions with the appropriate conditions and to focus more attention on examples in a text. A third approach is group discussion, which has been shown recently to improve learning in the classroom (Brown and Palincsar, 1989; Lampert, 1986; Minstrell, 1989).

Computer-Aided Support Systems

Numerous efforts have been applied to the development of computer-aided tools or systems for instruction. This approach has its obvious promise in its ability to record a student's responses, to replay the student's solution trace, and to display motion and invisible mechanisms on the screen, to name a few. It is also believed that evolving interactive learning environments and intelligent tutoring systems can be adapted to instruction of individual students. Three types of computer-based instruction are practice environments, embedded expert systems, and intelligent tutoring systems.

Computers can be used to create a variety of practice environments for simulation-based training. The most common kind are direct simulations of a real-world environment, such as a flight simulator. These simulations possess physical fidelity: they can look and feel like the real situation. Such simulations provide risk free and inexpensive practice. Simulations that forgo physical fidelity but retain cognitive fidelity have also been implemented. "Steamer," for example, simulates the operation of a steam plant (Williams et al., 1981). Although it does not preserve physical fidelity, its cognitive fidelity exposes the processes of a steam plant, such as the flow of the fluids. Finally, one can implement practice environments that present abstracted alternatives, such as navigating a rocket in a different gravitational field (Abelson and diSessa, 1980).

Practice environments can be made more sophisticated by incorporating an expert system. Such a system not only provides simulation of an environment, but can also solve problems within that environment. This kind of system can have different types of intelligence. For example, a system such as SHERLOCK (Lajoie and Lesgold, 1989) can solve a specified set of problems, and a system such as the Intelligent Maintenance Training System (Towne and Monroe, 1988) can troubleshoot any problem that the student poses to it. Thus, the effect of having a built-in expert system is that it can provide feedback (the solution) to the student. A drawback, however, is that the feedback is not sensitive to the student's understanding.

A full-fledged intelligent tutoring system has four components: a practice environment for solving problems, an expert system that knows how to solve all the problems, a model of the student (in terms of understanding how the student solves a problem, rather than whether the student's solution approximates the expert's solution), and a system for pedagogy. At the present time, there is no system that completely incorporates all these components. The best approximations are Burton and Brown's (1982) "How the West Was Won" system, and Clancey's (1983) Guidon system. Burton and Brown's system is designed to teach children basic arithmetic operations in the context of a game that is a variant of Chutes and Ladders. The system observes students as they play the game and gives them hints or advice at critical moments. Since it is a very simple game, the essence of the system is based on an analysis of the task, which divides it into subskills. The subskills are arranged in an hierarchy and each player's move is analyzed to determine the subskill to which it corresponds. Erroneous moves are compared with the subskills to see which one has been overlooked. Thus, the computer coach delivers feedback as a function of the match or mismatch between the student's moves and the subskill hierarchy. The coach also has heuristics for how to deliver instruction. Such pedagogical heuristics include rules of thumb, such as only give unsolicited advice when the player has made three or four moves without asking for advice. Hence, the system contains a practice environment; an expert system, in that the system knows how to play the game; a simple student model; and a pedagogy system, in its ability to monitor students' "understanding" of the game and deliver feedback selectively on the basis of the student's moves.

Cognitive Apprenticeship Revisited

In the first section of this chapter we noted that apprenticeship training is a popular method of instruction that embodies cognitive modeling. It relies on the teacher or the expert exposing the cognitive processes he or she is undertaking while solving a problem, making a decision, or diagnosing a fault. As we noted, certain strategies of learning can be easily modeled, and thereby perhaps learned by students with relative ease. But the rationale for an expert's choices of strategies or solution routes may not be obvious, especially if a great deal of content knowledge is needed. Furthermore, monitoring a student's own understanding demands complex processing, and it is not clear that this is undertaken normally by tutors. Indeed, there is some evidence that teachers in a tutoring situation do not necessarily provide "intelligent" coaching and scaffolding, presumably because they have not monitored the student's understanding accurately. In fact, Putnam (1987) observed six teachers tutoring students in a one-on-one situation and found that they did not systematically diagnose students' misunderstanding and tailor feedback accordingly. Instead, they seemed to follow a structured and prescribed sequence of presenting subject-matter content to their students.

Despite the lack of complete understanding of the processes undertaken by the tutor or expert, it appears that modeling in cognitive apprenticeship has had some success in teaching reading and writing, perhaps because it encourages students to engage in guided participation, actively articulating, reflecting, and exploring the skill that they are learning. There is evidence to suggest that these activities may be the critical source of learning in the apprenticeship situation. These activities can be viewed as self-construction, including self-explaining, asking questions, summarizing, providing critiques, posing problems, formulating hypotheses, and revising and editing. We noted above that there is evidence that these activities may facilitate learning and problem solving. There are also research findings that can be interpreted as providing indirect evidence that these activities are beneficial. For example, it is often noted that students improve their problem-solving performance if they participate in pairs. The most profitable dyadic situations are ones in which one member is more expert than the other (Radziszewska and Rogoff, 1988). It appears that the less expert partner offers self-explanations in these dyadic situations more than in the control situations in which each partner solves problems alone (Azmitia, 1988). It is tempting to speculate that what promotes the improvement of the less expert partner in the dyadic situations is the opportunity to construct new knowledge through articulation. Thus, to the extent that modeling promotes self-construction, it can be an effective instructional tool for cognitive skills.

SUMMARY AND CONCLUSIONS

An expert's knowledge is not only extensive, but much of it may be tacit, so that it takes a considerable amount of effort to elicit it. Experts may not always be aware of what their knowledge entails nor why they proceed in a specific way. The tacitness of expert knowledge may pose a problem for the utility of cognitive modeling for complex tasks requiring a great deal of domain knowledge. However, it has been shown to be quite effective in enhancing the learning of basic skills, such as reading (Palincsar and Brown, 1984) and writing (Scardamalia et al., 1984). In the context of a complex task, modeling in the sense of simply exposing an expert's own cognitive processes may present two additional complexities from the standpoint of instruction: to what extent does the student understand the expert's processes and to what extent should the expert attempt to understand the student's cognition in order to resolve the discrepancies between the two sets of processes. For example, it is often not clear to a student why his or her own approach to solving a problem is faulty or inappropriate. It appears that in order for cognitive modeling to work in a knowledge-rich complex domain, the expert has to be sensitive not only to his or her own cognitive processes, but also to how the student thinks and approaches a problem and to be able to explain in those terms why the student's approach may not work. To do so requires that an expert simultaneously is aware of and can articulate his or her own problem-solving processes and actively monitors his or her model of the student. Without further research on the cognitive processes of a tutor, it is not clear how successfully a tutor can achieve this dual role in a complex domain.

Although the idea of cognitive apprenticeship is promising and enticing, we cannot determine at this time whether the expert-modeling component is the critical one, since cognitive apprenticeship involves many other components, such as the requirement that instruction be situated in context and that students participate actively. Cognitive modeling also involves extensive explanations, and it seems safe to conclude that the nature of explanations is critical in assuring how well students can learn from an expert. Moreover, the self-constructions undertaken by the students while engaged in cognitive apprenticeship may also be an effective factor. Nevertheless, the success of cognitive apprenticeship for reading comprehension and writing suggests that cognitive modeling may be a feasible approach to explore for training basic skills.

REFERENCES

Abelson, H., and A.A. diSessa
  1980 *Turtle Geometry: The Computer as a Medium for Exploring Mathematics.* Cambridge, Mass.: MIT Press.
Anderson, J.R.
  1974 Retrieval of propositional information from long-term memory. *Cognitive Psychology* 6:451-474.
Azmitia, M.
  1988 Peer interaction and problem solving: when are two heads better than one? *Child Development* 59:87-96.

Brown, A.L., and A.S. Palincsar
    1989 Guided, cooperative learning and individual knowledge acquisition. Pp. 393-452 in
          L.B. Resnick, ed., *Knowing, Learning, and Instruction: Essays in Honor of Robert
          Glaser.* Hillsdale, N.J.: Erlbaum.
Burton, R.R., and J.S. Brown
    1982 An investigation of computer coaching for informal learning activities. Pp. 79-98 in
          D. Sleeman and J.S. Brown, eds., *Intelligent Tutoring Systems.* New York: Aca-
          demic Press.
Charness, N.
    1979 Components of skill in bridge. *Canadian Journal of Psychology* 33:1-16.
Chase, W.G.
    1983 Spatial representation of taxi drivers. Pp. 391-411 in D.R. Rogers and J.A. Sloboda,
          eds., *The Acquisition of Symbolic Skills.* New York: Plenum Press.
Chase, W.G., and K.A. Ericsson
    1981 Skilled memory. In J.R. Anderson, ed. *Cognitive Skills and Their Acquisition.* Hillsdale,
          N.J.: Erlbaum.
Chase, W.G., and H.A. Simon
    1973 Perception in chess. *Cognitive Psychology* 5:55-81.
Chi, M.T.H.
    1978 Knowledge structures and memory development. In R.S. Siegler, ed., *Children's
          Thinking: What Develops?* Hillsdale, N.J.: Erlbaum.
Chi, M.T.H., and R. Koeske
    1983 Network representation of a child's dinosaur knowledge. *Developmental Psychol-
          ogy* 19:29-39.
Chi, M.T.H., and K.A. VanLehn
    1991 The content of self-explanations. *Journal of the Learning Sciences.* In press.
Chi, M.T.H., R. Glaser, and E. Rees
    1982 Expertise in problem solving. Pp. 7-76 in R. Sternberg, ed., *Advances in the Psy-
          chology of Human Intelligence.* Vol. 1. Hillsdale, N.J.: Erlbaum.
Chi, M.T.H., R. Glaser, and M.J. Farr, eds.
    1988 *The Nature of Expertise.* Hillsdale, N.J.: Erlbaum.
Chi, M.T.H., J. Hutchinson, and A.F. Robin
    1989a How inferences about novel domain-related concepts can be constrained by struc-
          tured knowledge. *Merrill-Palmer Quarterly* 25:27-62.
Chi, M.T.H., M. Bassok, M. Lewis, Reimann, and R. Glaser
    1989b Self-explanations: how students study and use examples in learning to solve prob-
          lems. *Cognitive Science* 13:145-182.
Chiesi, H.L., G.J. Spilich, and J.F. Voss
    1979 Acquisition of domain-related information in relation to high and low domain knowledge.
          Journal of Verbal Learning and Verbal Behavior 18:257-273.
Clancey, W.
    1983 Guidon. *Journal of Computer-Based Instruction* 10:8-14.
Collins, A., and A.L. Stevens
    1983 A cognitive theory of interactive teaching. In C.M. Reigeluth, ed., *Instructional
          Design Theories and Models: An Overview.* Hillsdale, N.J.: Erlbaum.
Collins, A., Brown, J.S., and S.E Newman
    1989 Cognitive apprenticeship: Teaching the crafts of reading, writing, and mathematics.
          L. Resnick, ed., *Knowing, Learning, and Instruction: Essays in Honor of Robert
          Glaser.* Hillsdale, N.J.: Erlbaum.
Cooke, N.M., and J.E. McDonald
    1987 The application of psychological scaling techniques to knowledge elicitation for

knowledge-based systems. *International Journal of Man–Machine Studies* 26:533-550.

Egan, D.E., and B.J. Schwartz
1979 Chunking in the recall of symbolic drawings. *Memory and Cognition* 7:149-158.

Flanagan, J.C.
1954 The critical incident technique. *Psychological Bulletin* 51:327-358.

Hanisch, K.A., A.F. Kramer, C.L. Hulin, and R. Schumacher
1988 Novice–expert differences in the cognitive representation of computing systems: mental models and verbalizable knowledge. Pp. 219-223 in *Proceedings of the Human Factors Society 3rd Annual Meeting*. Santa Monica, Calif.: Human Factors Society.

Hoffman, R.R., ed.
1991 *The Psychology of Expertise: Cognitive Research and Empirical AI*. New York: Springer-Verlag.

Jeffries, R., A. Turner, P. Polson, and M. Atwood
1981 The processes involved in designing software. Pp. 255-283 in R.J. Anderson, ed., *Cognitive Skills and Their Acquisition*. Hillsdale, N.J.: Erlbaum.

Johnson-Laird, P.N.
1983 *Mental Models*. Cambridge, England: Cambridge University Press.

Klein, G.A.
1990 Knowledge engineering: beyond expert systems. *Information and Decision Technologies* 16:27-41.

Lajoie, S.P., and A. Lesgold
1989 Apprenticeship training in the workplace: computer-coached practice environment as a new form of apprenticeship. *Machine-Mediated Learning* 3(1):7-28.

Lampert, M.
1986 Knowing, doing, and teaching multiplication. *Cognition and Instruction* 3:305-342.

LeFevre, J., and P. Dixon
1986 Do written instructions need examples? *Cognition and Instruction* 3:1-30.

Lesgold, A.M., H. Robinson, P. Feltovich, R. Glaser, D. Klopfer, and Y. Wang
1988 Expertise in a complex skill: diagnosing X-ray pictures. Pp. 3121-3142 in M.T.H. Chi, R. Glaser, and M.J. Farr, eds., *The Nature of Expertise*. Hillsdale, N.J.: Erlbaum.

Minstrell, J.
1989 Teaching science for understanding. In L.B. Resnick and L.E. Klopfer, eds., *Toward the Thinking Curriculum: ASCD Yearbook*. Alexandria, Va./Hillsdale, N.J.: Association for Supervision and Curriculum Development/Erlbaum.

Newell, A., and H.A. Simon
1972 *Human Problem Solving*. Englewood Cliffs, N.J.: Prentice-Hall.

Norman, G.R., D. Rosenthal, L.R. Brooks, S.W. Allen, and L.J. Muzzin
1989 The development of expertise in dermatology. *Archives of Dermatology* 125:1063-1068.

Palincsar, A.S., and A.L. Brown
1984 Reciprocal teaching of comprehension-fostering and monitoring activities. *Cognition and Instruction* 1:117-175.

Pirolli, P.L., and J.R. Anderson
1985 The role of learning from examples in the acquisition of recursive programming skills. *Canadian Journal of Psychology* 39:240-272.

Putnam, R.
1987 Structuring and adjusting content for students: a study of live and simulated tutoring of addition. *American Educational Research Journal* 24:13-48.

Radziszewska, B., and B. Rogoff
1988 Influence of adult and peer collaborators on children's planning skills. *Developmental Psychology* 24:840-848.

Reitman, J.
1976   Skilled perception in GO: deducing memory structures from inter-response times. *Cognitive Psychology* 8:336-356.

Rogoff, B.
1986   Adult assistance of children's learning. In T.E. Raphael, ed. *The Contexts of School-Based Literacy*. New York: Random House.

Rosch, E., C.B. Mervis, W.D. Gray, D.M. Johnsen, and P. Boyes-Graem
1976   Basic objects in natural categories. *Cognitive Psychology* 8:382-440.

Scardamalia, M., C. Bereiter, and R. Steinbach
1984   Teachability of reflective processes in written composition. *Cognitive Science* 8:173-190.

Schauble, L., K. Raghavan, R. Glaser, and M. Reiner
1989   Causal Models and Processes of Discovery. Technical Report. Learning Research and Development Center, University of Pittsburgh.

Schoenfeld, A.H.
1983   Problem Solving in the Mathematics Curriculum: A Report, Recommendations and an Annotated Bibliography. The Mathematical Association of America, MAA Notes, No. 1.

Schuell, T.J.
1991   Designing instructional computing systems for meaningful learning. In P.H. Winne and M. Jones, eds., *Foundations and Frontiers in Instructional Computing Systems*. New York: Springer-Verlag.

Sharples, M.
1980   A Computer Written Language Lab. DAI Working Paper No. 134. Artificial Intelligence Department, University of Edinburgh, Scotland.

Simon, H.A., and M. Barenfeld
1969   Information-processing analysis of perceptual processes in problem solving. *Psychological Review* 76:473-483.

Towne, D.M., and A. Monroe
1988   The intelligent maintenance training system. Pp. 479-530 in J. Psotka, L.D. Massey, and S.A. Mutter, eds., *Intelligent Tutoring Systems: Lessons Learned*. Hillsdale, N.J.: Erlbaum.

Voss, J.F., J.R. Greene, T.A. Post, and B.C. Penner
1983   Problem solving skill in the social sciences. Pp. 165-213 in G.H. Bower, ed., *The Psychology of Learning and Motivation: Advances in Research and Theory*, Vol. 17. New York: Academic Press.

Vygotsky, L.S.
1978   *Mind in Society: The Development of Higher Psychological Processes*. Collected writings by Vygotsky. Edited and transcribed by M. Cole, V. John-Steiner, S. Scribner, and E. Souberman. Cambridge, Mass.: Harvard University Press.

Williams, M., J. Hollan, and A. Stevens
1981   An overview of STEAMER: an advanced computer assisted instructional system for propulsion engineering. *Behavior Research Methods and Instrumentation* 13:85-90.

Wood, D., and D. Middleton
1975   A study of assisted problem-solving. *British Journal of Psychology* 66:181-191.

Zhu, X., and H.A. Simon
1987   Learning mathematics from examples and by doing. *Cognition and Instruction* 4:137-166.

5

Developing Careers

Managers in large organizations increasingly require complex cognitive and social skills to deal with rapidly changing situations, and there is correspondingly increasing interest in career development programs that teach the relevant skills. One such organization is the U.S. Army, whose officers make decisions that involve vast resources and have worldwide implications. Current Army officer training at each level provides knowledge and skills to meet the needs at that level. However, early development for individuals with the desire to do well in advanced positions could contribute to successful performance at that level as well as to career mobility. As one of its tasks, the committee agreed to formulate an approach to careers based on concepts from the career-development literature (e.g., the Jossey-Bass series on career development resources). This approach is intended to contribute to ways of thinking about how career planning can be incorporated in training programs to meet the needs of the Army and similar large organizations.

Central to many training programs is the assumption that self-insight is a necessary first step to career planning. It is assumed that a person's performance can be improved through increased insight into one's needs, motives, strengths, and weaknesses, and that this process can be aided by structured self-assessment techniques. The Army's interest in these techniques coincides with a growing industry of inventories marketed to organizations and individuals interested in leadership training, developing interpersonal influence skills, team building, improving communications, time management, or decision making and creative problem solving.

Many of the techniques are in widespread use in public and private organizations. However, there has been little research on their effectiveness for either improving performance or changing behavior, in either the short or the long term. Nor have the techniques been placed within a broader framework of career development. Until such evaluations have been done, the use of those techniques can only be considered experimental. Thus, this chapter does not include an evaluation of a wide range of techniques or review of literature. Instead, we present an approach to the evaluation of self-report instruments and a way of thinking about career development issues, taking into account recent work on managerial development and performance in organizations.

The first section proposes a framework for studying and assessing career development, with attention to the role of self-report instruments in a broad context. The second section briefly describes existing Army career programs and the results of a questionnaire survey of instruments used at the Army War College. The third section discusses an evaluation of one popular instrument, the Myers-Briggs Type Indicator (MBTI). The chapter concludes with recommendations for research and applications that would contribute to a broadening of the career development concepts that guide many current counseling programs.

A FRAMEWORK FOR CAREER DEVELOPMENT

The framework presented in this section is intended to provide ideas for improving the career development process and for generating further research that would assist in achieving that goal. The discussion uses concepts and findings from the relevant behavioral science scholarly and research literature dealing with careers and career development in organizational settings.[1] It is relevant to the Army and its commissioned officers as well as virtually all large organizations.

Propositions

The research literature points to seven basic propositions that should undergird any set of programs aimed at strengthening career development processes.

1. *Each successively higher organizational level imposes new and broadened demands on knowledge and skills.* It has long been known that upper-level executives formulate broad strategies, middle-level managers translate those strategies into operational goals, and lower-level managers or supervisors implement methods to achieve those goals. A recent IBM study, for example, found that top-level executives spend a great

deal of time monitoring the environment, managers at the middle levels concentrate on planning and allocating distributions of resources and on providing for coordination among various groups, and the lowest echelon managers spend the bulk of their efforts on relationships with subordinates and motivating and assessing individual performance (Kraut et al., 1989). Likewise, in the Army context, Jacobs and Jacques (1987) have shown that the higher the level of the job, the greater the need for the individual to demonstrate cognitive complexity—to be able to deal with increasingly abstract and ambiguous situations through both analysis and synthesis.

Unfortunately, there is no single and straightforward approach to determining individual requirements for different levels and different functional areas. Rather, it appears that there is a need to consider a wide range of individual characteristics: cognitive, interpersonal, and managerial skills; personality dimensions; interests; values; and motivation. Thus, as London (1990:9) notes: "a comprehensive view of the individual must match the complex nature of Army Officer positions." It therefore follows that Army officers will need considerable assistance to gain an understanding of both their own characteristics—their strengths and relative weaknesses—and career aspirations in relation to the needs and demands of higher-level positions, and the role of training and on-the-job experiences in furthering their development for those positions.

2. *Early career experiences are crucial for strengthening subsequent capabilities.* Considerable research demonstrates the critical importance of initial job experiences—especially the types of assignment received and the types of supervision and mentoring provided to the person—for determining the course and speed of later career development (Bray et al., 1974; Bray and Howard, 1980; London, 1985; McCall et al., 1988). For example, McCall et al. (1988) identified several early career events that prepared executives-to-be for later career success: the first supervisory job; key project or task force assignments; rotation from line to staff positions, and vice versa; initiating an operation from scratch; turning a failed operation into a success; and coping with various hardships (e.g., sudden job changes, making a mistake, or dealing with a difficult subordinate). The import of these and other related findings is that career development and career planning—on the part of both the individual and the organization—should not be delayed until higher-level positions are attained but should begin at the very outset of a person's career and should continue.

3. *Career motivation is a multidimensional construct and is a major factor in career success.* Career motivation is one of a number of characteristics that are believed to contribute to an individual's perfor-

mance across a series of jobs and positions. The concept is multidimensional and includes needs, interests, and personality characteristics, which together influence the development of career resilience, insight, and identity (London, 1985; London and Bray, 1984). According to motivation theory, as applied to careers, "career resilience" is the maintenance component of motivation and refers to the ability to overcome career barriers and obstacles and take a proactive approach to accomplishing career objectives. "Career insight," which, according to this theory, is the "energizing component" of motivation, refers to an understanding of one's strengths and weaknesses and an awareness of the social and political environment within one's organization. "Career identity," representing the direction of motivation, encompasses one or more foci of one's energy and goals.

Together, these three dimensions form a pattern of career motivation. Resilience provides a foundation for forming a meaningful sense of insight, and insight forms the basis for developing career identities. Career motivation theory (London, 1983), therefore, argues for the continuous strengthening of career resilience and for efforts to develop insight and identity. It implies that those early in their careers, such as junior officers, need to experience tasks, jobs, supervisors, and work environments that will help them build confidence in themselves (resilience). They also need to begin to acquire information and feedback on their performance that will help them understand their personal strengths and capabilities, their areas of relative weakness or underdevelopment, and the operating environments in which they function (insight). Finally, they will need early on to establish some defined career targets, even though these may change over time (identity).

4. *Although development occurs throughout a career, individuals are most receptive to learning during times of "frame-breaking change."* The concept of frame-breaking change refers to change that creates uncertainties about the continued effectiveness of current repertories or modes of behavior. Individuals undergoing these kinds of changes are assumed to be motivated to search for behaviors, new and old, that will be effective in the new environment. Research shows (e.g., Berlew and Hall, 1966) that the first year of an individual's career is one critical period for new learning. Similar periods also occur when a person begins a major new assignment or transfers to a significantly different geographical or work environment. All of these and similar situations provide opportunities for career development programs in which the person will be maximally receptive to feedback and to encouragement for undertaking efforts to add new capabilities or enhance existing ones. Thus, any organization, including the Army, needs to be alert to how

these critical junctures can best be used for career development that will benefit both the individual and the organization.

5. *Individuals need at least some information about the requirements of positions at least two levels above their current position in addition to information about their current and next-level positions.* This proposition argues that if individuals are to formulate realistic plans for their career development they need to receive information not only about their current jobs and those immediately ahead at the next level, but also about jobs and positions at least one level beyond that. In this way, they should have an improved perspective about how their current activities relate to the kinds of demands and requirements that will have to be met if they are to be promoted. Thus, ideally, both current and future job performance are enhanced.

The Army, like many organizations, already provides considerable training for positions at the current level in the organization and, often, the immediate next level. This proposition suggests that additional information on the types of capabilities, knowledge, and skills that may be required in the future be provided at relatively early stages in a person's Army career. This would permit the individual to engage in more long-range and effective planning for his or her career. While obviously not all officers will advance two levels from their current level, such information would help all officers better understand the organization of which they are a part and how their current assignment relates to it. Research on career motivation indicates that such motivation is higher in organizations that treat individuals as resources for the future as well as for the present (Bray et al., 1974; Hall, 1976; London, 1985).

6. *When individuals plan ahead in making career decisions, they make better decisions.* The more thought individuals give to making future career decisions, the better will be the quality of those decisions. This proposition implies obtaining as much relevant information as possible in advance of a career decision about one's self in relation to future job and organizational requirements. It also implies that it will be necessary to analyze and interpret such information so that it can be used effectively. Clearly, therefore, in the Army context there is a joint role for both an individual officer and the Army: both parties need to understand their complementary obligations to be as thoughtful as possible in career decisions. Uninformed or ill-informed career aspirations and decisions help neither an individual nor the organization.

7. *Self-assessment is a potentially valuable aid in making informed career decisions.* Self-assessment (in the context of this chapter) can be thought of as the systematic process of generating data about oneself

and analyzing those data to provide guidance for career decisions. It is a counterpart to systematic assessment of individuals by other means and other sources, such as performance appraisals involving assessment by superiors or assessment of performance in simulated work situations by trained observers. As noted by Sundberg (1977:299):

People need an understanding of their own values, resources and priorities to help them choose how they want to live. Tests and other assessment procedures can help. . . . They can become instruments not just for decisions and descriptions, but for learning about one's self or a special area of knowledge or skill . . . such methods can enable individuals . . . to move toward goals they devise.

The goal of self-assessment in career decisions is to facilitate a better match between an individual and particular types of work or positions. Potentially, self-assessment can improve the likelihood of individuals seeking jobs or vocations that match their skills and personality characteristics (Stumpf and Colarelli, 1980). Indeed, a well-known theory of vocational choice (Holland, 1973) offers considerable evidence supporting the usefulness of such matches. However, accurate and meaningful self-assessment is not easy because the generator of such information, the individual, is so close to and involved in the information supplied. Ideally, self-assessment methods and instruments should produce agreement between self and others and should be able to discriminate among different performance and skill dimensions (London and Stumpf, 1982). If they do, then they can play an important role in career development programs.

Objectives

In this section we outline five major objectives, or action steps, for a systematic approach to career development programs. These action steps are based on the seven propositions identified in the preceding pages and current scientific knowledge about career development in organizations. They form a logical sequence, starting with an analysis of current skill requirements and career programs and ending with on-going and future evaluation of the entire process. (These steps in turn lead to the section on research priorities.)

Objective 1. Analyze current skill requirements and career programs. In the Army, a comprehensive review of current skill requirements and career programs would involve the following kinds of actions: an analysis of key technical skills required of officers at different levels and in different functional areas; an analysis of the current levels of skill of officers; and an inventory of existing career planning programs, assessment procedures, and career paths. The intent of this first objective is to determine how well current needs are being met and to provide benchmarks for evaluating gaps between current and future required skills. Meeting this first objective would clarify the extent of integration among current approaches to skill development and career planning in the Army and, likewise, the extent to which there are gaps and discontinuities.

Objective 2. Identify skills and leadership styles that will be needed to a greater extent in the future in the Army. This objective is designed specifically to take into account the changing political, economic, and social conditions that will exist in the 1990s and beyond. Expected and desired skills and leadership styles appropriate to the future need to be identified and then compared with existing skills and requirements so that they can be incorporated into career development programs. Some skills and styles that may be relatively more emphasized in the future might include, for example: understanding world economic and political conditions; analyzing ambiguous situations that have no "right" or "wrong" answers; empowering subordinates; negotiating; resolving conflicts; building intergroup relations; and making complex resource allocation decisions. The relevance of each of these (and other similar skills and approaches to leadership) to positions at different organizational levels and functional areas need to be analyzed as a basis for communicating and incorporating them into career planning and development programs, as well as used as a basis for training, appraisal, and reward systems.

Objective 3. Design a systematic and continuous career planning and development process. On the basis of the results of achieving the first two objectives, the Army should proceed to design a set of career planning and development programs that are both systematic and continuous. This process assumes that officers themselves should have the central role and responsibility for their own career planning and development while the institution, the Army, provides the enabling resources. Guidelines for designing such a comprehensive and continuous process might include the following: assessment and self-assessment methods that cover a wide range of individual characteristics; information that is available to the officer concerning a range of specific career opportunities in the Army and the leadership and management skills requirements associated with each opportunity; the encouragement and expectation that officers will use that information to set their own educational and top experience goals; an explicit career planning process that can be applied to each major function and level of the Army; and reasonable opportunity for officers to determine their career directions within the limits of Army needs and requirements.

Objective 4. Identify and develop mechanisms to support the role of an officer as coach, developer, and mentor of subordinates. This objective sets the specific goal of emphasizing the necessity for coaching, developing, and mentoring activities by superiors as part of any effective career development process. To convert this objective into reality may require additional or special training programs as well as explicitly considering the performance of these activities in evaluation and reward systems. One such type of program would be tutoring or expert modeling along the lines discussed in Chapter 4. More generally, expert officers should be a good source of guidance about how careers can be best developed. Some of the expert modeling methods discussed in Chapter 4 can be used to elicit information on what officers do. Advantages and disadvantages of these methods are outlined in that chapter.

Objective 5. Conduct continuous and systematic evaluations of the various elements of the career planning and development process. This objective recognizes that setting up and establishing a sound career planning and development process is not enough. In order for it to remain effective, there must be planned systematic evaluations of its various components. Comparisons will need to be made between different approaches and programs to determine their relative efficacy and payoffs: the programs that are not meeting the criteria set for them need to be phased out or modified; those that are contributing to improved individual and organizational performance need to be supported. This objective also implies that research on various facets of the overall process should play a vital role, as will experimentation with new or innovative methods.

Future Research Priorities

This section presents some future research projects that could facilitate the goal of improving the Army's overall career development process. This list is meant to be suggestive rather than exhaustive and takes into account the reality of a limited resource base to undertake such research.

Longitudinal Studies of the Effects of Intensive Career Development Activities Particular cohorts of junior-level officers could be followed over time to compare the effects (e.g., performance, officer career satisfaction) on those given relatively greater amounts of intensive career development attention by means of various self-assessment and other assessment procedures, career counseling, and so forth in comparison with those given lesser amounts of career development attention. Such research studies would help provide an objective basis for the amount of resources—direct and indirect—that the Army should devote to career development for officers.

Comparisons of the Effects of Particular Career Intervention Activities at Particular Times   Given limited resources, it is probably not feasible to provide equally intense career development activities for all officers on a continuous basis. Thus, it will be important to determine, through research, at what specific point in an officer's career certain developmental activities or assessments will have their greatest subsequent impact. Research of this type could compare the relative effects of the use of a given instrument or development exercise administered to different groups at different times.

Comparisons of the Effects of Specific Career Development Methods and Instruments   Again, given limited resources of both the Army and of officers themselves in terms of their time and energy, choices will need to be made concerning which methods, procedures, and instruments should be used on a regular basis. Well-designed rigorous research involving direct comparisons between particular methods will be a cost-effective way to weed out those that are relatively ineffective, even if most or all of them may have a great deal of apparent validity and popularity.

Studies on How to Motivate Officers to Follow Up and Take Personal Action to Implement Further Skill Development Based on Information Provided by Career Assessment Activities   As noted above, receiving useful information about one's self and about the requirements of potential future positions in a career sequence in an organization is only a first step. An individual must then act on this information if career development is to take place. Relatively little is known about how individuals use the career information they receive and what factors motivate them to take action. Research could test several different approaches to motivating follow-up action to see which are most effective. The criteria for determining the effectiveness of different motivational methods or approaches would be the extent and frequency of the concrete career development activities subsequently undertaken by officers within a given time.

Studies of the Effects of Career Coaching and Mentoring by Superiors   Research could be conducted to determine the relationship between different amounts or types of career coaching and mentoring and subsequent career development behavior and career satisfaction.

ARMY PROGRAMS

Like many institutions, the Army has recognized the importance of considering the development of careers as a part of its approach to training. Although there is no system-wide program, a number of Army training facilities and bases have developed programs that include goal setting and self-reflection for career guidance. While sharing the overall objective of facilitating career planning, the programs vary in emphasis placed on particular techniques or procedures. These programs have been developed at the initiative of the local commanding officer; they offer alternatives to the traditional one-on-one counseling conducted between a soldier and his or her immediate supervisor. Four centers have established programs: the Army War College (AWC) at Carlisle, Pennsylvania; the National Defense University (NDU) in Washington, D.C.; Fort Bliss near El Paso, Texas; and Fort Leavenworth in Leavenworth, Kansas. Participation at all the locations is intended only to help students expand their own self-awareness; the evaluations are not retained by the organization for administrative use.

Self-Assessment Instruments

Career counseling programs use several instruments intended to provide students with a variety of ways to view themselves on certain dimensions of intrapersonal and interpersonal styles. Five instruments are used in many of these programs: the Myers-Briggs Type Indicator, the Kirton Adaption-Innovation Inventory, the Leader Effectiveness and Adaptability Description, the Terminal and Instrumental Values Surveys, and the Organizational Values Survey.

Myers-Briggs Type Indicator (MBTI) The MBTI uses four indices, which are said to represent personality tendencies: "extraversion-introversion" (E-I), which is the distinction between whether a person prefers the external world of people and things or the internal world of ideas; "sensing-intuition" (S-N), which distinguishes between whether a person pays more attention to realistic, practical data or to one's imagination and the possibilities of a situation; "thinking-feeling" (T-F), which is the difference between valuing impersonal logic or personal values and emotions when processing information or making decisions; "judging-perceiving" (J-P), which distinguishes between analyzing and categorizing the external environment and responding to it flexibly and spontaneously. The questions used to develop the four indices take the following form: "When you go somewhere for the day, would you rather (A) plan what you will do and when, or (B) just go?" The combination of the four indices is a type or representation of how one operates in the world (e.g., ENTJ or ISFP). The type indices serve as a basis for guided discussions that usually take place in small groups.

Kirton Adaption-Innovation Inventory (KAI) This instrument is designed to measure different approaches to creativity, problem solving, and decision making. It provides a score on a continuum ranging from highly adaptive to highly innovative. "Adaptors" are regarded as those who produce ideas based on stretching existing agreed parameters, that is, improving and doing better. "Innovators" are assumed to be more likely to reconstruct the problem, expanding beyond current paradigms, that is, doing things differently. The questions take the following form: "How easy or difficult do you find it to present yourself, consistently, over a long period as a person who is patient?"

Leader Effectiveness and Adaptability Description (LEAD-Self) This instrument is designed to measure self-perception of three aspects of leadership behavior: style, style range, and style adaptability or effectiveness. It is based on the Hersey-Blanchard (1977) situational theory of leadership that distinguishes between the amount of task direction and the amount of socio-emotional support a leader provides, given the situation and the responsiveness of the followers or group. A companion to the LEAD-Self is the LEAD-Other instrument, which asks a respondent to describe the leadership behavior of another person.

Terminal and Instrumental Values Surveys Designed by Rokeach (1973, 1979), these surveys present students with lists of terminal values (states of existence, e.g., a comfortable or exciting life) and instrumental values (modes of conduct, e.g., active, ambitious, broadminded). The instruments are designed to identify the guiding values in a student's life. Respondents are asked to compare the values, arranged alphabetically, in terms of importance to them as guiding principles in their lives.

Organizational Values Survey This survey presents students with a list of values that might exist in an organization and form the climate of that organization, e.g., achieving, balanced, caring. Students are asked to put the alphabetically arranged values in priority order, in terms of whether they are reflected in the organization in which they work and whether the organization orders them in the same way.

The Army War College

The AWC has constructed a highly organized program intended to aid career planning for officers faced with mid-career decisions. The program is implemented during the first weeks after the student-officers arrive for their year-long stay in Carlisle. It is guided by a career planning philosophy rooted in the idea of time management. Since time management assumes that a person knows what he or she wants, it is important to address the issue of goals: professional, family, community, and personal. To define this set of goals, the program uses self-assessment devices as a means for encouraging students to reflect on their goals and plans to achieve them.

Students are given a development guide that introduces them to the purposes of the program, its philosophy, and its steps. Organized in the form of a flow chart, the steps consist of data gathering and self-reflection (Where am I now? Who do I think I am?), goal setting (What is most important to me?), a learning plan (How can I achieve my life goals, and how will this year at the college contribute to them?), feedback (Is my learning plan realistic?), and periodic review. Each step consists of specific activities that are described in the guide. The first step, data gathering and self-reflection, includes writing narrative descriptions of the self-assessments of personal style (the MBTI), leadership style (LEAD-self), problem-solving style (the KAI), and values (Rokeach terminal, instrumental, and organizational values), as well as personal health and fitness. (Results obtained from a survey of the effects of these instruments are presented in the next section.) The second step, goals statement, asks students to rate the importance and assess the feasibility of goals organized by life areas. The third step consists of developing a learning plan designed to accomplish their goals at the college. The fourth step, feedback, asks students to review with a faculty adviser the goals and plans they have developed. Periodic review takes into account possibilities for changes as the year at the AWC unfolds. And, finally, the development guide reinforces a sense of commitment to time management by asking students to organize their activities through careful scheduling with the help of a daily calendar.

The National Defense University (NDU)

The NDU program is an abridged version of the program at the AWC. What the AWC program contributes in depth of understanding of the self-evaluation process, the NDU program contributes in breadth of participation: at the AWC, only 10 percent of the students participate in the semester-long elective course; at the NDU, 98 percent of the students participate in a self-assessment workshop lasting a few hours. Like the AWC program, the NDU program also includes a battery of self-assessment surveys and a goal-setting exercise during the first few weeks of attendance at the university and uses the MBTI, the KAI, and a health-fitness survey. A learning style inventory, an assessment of learning environmental preferences, the Campbell work orientation survey, and a personal opinions survey are administered only in the NDU program.

Although counseling is provided to aid students through the process of articulating their goals and work plans, the step-by-step procedures used at the AWC are not implemented in the NDU program. A smaller program at NDU, the Industrial College of the Armed Forces, is organized primarily around the MBTI and its interpretation in relation to group dynamics and team building. The NDU also offers stress-reduction clinics.

Fort Bliss

At Fort Bliss two general training courses, officer basic training and officer advanced training, are preceded by several self-assessment inventories. A nurse administers a health risk assessment survey and a chaplain administers a life expectancy stress test and the MBTI. Results are discussed on a one-on-one basis with each student, who also takes diagnostic tests for skills in such technical areas as computer literacy and map reading.

Fort Leavenworth

The Fort Leavenworth approach to career development is based on performance assessments that are part of a Leadership Assessment and Development Program (LADP). The LADP combines self-assessment with the assessments made by peers and trained assessors in nine areas: technical and tactical proficiency, communications, professional ethics, planning, management technology, decision making, teaching and counseling, supervision, and soldier team development. The assessor ratings are based on actual task performances (identified with various types of leadership positions), repeated for diverse tasks performed by students throughout the duration of the course, and also are made by different assessors. Some assessments are made quickly, for example, reactions to situations can be assessed in 10 minutes; other assessments are made over a longer period of time, for example, performing as a platoon leader on a tactical mission. The information gathered from these assessments are consolidated by senior assessors who prepare final assessment reports that serve as a plan for self-development. Like students at the AWC program, students at Fort Leavenworth engage in goal-setting exercises after a data-gathering phase. Unlike the students at the AWC, these students are provided with performance-based information that they can take into account in setting their goals. They are also given an opportunity to consider performance requirements for tasks at higher levels in the organizational hierarchy. (The issue of anticipating possible future performance requirements is discussed above in conjunction with a new framework for career development.) As in the programs described above, care is taken to ensure that the evaluations are used only by the students for development purposes, without any implications for administrative decisions.

Survey of Effects

The four programs are similar in some respects, but they also differ. Although they all use self-assessment and goal-setting exercises, a key difference is between the programs that rely exclusively on self-assessment information for counseling (AWC, NDU) and the programs that use this information as part of a comprehensive performance evaluation that provides the basis for goal setting and planning (Fort Leavenworth).

The committee did not undertake an evaluation of these programs. It did, however, develop an approach to program evaluation that could serve as a model for systematic appraisal of effects. The approach entailed a questionnaire designed to assess several types of impacts: memory of feedback from instruments, relative value of various parts of the program or instruments, insights about self and others, follow-up actions in the short and long term, and overall impact on behavior and decisions. The questionnaire was divided into several parts, including questions about the program in general and about each of the self-assessment instruments used in the program in particular.

A pilot study was conducted with a sample of students in the 1989-1990 class at the AWC. These students participated in the AWC career development program during the latter part of August 1989. The questionnaires were administered in early February 1990, permitting sufficient time for assessments of memory and impact. The six parts consisted of questions about the overall program and memory and impact questions about each of the instruments used in that program and described above: the MBTI (Myers and McCaulley, 1985); LEAD-Self (Hersey and Blanchard, 1977); KAI (Kirton, 1984); terminal and instrumental values surveys (Rokeach, 1973, 1979); and values sought in the organization. The set of questions asked about each instrument was roughly parallel and concluded with a rating on a five-step scale of its impact on behavior and decisions, ranging from "very much" to "none." Results are summarized in terms of percentages of responses in each of the areas assessed, followed by concluding observations.

On Memory Virtually all respondents (97 percent) remembered having taken the MBTI, as well as the letter symbols (97 percent) and where they "scored" on each type scale as defined by the instrument (87 percent). This contrasts with 61, 68, and 68 percent recall for having taken the LEAD-Self, the KAI, and the Rokeach inventories, respectively.[2] The contrast between these instruments in recall is more evident with regard to specific results, with only 26, 13, and 13 percent of the respondents recalling their specific leadership style, style range, and style effectiveness, respectively. Of the respondents, 65 percent did not remember the values they listed on either the instrumental or terminal values survey, while very few recalled the values listed on the instrument "values I seek in my organization" (87 percent had no recall for any of the values listed). Specific memory for scores obtained on the KAI was better, with 65 percent of the respondents remembering where they fell on a continuum between "highly adaptive" and "highly innovative."

On New Insights A large number of the respondents indicated that the results confirmed what they already knew about themselves: 84 percent on the MBTI feedback; 55 percent on LEAD (48 percent indicated that the results were consistent with what supervisors or peers said about them); 65 percent on the KAI (58 percent indicated that these results were consistent with what supervisors and/or peers said about them); 26 percent for the Rokeach inventories (74 percent had no answer to this question) and 48 percent for organizational values. Few respondents indicated how any of the instruments, other than the MBTI, were of value to them; about half of the respondents had no answer to each of the questions asked about the specific instruments.

On Impact Eighty percent of the respondents indicated that the MBTI had either "very much" or "some" impact on their behavior. This contrasts to 33, 29, 33, and 39 percent for the other instruments. Equally compelling are the differences between the instruments on answers indicating "very little" or no impact: 12 percent for the MBTI compared with 28, 36, 36, and 35 percent for each of the other instruments. Virtually all the respondents indicated that the MBTI made them more aware of themselves and others, with 74 percent indicating that it caused them to change their behavior in relating to others, although they did not indicate what changes occurred. Few respondents indicated that any of the other instruments would lead them to make changes in their behavior: 16 percent on the LEAD, 16 percent on the KAI, 23 percent for the Rokeach values, and 23 percent for organizational values.

On the MBTI Clearly, this instrument had the strongest impact, with 61 percent of the respondents indicating that it was the aspect of the overall program that they found to be most helpful. While 71 percent found the follow-up discussion to be the most valuable part of the process, 23 percent thought that it was this part in particular that needed to be improved. Interestingly, however, the MBTI made more respondents uncomfortable (26 percent) than the other instruments (3, 3, 13, and 6 percent). Yet this did not prevent a large number of the respondents from indicating that they plan to take specific actions in the future based on the MBTI information (61 percent). However, further probes did not reveal what these actions were, despite the 42 percent of respondents who indicated that they actually did take some actions in the period between participation in the program and administration of the questionnaire. (It is noted that this may be an inflated figure, since many of the respondents may have been motivated by social desirability or a need for self-justification.)

On the Program Practically all respondents (97 percent) indicated that the program should be continued, with few specific suggestions about how it might be improved (23 percent said that an MBTI "follow-up" should be undertaken). While seeming to be satisfied with the program, few respondents indicated specific actions that they plan to take as a result of participation. With regard to aspects of the program that they viewed as being least helpful, about half had no answer; 16 percent said the Rokeach surveys, 13 percent said the LEAD survey, and 9 percent said that the KAI was least helpful.

These results suggest several conclusions. First, the MBTI had a very different effect on respondents than all the other instruments: on memory, on self-insights, and on short- and long-term planning and actions (although the specific behavior changes were not identified). So influential was this instrument that a number of respondents indicated that some kind of follow-up (or periodic discussions) would be the best way of improving the program. Although probes on the meaning of "follow-up" were not made, it would appear that it refers to guidance on ways to use the feedback.

Second, an inconsistency in responses about the MBTI is its apparent impact on the one hand and the indication by most respondents that it confirmed what they already knew on the other. Perhaps it is that very confirmation that leads to action. Dissonant or inconsistent information may have the effect of producing either inaction or no change from previous behavior.

Third, the other instruments seemed to have little impact and unimpressive recall. It would be interesting to probe further for explanations: for example, are the results due to a lack of saliency of the content and topics addressed by the instruments or due to the way they are administered and discussed in class?

Fourth, while almost all respondents found the overall AWC program to be valuable, few were able to be specific, especially with regard to impact on actions or decisions.

It must be cautioned that these results may not be representative of other populations or programs. The sample was small, from one program, and drawn entirely from the classes taught by the program's administrator, who may have conveyed either more or less enthusiasm for the MBTI than for other instruments.

Despite the preliminary nature of this survey, however, it does appear that the MBTI is a very popular instrument that leads people to consider taking actions. It is also a widely used instrument that enjoys a large market throughout the United States and elsewhere. For this reason, the committee decided to devote additional attention to this instrument, the underlying theory, issues of reliability and validity, and research on various populations and uses.

AN APPRAISAL OF THE MBTI

The committee's survey results highlight the value of the experience of taking the MBTI from the perspective of the respondent. These remarks underscore a wider popularity as documented in several recent publications. For example, McCaulley (1988) estimates that the MBTI is used as a diagnostic instrument by 1,700,000 people a year in the United States, and Moore and Woods (1987) lists the wide variety of organizations in business, industry, education, government, and the military that use it. It is probably fair to say that the MBTI is the most popular "self-insight, insight into others" instrument in use today. Unfortunately, however, the popularity of the instrument is not coincident with supportive research results. This section summarizes available research and addresses the question of why there is a discrepancy between its popularity and the lack of evidence for its validity. Specifically, we focus on issues of reliability, validity, and effectiveness of applications; for a more detailed treatment of these and related issues, see Thayer (1988).

Reliability

A number of reliability studies of the MBTI have been conducted. Corrected split-half and alpha reliability coefficients for continuous scores on each of the attitudes and functions typically range from .75 to .85, with some variation on the different scales (Bittle, 1987; Carlson, 1985; Myers and McCaulley, 1985; DeVito, 1985; Carlyn, 1977). While these results are acceptable, they do not address the key theoretical issue of the MBTI, which is stability of type. Test-retest reliabilities of type designations are more relevant. Myers and McCaulley (1985) report test-retest reliabilities from 11 different samples. In these samples, between 24 and 61 percent of the respondents showed stability of type, with a median of 40 percent. A change in only one of the four categories in the type designation occurred in 27-44 percent of the respondents in these samples, with a median of 37 percent. McCarley and Carskadon (1983) report only 47 percent of their respondents retained their initial types over a period of 5 weeks. Changes in the type designations of these magnitudes suggest caution in classifying people in these ways and then making decisions that would influence their careers or personal lives. A more plausible approach would be based on the assumption that most people change over time as a result of new experiences. Self-assessment instruments like those represented by the MBTI are likely, at best, to capture a person's current state and, therefore, should not be considered typologies.

With regard to scale independence, Carlyn (1977) found that three of the four MBTI scales—extraversion-introversion (I-E), sensing-intuition (S-N), and thinking-feeling (T-F)—are relatively independent. The fourth scale, judgment-perception (J-P), was related to the sensing-intuition scale with correlations ranging from .23 to .48 in 11 samples: sensors tended to be judgers, while intuitors tended to be perceivers in these samples. She interprets these results as support for the theory on which the instrument is based, which posits only three dimensions.

Validity

A number of different types of studies address the issue of validity: correspondences with self-typing, correlations with other instruments, behavior in experimental situations, and differences in MBTI profiles by occupation. The evidence from these studies is particularly relevant to the type of validity referred to as "construct validity."

One approach to validation consists of comparing judgments made by analysts who are familiar with the Jungian philosophy underlying the instrument with analysts who are unfamiliar with that philosophy. Bradway's (1964) study showed differential correspondences between the self-typing and MBTI-typing for a sample of Jungian analysts: 100 percent agreement for the I-E comparisons, 68 percent for the S-N comparisons, 61 percent for the T-F comparisons, and 43 percent on all three dimensions in one study; 96, 75, 72, and 43 percent, respectively, in another study. Similar results were obtained in the correlational study reported by Stricker and Ross (1964). Less impressive results were obtained in studies using subjects who were less familiar with Jungian theory. Low correlations between self-typing and MBTI-typing were reported in the studies reviewed by Cohen et al. (1981). Subjects in these studies were graduate students trained to use the Jungian typology for conducting interviews with other students.

Myers and McCaulley (1985) present correlational data from 20 studies showing relationships between MBTI scales and a wide variety of other instruments. They concluded that the I-E scale has good construct validity: it has high correlations with comparable scales of other instruments and low correlations with instruments designed to represent other constructs. In contrast, the S-N and T-F scales show relatively weak validity, with only moderate correlations with other instruments designed to measure similar constructs. Since these findings are based largely on high school and college student samples, however, caution is advised in attempting to generalize from them.

Several studies examined relationships between the I-E scale and observed behavior in experimental situations. The Carskadon (1979) study found differences between extraverts and introverts on some aspects of self-presentation during a "political talk," but these findings were not replicated in another study that was done more carefully by the same author and colleagues (Vargo et al., 1986). Two other behavioral studies show partial support for the I-E scale: Moore and Carskadon (1984) found that their extraverts were more likely than introverts to observe people in the environment but not things. And Shapiro and Alexander (1969) found that extraverts preferred to wait with others for the occurrence of a fearful situation while the introverts preferred being alone.

Large data sets have been developed by Van Velsor (1988) and Myers and McCaulley (1985) on type preferences for people in different occupations. In general, sales people, entertainers, counselors, and managers and administrators have higher percentages of extraverts, while librarians, archivists, computer specialists, and medical doctors have higher percentages of introverts; farmers, clerical workers, and military personnel have higher proportions of sensors while social scientists, artists, counselors, and lawyers have higher proportions of intuitors. Some of the comparisons are presented as combinations of types: for example, INFPs have higher than expected proportions of counselors, clinical psychologists, writers, and journalists, or ENTJs will attract attorneys, managers, sales personnel, and engineers.

The temptation to use these data for vocational counseling should be tempered by three methodological problems. First, there is weak discrimination among occupations due to an overlap between the types and preferred occupations. Second, there is a lack of attention to normative data: for example, 12.4 percent of elementary teachers are ESFJs, but the same percentage of a random sample of U.S. women are also ESFJs. Third, no evidence has been presented on relationships to performance in those occupations. Given these problems, the types may simply be an example of stereotypes. Despite these problems, the MBTI is becoming increasingly popular as a tool for vocational guidance.

The evidence summarized in this section raises questions about the validity of the MBTI. However, many users of the instrument have claimed that its value lies not in its diagnostic accuracy, which is problematic, but in its probative guidance. Respondents often emphasize the increased sensitivity gained from the discussions generated by MBTI feedback. It would seem that such gains could contribute to enhanced performance. Unfortunately, neither the gains in sensitivity nor the impact of those gains on performance have been documented by research. Nor has the instrument been validated in a long-term study of successful and unsuccessful careers. Lacking such evidence, it is a curiosity why the instrument is used so widely, particularly in large organizations.

Effectiveness of Applications

On the basis of a review of the published literature, Thayer (1988) concludes that most studies of the MBTI are inadequate and that, overall, there is a lack of systematic research on the many applications of the MBTI in organizations. His review covers studies on educational applications, training and development applications, and team-building applications. He notes three methodological criticisms of the research: the reporting of data is inconsistent and incomplete; statistical analyses are often incompletely described and may violate convention (e.g., no overall test of significance is calculated before detailed comparisons are made and no attention is given to appropriate baseline data in the analyses); and subjects or judges are often made aware of the hypotheses being tested. These problems prevent drawing conclusions from the studies, many of which are published in the Journals of the Center for the Applications of Psychological Type, Inc. (*Journal of Psychological Type and Research in Psychological Type*); we also note that, to date, few studies appear in mainstream research journals.

It may well be the case, however, that a more complete picture would be presented by taking into account the unpublished literature, such as technical reports, presentations, and dissertations. While such a review may indeed present a more complete assessment of the instrument, it is unlikely to offer a more optimistic appraisal. Thayer concluded that the relatively small community of MBTI researchers visible in the published literature are likely to have been also involved in the unpublished work. In most cases, a carefully designed and executed dissertation study or technical report would become a published article or be cited in the literature. Rather than search for more literature, it would seem more prudent to encourage better research on these issues.

Despite this overall appraisal, there are a few promising lines of research on the MBTI that could be further developed. Studies by Hoffman et al. (1981) and by Eggins (cited in Lawrence, 1984) suggest that the MBTI might be regarded as a measure of "learning style": the Hoffman et al. (1981) study shows that the dropout rate of extraverted students in a computer-assisted military course could be reduced by adding more group discussion sessions and providing minilectures; the Eggins' study shows that different types performed better when concepts were structured according to one or another approach referred to as inductive, deductive, or concrete. Studies by Blaylock (1983) and Brocato and Seaberg (1987) show that teams composed of mixed or complementary types performed better on various simulated tasks than teams of the same type. Since no attempt has been made to replicate these studies, the results must be regarded as only suggestive. Another line of investigation, developed by Yeakley (1982, 1983), indicates that similar styles communicate more effectively than dissimilar styles. More recent work by the same investigator (Yeakley, 1985) failed to replicate the earlier results, leading him to suggest that further tests of this hypothesis await reconciliation of the different results.

The lack of a supportive research foundation for the MBTI leads the committee to recommend that the instrument not be used in career counseling programs until its validity is supported by research. A positive recommendation would thus depend on the accumulation of evidence from studies designed according to rigorous methodological standards and conducted by a broad base of researchers from psychology, organizational behavior, and education. And even if the evidence is negative, the instrument could serve useful purposes: for example, it might be used to teach about the uncertainty of the category assignments and other deficits uncovered by the research.

Finally, it would seem appropriate to address the troublesome discrepancy between research results (a lack of proven worth) and popularity. What accounts for the popularity of an instrument that is not yet supported by research? Several reasons can be suggested. From the respondents' perspective, the MBTI provides generally positive feedback: the descriptors do not have clinical implications, they are presented as unique positive attributes, and they are sufficiently vague to apply to a large number of people in a wide variety of situations. Moreover, the opportunity to learn more about oneself and others in a nonthreatening environment (or to *believe* one is doing so) is an incentive for participation. It is not difficult to understand how such positive experiences can be a basis for popularity. From the perspective of organizational development, the instrument is a vehicle for addressing problems that can be resolved through guided discussion. Many professionals assume that the changes they observe during the sessions will transfer to the job setting and persist over time. And from the perspective of the instrument's developers, the profits from an audience eager for self-improvement encourages them to market the instrument aggressively; aggressive marketing—complete with type coffee mugs, t-shirts, pins, license plates—has apparently increased the number of consumers worldwide.

This phenomenon is not new to the committee and has been discussed in some detail with regard to other techniques that purport to enhance performance (see Druckman and Swets, 1988). Nonetheless, the popularity of this instrument in the absence of proven scientific worth is troublesome. As with the other techniques considered, career counselors are advised to take into account the reservations discussed in this section when considering the MBTI as part of a counseling package.

CONCLUSIONS

Career Planning Decisions on the use and value of specific career counseling and self-assessment instruments in organizational settings should be made within the context of a planned and systematic, organization-wide approach to career development. This applies to the Army as well as any other large, complex organization. The framework outlined in this chapter should be developed further in conjunction with relevant research: the longitudinal and cross-sectional studies suggested in the chapter are recommended with special attention to the structure of military organizations. Evaluations should be made of the cost-effectiveness of alternative career intervention activities with regard to the timing of the intervention and the methods used by the intervenors.

The Myers-Briggs Type Indicator At this time, there is not sufficient, well-designed research to justify the use of the MBTI in career counseling programs. Much of the current evidence is based on inadequate methodologies. Better evaluation studies, conducted according to rigorous methodological standards, are recommended. One type of useful evaluation would be to compare "successful" and "unsuccessful" careers. Positive results obtained from these studies, if replicated with different samples, could justify the use of the MBTI instrument in career counseling programs. Other self-assessment instruments currently in use or contemplated for use in counseling programs should also be subjected to the same rigorous evaluation.

Research on the effects of guided discussion, such as the discussions held on feedback from the MBTI or other self-assessment instruments is recommended. Such research should distinguish between subjective reactions to the experience and observed effects on subsequent actions and career performance.

We must, however, conclude this chapter on a cautionary note with reference to the Army. The type of career planning recommended by the committee emphasizes opportunities for crucial career experiences, especially early in a career (see proposition 2, above), but the transient character of most jobs in the Army, due largely to incentives for promoting officers with many different jobs, may militate against such opportunities. Frequent job changes may also lead to both job and career dissatisfaction and to personal or family disruptions. It will be necessary to take into account the impact of these factors on decisions made for long-term career development.

NOTES

1. Substantial portions of this section are based on a commissioned paper by London (1990).

2. Respondents' actual scores could not be obtained. The remembered scores, used in the analysis, may not be the same as the actual scores.

REFERENCES

Bittle, S.Y.
    1987 Psychometric Properties of the Myers-Briggs Type Indicator. Unpublished manuscript, Psychology Department, North Carolina State University.
Berlew, D.E., and D.T. Hall
    1966 The socialization of managers: effects of expectations on performance. *Administrative Science Quarterly* 11:207-223.
Blaylock, B.K.
    1983 Teamwork in a simulated production environment. *Journal of Psychological Type* 6:58-67.
Bradway, K.
    1964 Jung's psychological types: classification by test versus classification by self. *Journal of Analytical Psychology* 9:129-135.
Bray, D.W., R.J. Campbell, and D.L. Grant
    1974 *Formative Years in Business: A Long-Term AT&T Study of Managerial Lives.* New York: Wiley.
Bray, D.W., and A. Howard
    1980 Career success and life satisfaction of middle-aged managers. In L.A. Bond and J.C. Rosen, eds., *Competence and Coping During Adulthood.* Hanover, N.H.: University Press of New England.
Brocato, F.C., and J.J. Seaberg, Jr.
    1987 Psychological Type and Task Accomplishment in the Public School Management Team. Paper presented at the annual meeting of the American Education Research Association, Washington, D.C.
Carlson, J.G.
    1985 Recent assessments of the Myers-Briggs Type Indicator. *Journal of Personality Assessment* 49:356-365.

Carlyn, M.
  1977   An assessment of the Myers-Briggs Type Indicator. *Journal of Personality Assessment* 41:461-473.
Carskadon, T.G.
  1979   Behavioral differences between extraverts and introverts as measured by the Myers-Briggs Type Indicator. *Research in Psychological Type* 2:78-82.
Cohen, F.D., M. Cohen, and H. Cross
  1981   A construct validity study of the Myers-Briggs Type Indicator. *Educational and Psychological Measurement* 41:883-891.
DeVito, A.J.
  1985   Review of MBTI. In J.V. Mitchell, ed., *Ninth Mental Measurements Yearbook.* Lincoln, Neb.: University of Nebraska.
Druckman, D., and J.S. Swets, eds.
  1988   *Enhancing Human Performance: Issues, Theories, and Techniques.* Committee on Techniques for the Enhancement of Human Performance, Commission on Behavioral and Social Sciences and Education, National Research Council. Washington, D.C.: National Academy Press.
Hall, D.T.
  1976   *Careers in Organizations.* Santa Monica, Calif.: Goodyear.
Hersey, R., and K.H. Blanchard
  1977   *Management of Organizational Behavior: Utilizing Human Resources*, 3rd ed. Englewood Cliffs, N.J.: Prentice-Hall.
Hoffman, J.L., K. Waters, and M. Berry
  1981   Personality types and computer-assisted instruction in a self-paced technical training environment. *Research in Psychological Type* 3:81-85.
Holland, J.L.
  1973   *Making Vocational Choices: A Theory of Careers.* Englewood Cliffs, N.J.: Prentice-Hall.
Jacobs, T.O., and E. Jacques
  1987   Leadership in complex systems. In J.A. Zeide, ed., *Human Productivity Enhancement: Organizations and Personnel*, Vol. II. New York: Praeger.
Kirton, M.J.
  1984   Adaptors and innovators—why new initiatives get blocked. *Long Range Planning* 17:137-141.
Kraut, A.I., P.R. Pedigo, D.D. McKenna, and M.D. Dunnette
  1989   The role of the manager: what's really important in different management jobs. *The Academy of Management Executive* 3(4):286-293.
Lawrence, G.
  1984   A synthesis of learning style research involving the MBTI. *Journal of Psychological Type* 8:2-15.
London, M.
  1983   Toward a theory of career motivation. *Academy of Management Review* 8(4):620-630.
  1985   *Developing Managers.* San Francisco: Jossey-Bass.
  1988   *Change Agents: New Roles and Innovation Strategies for Human Resource Managers.* San Francisco: Jossey Bass.
  1990   Army Officer Career Development: Opportunities for Assessment, Planning, and Professional Growth. Unpublished manuscript, Harriman School for Management and Policy, State University of New York, Stony Brook.
London, M., and D.W. Bray
  1984   Measuring and developing young managers' career motivation. *Journal of Management Development* 3:3-25.

London, M., and S.A. Stumpf
    1982 *Managing Careers.* Reading, Mass.: Addison-Wesley.
McCall, M.W., Jr., M.M. Lombardo, and A.M. Morrison
    1988 *The Lessons of Experience: How Successful Executives Develop on Job.* Lexington,
          Mass: Lexington Books.
McCarley, N., and T.G. Carskadon
    1983 Test-retest reliabilities of scales and subscales of the Myers-Briggs Type Indicator
          and of criteria for clinical interpretive hypotheses involving them. *Research in
          Psychological Type* 6:24-36.
McCaulley, M.H.
    1988 The Myers-Briggs Type Indicator and Leadership: Working Paper. Paper prepared
          for the Conference on Psychological Measures and Leadership, San Antonio, Tex.
Moore, M.D., and T.G. Carskadon
    1984 Observing people, observing things: does the MBTI E-I scale measure what we
          assume it does? *Journal of Psychological Type* 7:41-45.
Moore, T., and W. Woods
    1987 Personality tests are back. *Fortune* (March 30):74-82.
Myers, I.B., and M.H. McCaulley
    1985 *Manual: A Guide to the Development and Use of the Myers-Briggs Type Indicator.*
          Palo Alto, Calif.: Consulting Psychologists Press.
Rokeach, M.
    1973 *The Nature of Human Values.* New York: Free Press.
    1979 *Understanding Human Values.* New York: Free Press.
Shapiro, K.J., and I.E. Alexander
    1969 Extraversion-introversion, affiliation, and anxiety. *Journal of Personality* 37:387-
          406.
Striker, L.J., and J. Ross
    1964 Some correlates of a Jungian personality inventory. *Psychological Reports* 14:623-
          643.
Sundberg, N.D.
    1977 *Assessment of Persons.* Englewood Cliffs, N.J.: Prentice-Hall.
Stumpf, S.A., and S.M. Colarelli
    1980 Career exploration: development of dimensions and some preliminary findings.
          Psychological Reports 47:979-988.
Thayer, P.W.
    1988 The Myers-Briggs Type Indicator and Enhancing Human Performance. Unpub-
          lished manuscript, Department of Psychology, North Carolina State University.
Van Velsor, E.
    1988 Database Analysis: Leadership Development Program, Center for Creative Leader-
          ship. Paper prepared for the Conference on Psychological Measures and Leader-
          ship, San Antonio, Tex.
Vargo, C., N. McCarley, and T.G. Carskadon
    1986 Extraverts and introverts: where are the differences? *Journal of Psychological
          Type* 12:46-49.
Yeakley, F.R.
    1982 Communication style preferences and adjustments as an approach to studying ef-
          fects of similarity in psychological type. *Research in Psychological Type* 5:30-48.
    1983 Implications of communication style research for psychological type theory. *Re-
          search in Psychological Type* 6:5-23.
    1985 Use of the communication style similarity scales: a cautionary note. *Journal of
          Psychological Type* 10:40.

PART III

Altering Mental States

IN THIS PART OF THE REPORT WE DISCUSS several approaches to the alteration of a person's mental state, presumably in order to enhance performance. The emphasis in this part is on changes in feelings and attitudes, rather than on changes in knowledge, as in Part II.

The four chapters represent a sampling of procedures or strategies intended to accomplish such changes. Each approach is the subject of a considerable body of research designed to evaluate effects or to provide an understanding of the underlying psychological mechanisms responsible for the effects. Each is also used widely in applied settings in which performance problems receive special attention. Much of the relevant research is summarized with an eye on implications for practice.

Of all the approaches to altering mental states, the one that is currently receiving the most attention is subliminal perception and learning. Chapter 6 addresses the idea of subliminal learning through audio cassette tapes, which has been widely marketed and promoted as a solution to a host of performance and attitudinal problems. In this chapter the committee evaluates these assertions in the context of psychological theory and available experimental evidence.

Chapter 7 considers meditation, a time-honored practice engaged in by millions of people who share the mystical religious traditions of Eastern countries. Meditation has also gained popularity in the West, where claims have been made for it as a technique that enhances performance. A number of studies have been conducted that address these claims. The evidence discussed in this chapter leads to conclusions about its effectiveness.

Pain as both a physiological and psychological reaction is the topic of Chapter 8. Encouraging evidence from psychological studies suggest ways to manage the feelings associated with acute and chronic pain. If effective, these strategies can increase a person's chances to survive under very difficult circumstances. They can also contribute more generally to an improved quality of life. In this chapter the committee surveys what is known about pain and its management, concluding with some guidance on approaches likely to be effective.

Chapters 9 and 10 deal with the intriguing topic of deception and its detection. We have learned quite a bit from experimental studies about the physical manifestations of deception. The literature surveyed demonstrates that a number of nonverbal behaviors signal when a person is lying. The review also calls attention to problems of detection and offers some strategies for improving accuracy. The insights derived from these studies may be quite useful for training people for positions in which sensitivity to possible dissimulation is essential. This is not to argue, however, that these insights are sufficiently definitive to be a basis for developing a training manual. Expanding the concept further, Chapter 10 discusses several broad frameworks for understanding the conditions under which individuals from different cultural backgrounds are likely to be caught lying.

Each of the chapters raises a number of interesting questions for research done in both laboratory or field settings.

6

Subliminal Self-Help

Building Self-Confidence is the title of an audio cassette tape manu-
factured and marketed by the Gateways Institute of Ojai, California.
When the tape is played at a comfortable listening volume, all one hears
is the rhythmic ebb and flow of a tropical ocean surf and the faint cry of
gulls circling the shoreline.

At least, that is all one hears consciously. According to an accompanying brochure, the tape also contains dozens of positive suggestions or
affirmations, such as: "I am a secure person. I believe in myself more
and more every day, and my confidence naturally rises to the surface in
every situation." Each of these statements is repeated hundreds of times
in the course of the 1-hour program. Because the suggestions are masked
by the ocean sounds, they cannot be perceived consciously. Nevertheless, according to the same brochure, these suggestions can be and are
perceived subconsciously, and therein lies their purported power. The
contention is that consciously imperceptible or subliminal messages

reach the subconscious mind, which is the seat of all memories, knowledge and
emotions. The unconscious mind has a powerful influence on conscious actions,
thought, feelings, habits, and behaviors, and actually controls and guides your life.
If you want to make real, lasting changes and improvements in any area of your life,
you must reach the subconscious mind where the changes begin.

For a busy person who lacks self-confidence and lives on a tight
budget, the *Building Self-Confidence* tape in question would seem to
have strong appeal. It retails for $12.95 in the United States and, like
several other Gateways Institute tapes, comes in a small carton carrying
the advertisement: "Subliminal tapes work, so you don't have to. . . .

Simply play the tapes while you work, play, drive, read, exercise, relax, watch TV, or even as you sleep. No concentration is required for the tapes to be effective. They work whether you pay attention to them or not." The brochure also notes:

A script is provided with each tape so you know the exact recorded subliminal message. It is not necessary to read the script while listening to the tape, although to enhance effectiveness, we suggest you use statements on the script as positive affirmations, repeating them to yourself from time to time. Many have found it very helpful to read the script aloud once each day just before going to bed at night.

To maximize results, play your subliminal tape at least once a day. The more often the tape is played, the faster and greater the effect. Because each person is unique, individual results will vary from person to person. Results are sometimes experienced within the first few playings, while in other cases it may take a few days or several weeks to see changes. Be assured that if you faithfully use the tape on a regular, daily basis, results will come.

Building Self-Confidence is but one of many subliminal self-help products sold by Gateways Institute, and Gateways is but one of many sources of such merchandise. According to one estimate (Oldenburg, 1990a), about 2,000 individuals or companies in America and Canada now produce subliminal self-help products for retail sale. That there is money to be made selling such products is suggested by a second estimate (Natale, 1988) that in 1987 American consumers purchased $50,000,000 worth of subliminal tapes intended for their personal improvement, a 10 percent increase over 1986 sales. Thus the subliminal industry is big and, by most accounts, getting bigger (see McGarvey, 1989; Moore, 1982; Natale, 1988; Oldenburg, 1990a).

It is easy to see why, for several reasons. First, the premise underlying subliminal suggestion—that a person can effortlessly accomplish in a matter of months or even weeks what others struggle but fail to do in a lifetime—is nearly irresistible (see Oldenburg, 1990a).

Second, as Oldenburg (1990a) has also pointed out, the promise of subliminal suggestion seems as inviting as its premise. To clarify, consider the catalog of products produced by Potentials Unlimited of Grand Rapids, Michigan. This catalog cites more than 100 subliminal programs that are claimed to aid people lose weight, stop smoking, quit drinking, think creatively, make friends, reduce pain (whether due to arthritis, migraines, or premenstrual syndrome), improve vision, restore hearing (a particularly difficult goal to attain through subliminal *auditory* suggestions, or so it would seem), cure acne, conquer fears (of death, driving, or flying, among others), read faster, speak effectively, handle criticism, alleviate depression, assuage guilt, project astrally, heal psychically, mentally travel through space or time or both (e.g., imagine visiting Atlantis or searching for hidden treasure in the Sphinx), and become a better bowler. Though this partial listing provides a sense of the remarkably broad range of problems and issues that are allegedly amenable to hidden messages, it does not capture the subtle yet seemingly crucial differences that exist among the various subliminal programs. For example, Potentials Unlimited offers two programs, *Divorce—Yes* ("If you seek the divorce, this tape can free you from the other person.") and *Divorce—No* ("If you don't want a divorce, yet have no choice, quiet your fears and regain confidence to live and love again."): one can only hope that the company exercises as much care and caution in filling customer orders as they presumably do in producing their subliminal tapes, for the consequences of a mix-up might be catastrophic.

Yet a third reason for the rapid growth of the subliminal industry is tied to both the proliferation of new products and the development of new technologies. Though "pure" subliminal audiotapes—those containing virtually no audible messages—remain a fixture in the marketplace, "mixed" tapes, featuring subliminal messages on one side and supraliminal suggestions for guided relaxation and visualization on the other, are becoming increasingly popular. In both cases subliminality is achieved either by the traditional method of masking suggestions with the sound of music or waves or by the newer technique of speech compression, whereby the voice track bearing the suggestions (as many as 100,000 per hour) is accelerated until it becomes an unintelligible high-pitched whine. Although speech-compression technology is disavowed by some companies, including Gateways Institute, it is endorsed by others, including the Psychodynamics Research Institute in Zephyr Cove, Nevada, a firm that is also notable for being among the first to sell subliminal programs for children, including a potty-training tape for toddlers (see Oldenburg, 1990a).

To complement their line of subliminal audio programs, many companies now also offer an array of subliminal video tapes, in which suggestions are shown so briefly that they cannot be consciously seen. This procedure is part of the latest high-tech subliminal innovation, called MindVision, that was introduced in November 1989 by Gateways Institute. As described by Oldenburg (1990b:C5):

. . . this "inconspicuous box" hooks into the television and VCR to flash visual subliminal messages "hundreds of thousands of times each hour" on the TV screen while repeating auditory subliminal affirmations all during regular TV shows. "The lazy man's answer to a better life," Gateways boasts.

But is it really? More to the point, what evidence is there that mass-marketed subliminal self-help products are effective in practice? Even more fundamental, is there any scientific evidence that such products, in principle, could be effective?

SUBJECTIVELY PERCEPTIBLE VERSUS
OBJECTIVELY DETECTABLE STIMULI

The question of effectiveness in principle has been addressed by Merikle (1988). In the introduction to his article, he remarks that, although the reality of subliminal perception continues to be a contentious issue in scientific circles, "recent research has led to a growing consensus that subliminal perception is a valid phenomenon that can be demonstrated under certain well-defined conditions (Merikle, 1988:357).[1]   The research to which Merikle refers has revealed two important observations that, taken together, provide strong support for subliminal perception. First, performance on a variety of psychological tasks—for instance, deciding whether a string of letters forms a word (e.g., Marcel, 1983), whether a word has a good or bad meaning (Greenwald et al., 1989), whether an ambiguously described person is friendly or hostile (Bargh and Pietromonaco, 1982), or whether a geometric shape seems light or dark (Mandler et al., 1987) is influenced by information that people *claim* they did not consciously perceive. Second, information presented above and below the level of *claimed* awareness has qualitatively different effects on performance (e.g., Dixon, 1971; Cheesman and Merikle, 1986; Groeger, 1984; Jacoby and Whitehouse, 1989). The importance of the second observation lies in the fact that, given the demonstration of differential (possibly opposite) outcomes, "one can be certain that effects observed in the supposedly unaware condition were not actually due to the subjects' being aware of an item without the experimenter's detecting that awareness" (Jacoby and Whitehouse, 1989:127).

Why the emphasis on claimed awareness? The answer is suggested by the results of a study by Cheesman and Merikle (1984) in which subjects were asked to name, as quickly as possible, a "target" color (a patch of blue, for instance) that was preceded by either a congruent or an incongruent color-word "prime" (the word *blue* as opposed to, say, *green*). In previous studies using visible color words as primes (e.g., Dyer and Severance, 1973), it had been shown that a target color is named faster if it is preceded by a congruent than by an incongruent prime. Whether color words rendered invisible by backward masking also produce a reliable "priming effect" in the color-naming task was an issue of central concern in Cheesman and Merikle's study.

To investigate this issue, Cheesman and Merikle measured color-naming latencies under three threshold conditions: suprathreshold, objective, and subjective. Each of these conditions comprised many individual trials, and every trial conformed to the same sequence of events in rapid succession: (1) presentation of a congruent or an incongruent color word prime, (2) presentation of a central mask composed of random letters, (3) display of the to-be-named target color.

The critical difference among the conditions was the duration of the interval separating onset of the prime from onset of the mask: a constant 300 milliseconds (msec) in the suprathreshold condition, an average of 56 msec in the subjective-threshold condition, and an average of 30 msec in the objective-threshold condition. Cheesman and Merikle settled on these intervals, or stimulus onset asynchronies (SOAs), by pretesting the subjects on the ability to detect which one of four color-word primes had been presented on a particular trial.

Results of this pretesting revealed that at the SOA corresponding to the suprathreshold condition, subjects stated that they could see the primes clearly, and they therefore estimated their performance on the test of four-alternative forced-choice target detectability would be perfect (100 percent)—which it was. At the SOA corresponding to the objective threshold, subjects indicated that they could not see the primes, and they therefore anticipated scoring at chance (25 percent)—which they did—on the test of target detectability. At the SOA corresponding to the subjective threshold, subjects again claimed that they could not consciously perceive the primes, and they therefore again anticipated scoring at chance as to which particular target color word had been presented on a particular trial. In actuality, however, their random "guesses" were, on average, 66 percent correct—a level of detection performance that plainly exceeds chance.

As the detectability of the primes varied across threshold conditions, so too did the size of the priming effect observed in the color-naming task. In the suprathreshold condition, a substantial priming effect was found (on average, target colors were named about 95 msec faster when primed by congruent than by incongruent color words); in the subjective-threshold condition, the effect was smaller but remained significant (mean difference of roughly 40 msec); and in the objective-threshold condition, the effect was virtually nonexistent (mean difference of less than 10 msec).[2] These results, in addition to those relating to tasks other than color naming (see Eriksen, 1960, 1986; Merikle, 1988), suggest that subjectively imperceptible but objectively detectable stimuli can affect certain actions. As such, these results are consistent with Merikle's (1988:360) conception of subliminal perception as "perception in the absence of subjective confidence."

There is one advantage of viewing subliminal perception this way (Merikle, 1988:360):

It eliminates much of the mysticism previously associated with the concept. No longer is it necessary to consider subliminal perception as implying the existence of some "supersensitive" unconscious perceptual system. Rather, the evidence simply suggests that we can sometimes discriminate among stimulus states, as indicated by our verbal responses, even when, based on our subjective phenomenal experiences, we have no confidence that sufficient stimulus information was perceived to guide response selection. Thus, according to this view, subliminal perception occurs whenever we can objectively discriminate among possible stimulus states but have no subjective confidence as to the correctness of our decisions.

A second advantage concerns the question, posed earlier, of whether it is possible in principle for mass-marketed subliminal self-help products to produce their intended effects. By Merikle's (1988:360) account:

When subliminal perception is viewed as a subjective state, there is a very clear specification of the minimum stimulus condition that must be satisfied before sufficient information is perceived, either consciously or unconsciously, to influence higher-level decision processes. Since, according to this view, subliminal perception reflects an absence of subjective confidence when responding discriminately to a stimulus, the minimum condition necessary for demonstrating subliminal perception is the presence of a detectable stimulus.

To determine whether subliminal self-help products, specifically, subliminal audio cassettes, meet this "minimum stimulus condition," Merikle (1988) performed two types of studies. First, if the cassettes actually contain covert messages, then frequency changes characteristic of spoken speech should be evident in spectrograms or "voice prints" derived from the tapes. Of the 40-odd spectrograms that Merikle culled from four subliminal audio cassettes (each produced by a different company), none showed any signs of hidden speech.

Though provocative, these null results are difficult to interpret because spectrographic analysis may not be capable of detecting very weak speech (e.g., at average signal-to-noise ratios of -10 to -20dB, see Borden and Harris, 1984). In addition, it is conceivable that in comparison with a sound spectrograph, the human auditory system is more sensitive to the detection and decoding of weak, degraded signals (i.e., embedded messages). In recognition of this possibility, Merikle (1988) performed a second type of study in which the human auditory system, rather than a sound spectrograph, served as the measuring instrument. In this psychophysical research, subjects were repeatedly tested for the ability to discriminate between two commercially produced cassettes that were identical except that, according to the manufacturer, one contained subliminal messages and the other did not. Merikle found that the subjects could not reliably distinguish between the "message" and the "no-message" cassettes, and he concluded (1988:370):

Taken together, the empirical results lead to the inescapable conclusion that the widely marketed subliminal cassettes do not contain any embedded messages that could conceivably influence behavior. This conclusion is supported both by the results of the spectrographic analyses indicating that these cassettes do not contain any identifiable embedded speech and by the results of the psychophysical studies indicating that these cassettes do not contain any embedded signals whatsoever that can be detected under controlled conditions. Given that consistent empirical support for subliminal perception has only been found under conditions that allow stimulus detection, these subliminal audio cassettes do not satisfy the most minimal conditions for demonstrating subliminal perception.

An ardent advocate of subliminal self-help might challenge this conclusion on two grounds: (1) some, perhaps many, of the vast number of the audiotapes (or any or all video tapes) that Merikle did not test do meet his minimum condition for demonstrating subliminal perception and thus could conceivably affect behavior as advertised; (2) some, perhaps many, of the people who buy and use these tapes say that "silent treatments" do them good (see McGarvey, 1989; VandenBoogert, 1984). We first consider in detail the second point and then discuss the implications of the first point.

MOBILIZATION, EFFORT JUSTIFICATION, AND EXPECTANCY EFFECTS

As noted by Oldenburg (1990a), many marketers of subliminal self-improvement products try to attract new customers by publicizing the ringing recommendations of past patrons. Oldenburg (1990a) cites several of these endorsements, and others may be found in *Discoveries Through Inner Quests*, a promotional magazine for the Gateways Institute. In the Winter-Spring 1990 issue of this magazine, a woman from Massachusetts writes: "Bless you! I'm listening to my tape on pain reduction. It is marvelous. I had almost instant relief from pain on first using it a few days ago. It's much cheaper than a doctor and much better than medication. Phenomenal is what it has done for my spirits." In the same issue, a California woman reports "dramatic results" in her eating habits after purchasing the subliminal tape titled Stop Eating Junk Food, and a man from Maine states that shortly after receiving the tape Wealth and Prosperity, he got a new job and tripled his old salary.

Though there is no reason to doubt the sincerity of these testimonials, there are several reasons to question the conviction that subliminal suggestions are in any way responsible for, or even play a part in, any self-perceived improvements in behavior. In the first place, by buying and using a subliminal self-help product, one demonstrates not only a desire for personal enhancement, but also a commitment to change one's ways. The very act of making such a commitment, of mobilizing oneself into action, may be therapeutic in its own right, in much the same way that some people realize marked improvements in behavior after they register for, but before they receive, individual psychotherapy (see Rachman and Wilson, 1980). Compared with undertaking psychotherapy, the commitment expressed through the purchase and use of a subliminal product is obviously much less. After all, such products are designed to work "so you don't have to," and its therapeutic potential is correspondingly much more modest in principle. Indeed, the commitment entailed in employing subliminal suggestions to, say, enhance one's popularity and make new friends seems comparable to the commitment involved in spending an hour every day for a month at the beach to accomplish these same goals. After visiting the beach on a regular basis, or following the steady use of a "be more popular" subliminal tape, one might in fact acquire some new friends. But surely this outcome is no more attributable to the properties of the beach than it is to the contents of the subliminal tape. Rather, responsibility rests with the person's decision to *do* something—go to the beach or play the subliminal tape—that might help him or her win friends. Consequently, the imaginary "beach therapy" might be every bit as effective, or ineffective, as the real "subliminal programs" that are purported to improve one's popularity.

A second, related reason that subliminal tapes, even those containing no detectable embedded messages, may seem salutary has to do with the social psychological phenomenon of effort justification: the finding that the harder we work at something, the more we like it (see Penrod, 1983). After buying a subliminal tape and using it daily for several weeks, as most manufacturers advise, many people would be reluctant to admit to themselves or others that they had wasted their time and money. Instead, they would be motivated to detect some sort of change in some aspect of their lives, in order to rationalize their investment (see Conway and Ross, 1984).

Yet a third reason for the possible effect of tapes without detectable messages, perhaps the most important, relates to expectancy effects. By way of background, most readers are familiar with the story of how, in 1957, an advertising expert named James Vicary subliminally presented the statements "Eat Popcorn and Drink Coke" to unsuspecting viewers of the film *Picnic*, resulting in an impulsive rush to the refreshment stand. Many readers may not know, however, that years later Vicary admitted that his study was a hoax intended to increase revenues for his foundering advertising firm (see Weir, 1984). Vicary's "demonstration" sparked a storm of controversy (see Moore, 1982, 1988; Pratkanis and Greenwald, 1988) and stimulated many investigations of subliminal advertising. One of these was a study, brought to our attention by Pratkanis et al. (1990), that was conducted by the Canadian Broadcast Corporation in 1958. As described by Pratkanis et al. (1990:5):

During a popular Sunday night television show viewers were told about the Vicary EAT POPCORN/DRINK COKE STUDY and were informed that the station would do a test of subliminal persuasion (although the content of the message was not revealed). The message "Phone Now" was then flashed subliminally on screen 352 times. Telephone company records indicated that phone usage did not increase nor did local television stations report an increase in calls. However, almost half of the nearly 500 letters sent in by viewers indicated that they felt compelled to "do something" and many felt an urge to eat or drink. It appears that expectations created by the Vicary study influenced what people believed had happened.

That subliminal methods of personal improvement, like those involved in public advertising, are susceptible to strong expectancy effects is a point made plain in a recent study by Pratkanis et al. (1990).[3] Through ads placed in local newspapers, these researchers recruited volunteers who were especially interested in the potential value of subliminal self-help tapes and who would probably be similar to those most likely to purchase such products.

On the first day of the study, the subjects completed a battery of tests to measure self-esteem and memory ability. Every participant was then given one or two commercially produced subliminal audiotapes: one claimed by the manufacturer to contain suggestions for improving self esteem (e.g., "I radiate an inner sense of confidence"), the other claimed to contain suggestions for improving memory (e.g., "My ability to remember and recall is increasing daily"). On both tapes, the suggestions were recorded behind background classical music, so as to render them subliminal. The intriguing aspect of this study was that only a randomly selected one-half of the subjects actually got the tape they thought they were getting, one-quarter received the memory enhancement tape mislabeled as one to improve their self-esteem, and one-quarter received a self-esteem tape mislabeled "memory improvement."

The subjects took their tapes home and listened to them every day for 5 weeks, the period recommended by the manufacturer for achieving maximum benefit. After 5 weeks, the subjects were asked to indicate whether they believed the tapes had been effective, and they also completed a second battery of self-esteem and memory tests.

The tests showed that the tapes had no appreciable effect, positive or negative, on any measure of either self-esteem or memory, but many of the subjects believed otherwise. Approximately one-half of those who thought they had received the self-esteem tape—regardless of whether they had actually received it or the memory tape—stated that their self-esteem had risen; similarly, about one-half of those who presumed, correctly or not, that they had received the memory tape maintained that their memory had improved as a result of listening to the tape. In light of those results, the title selected by Pratkanis and his associates to describe their study—"What you expect is what you believe, but not necessarily what you get"—seems most appropriate.

CONCLUSIONS

There are some well-documented psychological reasons that subliminal self-help products may appear to work, even if they contain no detectable embedded messages and thus fail to satisfy the "minimum stimulus condition" set by Merikle (1988) for demonstrating subliminal perception. It is possible, of course, that products now available in the marketplace do meet the criterion of detectability (after all, Merikle tested no video displays and only a handful of audio cassettes) or that such products could be engineered in the future. Suppose, for the sake of argument, that one were to identify or invent a subliminal self-help-product that complies with the minimum prerequisite. What then?

Clearly, the mere presence of objectively detectable messages would by no means ensure the product's effectiveness. Recent research does suggest that subjectively imperceptible stimuli may have short-term effects on the performance of such relatively simple tasks as color naming or lexical decision under controlled laboratory conditions. But one cannot and should not infer from this research that long-term changes in complex actions, cognitions, or emotions—such as smoking, self-confidence, or depression—can be effected by exposure to subliminal suggestions under such varied real-life circumstances as reading, relaxing, or even sleeping. Such effects, if any, remain to be conclusively established and rigorously explored.

Rather, as Merikle (1988) has remarked, the presence of detectable messages would only imply that it may be worthwhile to carry out carefully controlled studies of the possible effects of such messages. Such studies would need to address a very long list of questions, some of which have been raised in prior research on subliminal perception. For instance, are there significant individual differences in peoples' sensitivity to the embedded but detectable messages (e.g., Sackeim et al., 1977)? Might one's receptivity to such messages be enhanced by the adoption of a passive attitude or frame of mind (e.g., Dixon, 1971)? Do subliminal messages serve only to amplify preexisting tendencies or can they induce novel ways of acting, feeling, or thinking (e.g., Kihlstrom, 1987)? Are there demonstrable qualitative differences between the effects of presenting one and the same message above as opposed to below the subjective threshold of awareness (e.g., Cheesman and Merikle, 1986; Dixon, 1986)? Finding answers to these and many related questions will doubtless prove to be a difficult and demanding task, but perhaps a rewarding one as well. At this time, however, on the basis of the committee's review of the available research literature, we conclude that there is neither theoretical foundation nor experimental evidence to support claims that subliminal self-help audiotapes enhance human performance.

NOTES

1. In the interests of brevity and in keeping with our current focus on subliminal perception as a commercial means of promoting self-improvement, neither the history nor the current status of subliminal perception as a scientific concept is discussed in detail here. Readers interested in these issues should consult Adams (1957), Cheesman and Merikle (1984, 1986), Dixon (1971, 1981), Eriksen (1960), Goldiamond (1958), Greenwald et al. (1989), Holender (1986), and accompanying peer commentaries, Marcel (1983), Merikle and Cheesman (1987), Reingold and Merikle (1988), and Swets et al. (1961).

2. In addition to manipulating the prime-mask SOA, Cheesman and Merikle (1984) varied the prime-target color SOA, either 50, 550, or 1,050 msec. Because this latter variable did not significantly influence the size of the observed priming effects, the results for each prime-target color SOA have been averaged to yield the above priming data.

3. This study is also described in Greenwald et al. (1990), together with two successful replications.

REFERENCES

Adams, J.K.
   1957   Laboratory studies of behavior without awareness. *Psychological Bulletin* 54:383-405.
Bargh, J.A., and P. Pietromonaco
   1982   Automatic information processing and social perception: the influence of trait information presented outside of conscious awareness on impression formation. *Journal of Personality and Social Psychology* 43:437-449.
Bordon, G., and K.S. Harris
   1984   *Speech Science Primer: Physiology, Acoustics, and Perception of Speech*, 2nd ed. Baltimore, Md.: Williams & Wilkins.
Cheesman, J., and P.M. Merikle
   1984   Priming with and without awareness. *Perception and Psychophysics* 36:387-395.
   1986   Distinguishing conscious from unconscious perceptual processes. *Canadian Journal of Psychology* 40:343-367.
Conway, M., and M. Ross
   1984   Getting what you want by revising what you had. *Journal of Personality and Social Psychology* 47:738-748.
Dixon, N.F.
   1971   *Subliminal Perception: The Nature of a Controversy*. London, England: McGraw-Hill.
   1981   *Preconscious Processing*. Chichester, England: John Wiley.
   1986   On private events and brain events. *Behavioral and Brain Sciences* 9:29-30.
Dyer, F.N., and L.J. Severance
   1973   Stroop interference with successive presentations of separate incongruent words and colors. *Journal of Experimental Psychology* 98:438-439.
Eriksen, C.W.
   1960   Discrimination and learning without awareness: methodological survey and evaluation. *Psychological Review* 67:279-300.
Goldiamond, I.
   1958   Indicators of perception: subliminal perception, subception, unconscious perception: an analysis in terms of psychophysical indicator methodology. *Psychological Bulletin* 55:373-411.
Greenwald, A.G., M.R. Klinger, and T.J. Lui
   1989   Unconscious processing of dichotically masked words. *Memory and Cognition* 17:35-47.

Greenwald, A.G., E.R. Spangenberg, A.R. Pratkanis, and J. Eskenazi
    1990   Double-Blind Tests of Subliminal Self-Help Tapes. Paper presented at the American Psychological Association Convention, Boston, August 1990. Unpublished manuscript, Department of Psychology, University of Washington, Seattle.

Groeger, J.A.
    1984   Evidence of unconscious semantic processing from a forced error situation. *British Journal of Psychology* 75:305-314.

Holender, D.
    1986   Semantic activation without conscious identification in dichotic listening, parafoveal vision, and visual masking: a survey and appraisal. *Behavioral and Brain Sciences* 9:1-66.

Jacoby, L.L., and K. Whitehouse
    1989   An illusion of memory: false recognition influenced by unconscious perception. *Journal of Experimental Psychology: General* 118:126-135.

Kihlstrom, J.F.
    1987   The cognitive unconscious. *Science* 237:1445-1452.

Mandler, G., Y. Nakamura, and B.J.S. Van Zandt
    1987   Nonspecific effects of exposure to stimuli that cannot be recognized. *Journal of Experimental Psychology: Learning, Memory, and Cognition* 13:646-648.

Marcel, A.J.
    1983   Conscious and unconscious perception: experiments on visual masking and word recognition. *Cognitive Psychology* 15:197-237.

McGarvey, R.
    1989   Recording success. *USAir Magazine* February:94-102.

Merikle, P.M.
    1988   Subliminal auditory messages: an evaluation. *Psychology and Marketing* 5:355-372.

Merikle, P.M., and J. Cheesman
    1987   Current status of research on subliminal perception. Pp. 298-302 in M. Wallendorf and P. Anderson, eds., *Advances in Consumer Research*, Vol. 14. Provo, Utah: Association for Consumer Research.

Moore, T.E.
    1982   Subliminal advertising: what you see is what you get. *Journal of Marketing* 46(2):38-47.
    1988   The case against subliminal manipulation. *Psychology and Marketing* 5:297-316.

Natale, J.A.
    1988   Are you open to suggestion? *Psychology Today* 22:28-30.

Oldenburg, D.
    1990a   Hidden messages. *The Washington Post.* April 3:C5.
    1990b   Silent treatments. *The Washington Post.* April 5:C5.

Penrod, S.
    1983   *Social Psychology.* Englewood Cliffs, N.J.: Prentice-Hall.

Pratkanis, A.R., and A.G. Greenwald
    1988   Recent perspectives on unconscious processing: still no marketing applications. *Psychology and Marketing* 5:337-353.

Pratkanis, A.R., J. Eskenazi, and A.G. Greenwald
    1990   What You Expect Is What You Believe, But Not Necessarily What You Get: On the Effectiveness of Subliminal Self-Help Audiotapes. Paper presented at the annual convention of the Western Psychological Association, Los Angeles, California.

Rachman, S.J., and G.T. Wilson
    1980   Using direct and indirect measures to study perception without awareness. *Perception and Psychophysics* 44:563-575.

Reingold, E.M., and P.M. Merikle
    1988   Using direct and indirect measures to study perception without awareness. *Perception and Psychophysics* 44:563-575.
Sackeim, H.A., I.K. Packer, and R.C. Gur
    1977   Hemisphericity, cognitive set, and susceptibility to subliminal perception. *Journal of Abnormal Psychology* 86:624-630.
Swets, J.A., W. Tanner, and T.G. Birdsall
    1961   Decision processes in perception. *Psychological Review* 68:301-340.
VandenBoogert, C.
    1984   A Study of Potential Unlimited, Inc. Subliminal Persuasion/Self-Hypnosis Tapes. Potentials, Inc., Grand Rapids, Michigan.
Weir, W.
    1984   Another look at subliminal "facts." *Advertising Age* October:46.

7

Meditation

Meditation is generally defined as a class of techniques designed to influence an individual's consciousness through the regulation of attention. However, there is less agreement on its conceptualization than is commonly thought. Necessary procedural elements seem to be: (1) to lie quietly or to sit in a particular position, (2) to attend to one's breathing but not necessarily to try to slow it, (3) to adopt a passive attitude, (4) to be at ease, and, sometimes, (5) to repeat aloud or to oneself a word or phrase, referred to as a mantra. What is less clear is whether one's mind should be directed to an idea of a Supreme Being or to a less theistic notion of the universality of existence, or whether the mind should be "empty," except perhaps for the repetition of the mantra. An additional controversy is whether the practice of meditation has to be but one part of a particular life-style, as was and is the case on the Indian subcontinent, where yogic practices and philosophies originated.

One of the problems in evaluating the importance of an overall life-style is that those who are well practiced in meditation (of whatever kind, except perhaps for Westernized versions; see below) are generally the ones who serve as subjects in experiments. Perhaps that is as it should be, given that considerable dedicated practice is asserted to be necessary for doing it "right"; however, that characteristic makes it difficult to separate specific techniques from a firmly held belief system. In this respect, research on meditation is similar to research on such topics as psychoanalysis and related approaches to clinical treatment.

There are three streams in the history of meditation. First, meditation is central to various forms of eastern mysticism, especially Buddhism, the central principle of which is that God is knowable through proper meditation. An insight unknowable except to the faithful can also lead to greater physical strength, long life, and a general contentment ("Nirvana"). The proper practice of meditation, however, is said to require a withdrawal from the everyday world, although the dramatic experience of Buddhist Vietnamese monks immolating themselves with fire as a political protest in the early 1970s indicates that such priestly withdrawal is not incompatible with deep concern for everyday realities.

Second, in the late 1950s a wise man from India known as the Maharishi Mahesh Yogi introduced transcendental meditation to the West, especially the United States. The Maharishi stated that transcendental meditation was a method based on scientific principles that could be studied systematically, and that its conscientious practice could lead to a deep and complete understanding of nature and to general benefits for humankind (Maharishi Mahesh Yogi, 1966). Unlike Buddhist meditation, transcendental meditation did not require radical life-style changes or extended practice, and it placed greater emphasis on "destressing" people than it did on spiritual enlightenment or contact with a Supreme Being. The 1960s was conducive to the spread of transcendental meditation among both lay people and scientists; the work of the latter group is reviewed below.

A third stream in humankind's long-standing interest in meditation can be found in some Western mystical traditions, both Christian and Jewish. Among Hasidic Jews, for example, there is a tradition of dancing and chanting for long periods of time in order to achieve an altered state in which the teachings of God can be more readily received.

Thus, people in many parts of the world have for centuries been drawn to practices that, without drugs or other direct physical manipulations, are believed to lead to altered states of consciousness. These practices are also believed by some to put one in contact with higher truths or with God, and sometimes to bring more earthly benefits, such as better physical and emotional well-being.

SCIENTIFIC EVALUATIONS OF MEDITATION

Divine or spiritual revelation represents one time-honored way to know one's world and one's place in it. It is different from scientific ways of knowing, however, and it is the latter epistemology that guides our evaluation of meditation. Over the past 30 years considerable scientific attention has been directed to various meditative practices.

From a rational point of view, the practice of meditation may lead to psychological and physical benefits by distracting a person from stressors, whether they are environmental or self-generated. (There is a school of thought that an external event is a stressor only if it is appraised or evaluated as such; see Lazarus, 1966.) If a person seeks out a quiet place, closes his or her eyes, and repeats a mantra, there is every reason to expect that the person's cognitive apparatus will become less occupied with processing negative information. Generations of insomniacs have been instructed to lie quietly and count sheep. It is doubtful that this homespun remedy for sleeplessness would persist over the years if it did not help some people some of the time.

The problem, from a scientific perspective, concerns proper experimental controls. Controls for distraction or for just sitting or lying quietly and undisturbed are seldom found in the many studies that demonstrate positive benefits, such as reduction in respiration and heart rate, and in experiences of stress, such as anxiety or anger (Cheaper and Giber, 1978; Delmonte, 1985). Indeed, when resting-only controls are present, there is virtually no evidence that reductions in somatic arousal (heart rate, respiration rate, skin conductance fluctuations, blood pressure) are any less than those found in experienced meditators who are meditating (Holmes, 1984). There are some reports of benefits in blood pressure reduction for borderline hypertensives (e.g., Benson, 1975; Patel, 1973), but the combined use of other techniques, such as relaxation, in most studies precludes a clear attribution of any positive effects to meditation by itself (Delmonte, 1984, as cited in Brener and Connally, 1986). Patel (1976) for example, says that in addition to meditation, patients must make life-style changes to reduce conflict, a sensible enough conclusion and one that is consistent with the growing recognition that successful interventions must usually be multifaceted (Davison and Neale, 1990).

Overall, our assessment of the scientific research on mediation leads to the conclusion that it seems to be no more effective in lowering metabolism than are established relaxation techniques; it is unwarranted to attribute any special effects to meditation alone. The rest of this section discusses several kinds of studies that underlie our conclusions.

The Pit Burial Studies

The most striking presumed benefits of meditation are found in reports from "pit burial" studies. There is a tradition in India that certain highly regarded yogis can perform superhuman feats. One such feat is to be buried alive for 1 or 2 days. Special importance is attributed to the mystique of the meditation and the yogis' general life-style. In a pit burial, the person lies supine in a board-covered pit underground or in an airtight box above the ground. The longest recorded period survived by a human being was reported by Vakil (1950). After 62 hours, the man emerged stuporous but alive. So startling were these reports that in

1960 the government of India established a committee to study yogic practices as part of an investigation of indigenous medicine. Most controlled research in the West has been conducted in conjunction with this Indian effort.

Mammals, of course, produce carbon dioxide when they exhale, and it is normal for the respiration rate to increase as carbon dioxide concentrations increase. Thus, breathing in an airtight box gradually uses up oxygen at the same time it produces carbon dioxide; the trick is to breathe as slowly as possible, thus using up the least amount of oxygen, but this requires that one suppress the normal mammalian reflex to breathe more rapidly as carbon dioxide increases. In this connection, we note that evidence supports the assertion that meditation reduces metabolic rate, probably through a reduction in respiration rate.

In one study, an experienced yogi instructor had a lighted candle with him in an airtight box. The candle went out after 3 hours, but the yogi remained there for an additional 5 hours. On another occasion he spent 10 hours alone in the box. It was found that his oxygen intake decreased by 40 to 50 percent. At the end of his ordeal, the air he was breathing contained 15.8 percent oxygen and 4.4 percent carbon dioxide; the proportions for air at sea level are 20 percent and less than 2 percent, respectively. Thus, the actual air available for consumption was not very different from regular air. Another study showed that as long as carbon dioxide concentrations did not exceed 7 percent and as long as oxygen concentration was at least 12 percent, a person could remain alive in a box.

In our view the renowned yogic feat is probably due not to special properties of meditation, but rather to confidence in one's ability to slow down one's respiration rate and to the faith that one can survive the ordeal if only one does not panic (and thereby use up more oxygen than normal). For a nonmystical Westerner, it would seem that what is required is knowledge of the scientific facts as summarized above and a confidence in one's skills to lie still and reduce one's respiration rate. Faith in one's "captor" would also seem important, as would the availability of a "panic button" to gain early release if one felt the need to ask for it. It is well known and reported in the committee's earlier report (Druckman and Swets, 1988) that perceived control and predictability are inherently anxiety-reducing. Religious faith and patriotism may well be powerful forces that enable people to cope under highly stressful circumstances; these possibilities remain to be investigated.

The Generalization Problem

A central problem for any intervention is whether benefits such as reduced anxiety, achieved during a therapeutic or training session, generalize to everyday situations. Consideration of the value of any stress management method must include the conditions of its application. For example, if a person's task is to lie still in a confined space and "just" control his anxieties so that he does not panic after hours or days, then meditation, relaxation, or prayer can be useful. We have seen from the pit burial studies that enough oxygen is available even in an airtight space for a person to survive for hours—provided the person maintains a low respiration rate—and this goal is achieved more readily if the person does not panic. But if the situation calls for performing a complex sensorimotor task, such as firing a rifle or reading a radar screen, engaging in meditation would seem impossible if not counterproductive, and there are no data suggesting otherwise.

The most supportive data come from relaxation/meditation/biofeedback studies that show lasting reductions in blood pressure following proper training (DiTomasso, 1987). However, the issue here is what accounts for this generalization of effects: Does the person take time out during the day to relax or meditate, or is there some more enduring, systemic reduction in arousal level that does not require conscious attention and practice? Other explanations of lasting reductions would consider changes brought about by the person's lowered reactivity or anger and the positive social-environmental effects that such internal changes might cause. In addition, any consideration of meditation would have to include the religious component, at least insofar as it would seem to provide a strong motivation to practice and apply the techniques.

We conclude that data do not exist to answer the generalization question. The laboratory findings that do exist fail to demonstrate that meditation itself enhances a person's ability to reduce arousal from a stressor (Holmes, 1984). Similar criticisms can be made of the effects of relaxation alone, that is, training and encouraging people to relax their muscles and calm their minds. Although there is overlap with some meditation techniques, relaxation training is readily distinguishable insofar as it does not try to teach a person to gain philosophical-religious insights or to get close to a supreme being. But as with meditation, the interesting and still unanswered question is how generalization is achieved—perhaps a person must be taught to relax differentially in actual stressful situations (see Goldfried and Davison, 1976:98). Or, as with meditation, an answer might be found in the establishment of a more supportive environment and life-style. For example, learning to relax and to enjoy good feelings may prompt a person to make positive changes in his or her work and personal situation, thereby reducing the general stressfulness of the social environment.

Another possibility for most meditation practices relates to the philosophical context. It may be that meditation and relaxation, including

relaxation achieved with certain forms of biofeedback, effect cog
change. Recent evidence in support of this is available in a rep
Davison et al. (in press), who found that intensive relaxation training
reduced blood pressure in hypertensives more so than in a group given
nonpharmacological medical information and also reduced anger and
hostility in subjects' thoughts. Moreover, reductions in hostility and
anger were positively correlated with reductions in cardiovascular activity, which is consistent with the hypothesis that cognitive changes
brought about, in part, by relaxation training contribute to reductions
in hypertension.

Review of the Literature

In 1986 the Army Research Institute commissioned a review of the
literature on meditation by Brener and Connally of the University of
Hull in England. In this section we summarize the key conclusions
reached by the authors, note what research is needed, and discuss possible implications for performance. In the next section we present and
comment on a specially commissioned critique of the review.

Key Conclusions

The Brener-Connally review concentrates primarily on the role of
meditation in reducing stress and hypertension. They find that research
to date supports claims that meditation produces relaxation or stress
reduction. The effects of meditation are unlikely to be due to "exotic"
factors: subjective effects (e.g., relaxed feelings) may be the result of
alterations in blood chemistry brought about naturally through normal
bodily processes. They find it is difficult to separate the "unique" effects of meditative procedures from more general "atmosphere" effects
including the patient's (meditator's) beliefs and the therapist's (instructor's)
confidence. Overall, there are few cases in which meditation is shown
to be more effective than other treatments for stress and anxiety.

Brener and Connally conclude that reported feats of endurance such
as pit burials are likely to be due to the effect of meditation or deep
relaxation on metabolism. A lowered metabolism may allow for sur-
vival under conditions of restricted oxygen availability. Effects on metabolism can be produced by controlling respiration in the manner practiced by yogis.

Many promoters of meditation are more concerned with demonstrations of the experience than with experimental evaluations of the procedure. Little progress has been made in attempts to understand the underlying mechanisms for observed effects of meditation. Experimental

work to date is characterized by weak designs: a lack of control for subject selection, experimenter biases, expectancies, and atmosphere effects. Work on meditation has led to speculations regarding presumed links between psychological processes (e.g., states of nonanalytical thought) and physiological processes (e.g., neural activity, blood pressure).

Needed Research

Like the research literature on various forms of psychotherapy, the study of meditation would benefit from better experimental designs with proper controls and baselines for judging change. A promising area of investigation is an examination of the pathways through which psychological manifestations of meditation are produced. The better resolutions provided by new brain-scanning technologies may elucidate what happens in the brain during meditation.

Further work is needed on the psychological or institutional context for the practice of meditation. Particular attention should be paid to the Army context in relation to adoption of nontraditional training techniques. More attention should also be paid to the medically-relevant claims for the treatment of anxiety, pain, and disease as well as the medical implications of sustained attention. Finally, linkage between the documented effects of meditation and performance remains an uncharted topic: are there "unique" effects of meditation on performance that differ from those shown to result from other (nonmeditative) procedures that reduce stress?

Implications for Performance

The Brener-Connally review makes clear how little we know about relationships between physiological measures (e.g., electroencephalogram, heart rate) and psychological changes such as attitudes reported for meditation and performance in any situation. Experiments are needed that explore hypothesized relationships between changes in the physiological or psychological variables and changes in the way people perform on well-defined tasks. A start along these lines is the work done by Beatty and his colleagues in the 1970s (e.g., Beatty et al., 1974; Beatty and O'Hanlon, 1979). They focused on vigilance performance as manifested in such tasks as radar monitoring. They did not, however, examine links between meditation effects and motor or cognitive performance.

The review discusses the many complex issues that surround evaluations of meditative practices. It also points to the conclusion that a good deal of research is needed to document the possible links to performance. On the basis of this conclusion, it would seem appropriate to pursue a program of basic research designed to relate meditative practices to performances on relevant tasks. If the effects of meditation reviewed in the Brener and Connally paper are replicable, there is reason to believe that those effects would intervene between the procedures and observed performances. There may, however, be some gaps in their coverage of meditation as noted in the next section.

CRITIQUE OF THE LITERATURE REVIEW

In an effort to give as much consideration as possible to the military application of meditation, the committee commissioned David Shannahoff-Khalsa, a practitioner of yogic techniques, to write a critique of the Brener and Connally review paper.

The critique by Shannahoff-Khalsa (1990) contains four major points. First, the Brener-Connally paper covers only 300 of 1,200 published studies on meditation and relies on texts written by people who are not "masters." There is also too much focus in the review on the Buddhist meditation method. Second, Brener and Connally also lack familiarity with certain yogic practices, most especially Kundalini Yoga, as learned by Shannahoff-Khalsa from the Yogi Bhajan. Third, in an extended discussion and description of Kundalini Yoga techniques, Shannahoff-Khalsa notes that they are reported to be very effective for controlling stress, pain, and fatigue; it is claimed these techniques cure various mental disorders and generally enhance human performance through the development of a powerful mind and body. Included is a technique "for developing a penetrating force that cannot be matched by any contemporary techniques available in the military today" (1990:28). Fourth, Shannahoff-Khalsa makes proposals for research along with the caution that knowledge of the techniques not be disseminated widely because of their great power.

Overall Assessment

Great emphasis is placed by Shannahoff-Khalsa on a book by Murphy and Donovan (1988) that reviews more than 1,200 meditation studies, many more than those covered by Brener and Connally. Furthermore, the authors are self-labelled meditation devotees, while Brener and Connally avowedly are not. He goes on to say that another meditation expert, Deane Shapiro, asserts that the Murphy-Donovan book "gives a fair analysis of this literature."

Although Shannahoff-Khalsa says that Brener and Connally are fair in their appraisal, he asserts that they have overgeneralized from a limited source base, although he admits that no one can assimilate all the literature on meditation. One glaring weakness is in their treatment of the yogic perspective. According to Shannahoff-Khalsa, their coverage is adequate for Buddhist-Vipassana, transcendental, and Zen meditation, but not for Kundalini Yoga. Nevertheless, he tends to agree with Brener and Connally's overall judgment that there is no consensus on how to define meditation, how to do it, whether its results are superior to other psychological techniques such as relaxation, and whether the published studies contain too many methodological flaws to permit clear conclusions.

Shannahoff-Khalsa is critical, however, of Brener and Connally's reliance on transcendental meditation and related work by Benson (1975) on "the relaxation response." Both transcendental meditation and Benson's procedure, he asserts, make a person "overly sensitive" to the extent that they become passive and withdrawn. Yogi Master Bhajan concluded this from transcendental meditation practitioners who came to study with him, and Shannahoff-Khalsa agrees on the basis of his own 2-year experimentation with transcendental meditation, during which time he found himself becoming temperamental and touchy. He concludes that even if performed only 20 minutes a day, as the Maharishi and Benson suggest, such practice harms the person in that it induces a retreat into a silent realm, produces a passive attitude toward the external world, and reduces active coping. In general, he is critical of silent meditation and any form that does not require sitting with an erect spine and that is not more complex and structured than transcendental meditation. The problematic evidentiary bases of these conclusions are clear.

Kundalini Yoga

According to Shannahoff-Khalsa, the biggest omission of Brener and Connally has to do with yogic techniques from India and the Chi-gong (life-force) techniques from China. While there is no clear division between meditation and yoga, the former requires less motor activity. He says that the parent of all yogic practices is Kundalini Yoga as taught by Yogi Bhajan.   Much of Shannahoff-Khalsa's paper contains excerpts from his other writings that detail Kundalini techniques and physiological rationale and provide recommendations for their use by the military. In his paper on stress technology medicine, he argues that the nasal cycle is a simple parameter for assessing autonomic-central nervous system interrelationships as well as a means of determining left- and right-brain dominance. Stress, he asserts, results from how long and how frequently a swing in homeostatic imbalance is maintained. Moreover, nasal obstruction in the left or right nostril can be related to psychopathology and stress.

On the basis of these neurophysiological speculations, Shannahoff-

Khalsa proposes numerous exercises, many of which entail unilateral forced nostril breathing. He cites some of his own studies that purport to show that unilateral forced breathing could stimulate the contralateral hemisphere, producing relatively greater amplitudes in the electroencephalogram. He says that this effect is consistent with relationships of the nasal cycle and cerebral rhythm from yogic medicine. He also says recent data of his group purport to show that such breathing has predictable positive effects on cognitive performance by rectifying imbalance in the autonomic nervous system.

The committee finds these claims unwarranted. Specifically, the idea that too much left-brain activity and right sympathetic dominance may be what we think of as stress cannot be supported by any empirical data. Furthermore, this assertion is not consistent with contemporary scientific theories about the neuroendocrinology of stress (e.g., Weiner et al., 1989). One empirical study has attempted to address the possibility that one hemisphere may participate to a greater extent than the other in triggering the cascade of cognitive, affective, and biochemical events that we call stress. Using salivary cortisol secretion as a biologic marker of stress response, Wittling and Pfluger (1990) found that the right hemisphere (and not the left, as predicted by Shannahoff-Khalsa, 1991) is differentially active in producing the stress response.

Would the techniques recommended by Shannahoff-Khalsa, if indeed they had the proposed effect, influence the perception of stress and its biologic concomitants? There exists in the neuropsychology literature a small and inconclusive group of studies that have examined the relationship between unilateral forced nostril breathing and how it may influence behavior and indices of brain function (e.g., electroencephalogram). These empirical studies (Werntz et al., 1983; Werntz, 1987; Klein et al., 1986; Block et al., 1989) contain some support for the notion that unilateral nostril breathing may have an effect on cognitive performance and electroencephalogram activity. Overall, however, this literature raises many more questions than it answers.[1] Moreover, the committee queries whether the effects, if any, have application to complex behavioral tasks that are encountered in the real world.

Shannahoff-Khalsa also describes in some detail a number of yogic exercises taught to him by Yogi Bhajan. Though not yet proven valid by science, these exercises are effective for many purposes, he says, including stress management and control of some psychopathologies such as obsessive-compulsive disorder (one of the most difficult nonpsychotic disorders to treat). He believes that "our future holds the possibility for developing a near stress-resistant and disease-resistant individual" (1990:47) if such techniques are properly taught and faithfully practiced.

In another paper on advanced neuropsychological technology pro-

hoff-Khalsa (1987) asserts that Kundalini Yoga can make
edly resistant to the highest stress; he strengthens this as-
references to Tibetan monks carrying out extreme activities,
ing isolated for 3 years. He proposes training programs and
and sees Kundalini Yoga as the best way to prepare military
el for the extreme mental and physical challenges of modern and
fu.. warfare.

Shannahoff-Khalsa concludes by asserting that, of all the forms of meditation, Kundalini Yoga has the most promising implications for the military, that its skilled application can help develop "the soldier-saint" in whom is deeply instilled the desire to excel in the art of warfare. So convinced is he of the power of these techniques that he urges great caution in their dissemination. This caveat assumes that Kundalini Yoga is as powerful as he asserts. The committee does not find evidence to support that conclusion.

A CAUTIONARY NOTE ON EPISTEMOLOGY

It must be noted that it is very difficult for nonmeditation experts and thoroughly Western scientists like the members of the committee to evaluate many of the claims like those of Shannahoff-Khalsa. He is deeply immersed in Kundalini Yoga and conducts both his personal and professional life in keeping with the philosophical and procedural requirements of that practice. He asserts, as do some psychoanalysts, that one cannot know a complex and powerful system unless one experiences it in a deep and thoroughgoing way. No one on our committee has done this with Kundalini Yoga or, for that matter, with the other meditation practices we have reviewed. This epistemological issue has important policy implications. Contemporary science is but one way of knowing. It is, however, the way of knowing that characterizes the work of this committee. At the same time, it seems appropriate to be mindful of the constraints that science, as well as culture, background, and personal life experience, places on how the committee views the field of meditation.

CONCLUSIONS

The scientific literature on meditation indicates that controls for distraction or for just sitting or lying quietly and undisturbed are seldom to be found in the many studies that demonstrate positive benefits from meditation. When appropriate controls are present, no evidence supports the notion either that meditation reduces arousal any more than does simply resting quietly or that meditation permits a person to better cope with a stressor. When meditation has been found to be effective for such things as reducing hypertension, the combined use of other techniques, such as relaxation training, precludes a clear attribution of any positive effects to meditation itself. Life-style changes to reduce conflict are also apparently instrumental, a sensible enough conclusion and one that is consistent with the growing recognition that successful interventions must usually be multifaceted.

The highly publicized feats of some yogis who can remain buried for many hours without suffocating are probably due not to any special properties of meditation, but rather to confidence in their ability to slow down their respiration rate as well as faith that they can survive the ordeal if only they do not panic and use up more oxygen than normal. Consistent with findings from the committee's earlier report, perceived control and predictability are inherently anxiety-reducing. A related possibility concerns the philosophical context for most meditation practices. It may be that meditation and relaxation (and perhaps also relaxation achieved with certain forms of biofeedback) effect cognitive change, not the least of which may be an enhanced sense of self-efficacy, a belief that one can control one's stress reactions to some extent.

A particular challenge to those who advocate meditation is whether in-session benefits generalize to everyday situations or to conditions of special challenge. Does a person take time out during the day to meditate, or is there some more enduring, systemic reduction in arousal level which does not require conscious attention to practice? Perhaps interpersonal, social context changes are brought about by the person's lowered reactivity to challenge, and these positive social-environmental shifts present the individual with a less stressful environment. We do not believe that data exist to answer this question.

There is no scientific evidence to support the assertion that the proper application of Kundalini Yoga can help develop "the soldier-saint" in whom is instilled the superhuman desire and ability to excel in the art of warfare.

NOTE

1. Block et al. (1989) found that unilateral forced nostril breathing influences spatial and verbal performance, but with opposite results for males and females. Werntz and his colleagues (Werntz et al., 1983; Werntz, 1987) employed the unusual assumption that greater integrated electroencephalogram amplitude over a particular hemisphere indicates that it is dominant at the time. (The traditional interpretation is that fast, low voltage activity reflects decreased cortical activation.) Furthermore, in the Werntz et al. study, there were five subjects, only one of which showed shifts in EEG symmetry. Klein et al. (1986) found that free breathing subjects showed a small correlation between nostril dominance and cognitive performance and that unilateral nostril breathing does not influence cognitive performance. Based on this evidence it would seem premature to suggest that this approach be used for stress reduction.

REFERENCES

Beatty, J., and J.F. O'Hanlon
  1979 Operant control of posterior theta rhythm and vigilance performance: repeated treatments and transfer of training. In N. Birbaumer and H.D. Kimmel, eds., *Biofeedback and Self-Regulation*. Hillsdale, N.J.: Erlbaum.
Beatty, J., A. Greensberg, W.P. Diebler, and J.F. O'Hanlon
  1974 Operant control of occipital theta rhythm affects performance in a radar monitoring task. *Science* 183:871-874.
Benson, H.
  1975 *The Relaxation Response*. New York: Morrow.
Block, R., D. Arnott, B. Quigley, and W. Lynch
  1989 Unilateral nostril breathing influences lateralized cognitive performance. *Brain and Cognition* 9:181-190.
Brener, J., and S.R. Connally
  1986 Meditation: Rationales, Experimental Effects, and Methodological Issues. Paper prepared for the U.S. Army Research Institute for the Behavioral and Social Sciences, European Division. Department of Psychology, University of Hull, London, England.
Cheaper, D.M., and D. Giber
  1978 Meditation and psychotherapeutic effects. *Archives of General Psychiatry* 35:294-302.
Davison, G.C., and J.M. Neale
  1990 *Abnormal Psychology*, 5th ed. New York: Wiley.
Davison, G.C., M.E. Williams, E. Nezami, T. Bice, and V. DeQuattro
  In   Relaxation, reduction in angry articulated thoughts and improvements in borderline
  press hypertension and heart rate. *Journal of Behavioral Medicine*.
Delmonte, M.M.
  1985 Meditation and anxiety reduction. *Clinical Psychology Review* 5:1-12.
DiTomasso, R.A.
  1987 Essential hypertension: a methodological review. In L. Michelson and L.M. Ascher, eds., *Anxiety and Stress Disorders*. New York: Guilford.
Druckman, D., and J. Swets
  1988 *Enhancing Human Performance: Issues, Theories, and Techniques*. Committee on Techniques for the Enhancement of Human Performance, Commission on Behavioral and Social Sciences and Education, National Research Council. Washington, D.C.: National Academy Press.
Goldfried, M.R., and G.C. Davison
  1976 *Clinical Behavior Therapy*. New York: Holt, Rinehart, and Winston.
Holmes, D.S.
  1984 Meditation and somatic arousal reduction: a review of the experimental evidence. *American Psychologist* 39:1-10.
Klein, R., D. Pieton, S. Prossner, and D. Shannahoff-Khalsa
  1986 Hemispheric performance efficiency varies with nasal airflow. *Biological Psychology* 23:127-137.
Lazarus, R.S.
  1966 *Psychological Stress and the Coping Process*. New York: McGraw-Hill.
Maharishi Mahesh Yogi
  1966 *The Science of Being and Art of Living*. London: International SRM Publications.
Murphy, M., and S. Donovan
  1988 *The Physical and Psychological Effects of Meditation: A Review of Contemporary*

Meditation Research with a Comprehensive Bibliography 1931-1988. San Rafael, Calif.: Esalen Institute for Exceptional Functioning.

Patel, C.
1973 Yoga and biofeedback in the management of hypertension. *Lancet* 2:1053-1055.
1976 TM and hypertension. *Lancet* 1:539.

Shannahoff-Khalsa, D.S.
1987 Advanced Neuropsychological Technology Programs for Defense. Unpublished paper, Khalsa Foundation for Medical Science, Del Mar, Calif.
1990 A Commentary on the Jasper Brener and Samuel R. Connally Report. Paper prepared for the Committee on Techniques for the Enhancement of Human Performance, National Research Council. Khalsa Foundation for Medical Science, Del Mar, Calif.
1991 Stress technology medicine: a new paradigm for stress and considerations for self-regulation. In M. Brown, C. Rivier, and G. Koob, eds., *Neurobiology and Neuroendocrinology of Stress.* New York: Marcell Dekker Press.

Vakil, R.J.
1950 Remarkable feat of endurance by a yogi priest. *Lancet* 2:871.

Weiner, H., I. Florin, R. Murison, and D. Helhamer
1989 *Frontiers of Stress Research.* Toronto: Huber.

Werntz, D.A.
1987 Selective hemispheric stimulation by unilateral forced nostril breathing. *Human Neurobiology* 6:165-171.

Werntz, D.A., R.G. Bickford, F.E. Bloom, and D.S. Shannahoff-Khalsa
1983 Alternating cerebral hemispheric activity and lateralization of autonomic nervous function. *Human Neurobiology* 2:39-43.

Wittling, W., and M. Pfluger
1990 Neuroendocrine hemisphere asymmetries: salivary cortisol secretions during lateralized viewing of emotion-related and neutral films. *Brain and Cognition* 14:243-265.

8

Managing Pain

There is encouraging evidence that people can be taught nonpharmacological ways to cope with physical pain, particularly that which results from extreme psychological stress. This chapter examines the literature on pain management for clues about how to help people survive and function when environmental challenge is so severe that stress involves physical pain. (For this chapter the committee benefited from a commissioned paper by Laura Darke [1990].)

It is widely accepted that pain is worse when anxiety is high, and thus, that it can be controlled to an appreciable degree when anxiety can be diminished (Sternbach, 1966). Factors involved in the control of anxiety and stress (see Druckman and Swets, 1988) are similar to those important in the control of pain. It should be mentioned at the outset, however, that pain, like anxiety, has adaptive properties. People born congenitally incapable of experiencing pain often suffer serious injuries and even early death because they lack the capacity to take appropriate action cued by the experience of pain from a truly harmful stimulus. Our focus on the management or reduction of pain should not dismiss its beneficial nature under certain circumstances.

ASPECTS OF PAIN

To place pain management in context, it is useful to distinguish among four dimensions of pain (Loeser, 1980): nociception, pain, suffering, and pain behavior. It will quickly become evident that pain does not arise from a direct linkage between nerve stimulation and the cortex.

Nociception is defined as "mechanical, thermal or chemical energy impinging upon specialized nerve endings that in turn activate A-Delta and C fibers, thus initiating a signal to the central nervous system that aversive events are occurring" (Loeser, 1980:313). Thus, nociception is the basic physiological event that is presumed to create the conditions for the experience of pain. In practice it is inferred from a person's self-report. The fact that these afferent fibers travel in a complex fashion to many parts of the central nervous system provides an anatomical, although incompletely understood, basis for the modulating effects that higher mental processes have on the perception of pain (Gatchel et al., 1989).

Pain is defined as the perception of nociceptive stimulation. As with other kinds of perception, there may not always be a precise match between what is perceived and what actually exists. For example, in phantom limb pain, a patient perceives pain in an extremity that has been surgically or traumatically removed. Conversely, nociception can occur without the perception of pain, as when a soldier in combat is unaware for a period of time of a wound that is doubtless creating nociceptive input.

The theoretical basis of this view of pain is derived from Melzack and Wall's (1965) "gate-control" theory of pain, which proposes that there is a neurophysiological mechanism in the dorsal horn of the spinal cord that can increase or decrease the transmission of nerve impulses from the peripheral afferent nociceptive fibers. This gate is influenced by efferent nerve impulses *from* the brain, forming a physiological basis for the effects (reviewed below) that thought and emotion can have on the experience of pain (Gatchel et al., 1989). Conditions that "open the gate" and enhance pain perception are anxiety, depression, and focus on the pain; those that close the gate include relaxation, optimism, and distraction.

Suffering can be defined as the evaluative or affective response to the perception of pain, but it can be present also without pain, as when a loved one dies or withdraws. Indeed, loss or the threat of loss are believed central to the experience of suffering (Bakan, 1968). According to existential writings (e.g., Gendlin, 1962), suffering can be lessened if a person sees some meaning to the ordeal he or she is undergoing (see below). *Pain behavior* is defined as the observable behaviors associated with either pain or suffering. Thus, pain behavior may or may not always arise from nociception. Examples are moaning, teeth-clenching, guarded gait, irritability, and avoidance of activity (Turk et al., 1985).

The extensive work of Fordyce (1988; described in detail below) is based on the distinction between nociception/pain and suffering/pain behavior. In the former there is a physical input that cues the body to an aversive event that must be attended to in order to prevent or minimize bodily injury. In the latter, the person's reports of suffering from pain may not be entirely, or even importantly, related to organic nociception but rather may be associated with complex psychological factors having little to do with tissue injury.

Acute Versus Chronic Pain

Acute pain is linked to nociception. Chronic pain can evolve from acute pain and is said to be present when healing time is past, that is, when there is no nociception, generally regarded as a period of 6 months from an injury or event. It is more often associated with suffering and disability. Depression and anxiety magnify chronic pain more than they do acute pain (Kelly, 1986), and traditional medical treatments seldom help (Gatchel et al., 1989). The profiles of a well-known personality assessment instrument, the Minnesota Multiphasic Personality Inventory (MMPI), discriminate between acute and chronic pain patients, the latter showing elevations in the "neurotic triad," hypochondriasis, depression, and hysteria. This pattern is believed to be due to the constant wearing away of the person's energy from the ongoing pain, his or her preoccupation with it, and despair from not improving (Sternbach, 1974; Barnett, 1986).

Psychological Factors in Pain

Pain used to be considered strictly a function of physical injury, but in recent years there has been increasing appreciation of psychological factors. These factors (see Peck, 1986) lay the groundwork for consideration of pain management.

Fear, Anxiety, and Depression   In general, there is a linear relationship between anxiety and the experience or perception of pain (Cohen and Lazarus, 1973; Wilson, 1981), especially for acute pain. The nature of the anxiety usually relates to fear of death or of disability and fear of the unknown. Hospitalization generally brings with it radically new situations to be adjusted to, loss of one's normal freedom and control, separation from family and other social supports, and procedures that occasion nociception. It should also be mentioned that pain *behaviors* can serve as excuses to escape from or avoid fearsome situations, referred to by psychoanalysts as secondary gain; for many people, especially men, complaints of pain are more acceptable than reports of fear. Depression is also associated with the experience of pain (Halpern, 1978); some symptoms of depression, like sleep disturbance and lethargy, can themselves exacerbate pain over the long term or can contribute to chronic pain. Of course pain from a traumatic event like a serious injury often leads to depression that both causes and is itself caused by loss of occupational function, decreases in cognitive and sexual functioning, and changes in physical appearance.

Perceived Control Over Noxious Stimuli   As with fear and anxiety, pain perception seems to increase if a person does not believe he or she has some degree of control over the nociceptive stimulation (Averill, 1973; Geer et al., 1970; Glass et al., 1973). In addition, extended periods of helplessness can also contribute to depression.

Attention/Distraction   Distraction from a painful stimulus can decrease the perception of pain, and attention to it can increase pain (Blitz and Dinnerstein, 1971; Turk, 1978; Turk et al., 1983).

Cognitive Appraisal   Along the lines of Lazarus's (1966) classic work on appraisal and fear, the way a person construes his nociceptive pain can affect subsequent pain experience and behavior. A literary example is in Stephen Crane's *Red Badge of Courage*, in which a soldier during a Civil War battle wishes to be wounded so that his courage will not be questioned. Nonfictional wartime examples were reported by Beecher (1956), who found during World War II that soldiers about to be sent home because of their wounds reported far less pain than civilians with comparable wounds created by surgery. In general, the meaning of a nociceptive stimulus can affect how one reacts to it, whether one can continue to function and how much discomfort will be experienced; certainly, commitment and strong belief in a cause is a time-honored factor in coping with all sorts of ordeals, whether painful or not.

Coping Style   A person's cognitive coping style, in terms of avoiding or seeking information, has been shown to interact with the benefits of information provided prior to a painful or threatening event. Byrne (1964) originally classified styles of coping along a "repression-sensitization" continuum: repressors are said to prefer to cope by denial and avoidance; sensitizers prefer confrontation with the stressor. Some studies have found that sensitizers do better when information is provided than when it is not, while repressors show the opposite pattern. For example, Andrew (1970) found that repressors used more medication postoperatively. Shipley et al. (1978, 1979) similarly found repressors to have higher heart rates during a medical procedure and to require more tranquilizers than sensitizers when they had been given information about the procedure.

Learning Factors   Responses to nociceptive stimuli can be greatly influenced by observation of how others respond to them (Craig and Weiss, 1975). Such social modeling actually affects the experience of painful stimuli.

Pain behavior can be influenced by contingencies, like the presence of a solicitous spouse (Fordyce, 1976, 1978); this forms the basis of his work with chronic pain (described below).

TREATING ACUTE PAIN

Acute pain refers to relatively short-term suffering and disability resulting from trauma. The perception of acute pain is influenced by a number of psychological factors, and recovery is likely to be aided by several nonpharmacological approaches that enable people to manage the pain. A number of these approaches are described in the following paragraphs.

Placebo and Expectation   Placebo refers to the improvement based on expectation of gain rather than on the operation of a specifically effective therapeutic agent. (This distinction, of course, would not hold if one's theory of change postulated expectation of gain as itself an active therapeutic agent.)   There is some intriguing evidence that placebo-based improvement in pain perception has a biochemical basis: expectation of benefit may release beta-endorphins, endogenous opioids which inhibit transmission of pain signals (Levine et al., 1978).   Thus, in addition to being a response to a stressor, the release of endorphins might occur under the psychological conditions known to induce an expectation of benefit.

Psychological Support   Psychological support includes describing to patients how they can expect to feel following surgery or trauma (see appraisal section below) and other general psychotherapeutic efforts that reduce anxiety and depression.

Sensory and Procedural Information   Classic work by Janis (1958) showed that surgery patients with moderate levels of anticipatory fear suffered less pain postoperatively than patients with either low or high levels of such fear. His work was followed by Egbert et al. (1963, 1964), who found that providing patients with information preoperatively about their surgery led to their being released earlier and experiencing less pain.

Sensory information involves telling patients what sensations to expect during or after a medical procedure; procedural information entails telling them about the medical procedure itself. The former tends to be more helpful for most people than the latter (Johnson, 1983), probably because of lessened anxiety that comes from knowing that certain sensations are normal. Having been told that a certain kind and degree of pain is to be expected, a patient may be less concerned about the pain being experienced because it is not construed as a sign that something is wrong. When procedural information helps, it may be due to the opportunity it allows a patient to rehearse the upcoming event in his or her imagination and thus become desensitized to the anxiety associated with the event (Wolpe, 1958).

Relaxation Training Relaxation training is a powerful treatment for increasing pain tolerance in some situations. For example, patients instructed in breathing and relaxation prior to their first attempt to get out of bed after surgery reported less incisional pain and used fewer analgesics than control patients (Flaherty and Fitzpatrick, 1978). In the laboratory, relaxation has been effective for reducing cold pressor pain (pain produced by immersing the hand in ice water) and also for decreasing pain ratings (e.g., Stevens and Heide, 1977; Stone et al., 1977). This effect is likely due to reducing anxiety and increasing a sense of control (Peck, 1986).

Enhancement of Personal Control As already mentioned, people generally experience less pain and stress if they can exercise a degree of control. An intriguing and promising medico-psychological procedure is a patient-controlled analgesia (PCA) machine that allows a patient to administer his or her own pain killers with a preset upper limit. Such a device and procedure would be expected to impart a sense of greater control, and it has been found that patients achieve better relief from pain with the PCA and even use less analgesic medication (White, 1986). A recent study with labor pain showed that satisfaction was very high: patients preferred the PCA to techniques that actually reduce pain intensity more completely, such as epidural morphine. In general, being active rather than passive is better because activity can be distracting in itself (see Gal and Lazarus, 1975).

Many empirical findings support the notion that if patients do not believe that they can control or terminate an aversive event, it is perceived as more painful (e.g., Averill, 1973). A PCA machine allows a patient an increased degree of control over a noxious event, which theoretically should decrease both anxiety and perceived pain. Of course, having a PCA machine means a patient's attention must be engaged to administer the analgesia, and so must be focusing on pain. But this would be true in any case. In traditional nurse-administered analgesia, a patient is often very focused on the pain because the system requires that a patient wait until the pain is substantial before requesting medications. And even after a patient requests the medication, he or she must wait until the nurse has the time to fulfill the request. This alternative obviously does not allow the patient to be distracted from the pain. In fact, quite the opposite. Under certain conditions, distraction can be pain reducing, as discussed in the next section.

Cognitive Coping Skills Training   There are two main cognitive strategies proposed for pain relief (Turk et al., 1983), and they are more useful for mild to moderate pain than for extreme pain: to alter a person's appraisal of pain and to direct attention away from pain.

One strategy of cognitive coping involves providing information about painful medical procedures (Janis, 1958). Such information may lead to enhanced self-efficacy (Bandura, 1977) because a person acquires information that can be used to take effective coping action (Anderson and Masur, 1983). For example, a person about to have a dye injected for assessment purposes could be told that "When the dye is injected (procedural), you will feel a hot flash (sensory)" (Anderson and Masur, 1983:10).

Six types of diversion strategies can be distinguished:

• imagination-inattention: pleasant imagery incompatible with feeling pain, such as imagining something very positive during dental treatment (Horan et al., 1976);

• imaginative transformation of pain: reinterpreting pain into a sensation like numbness, something that is a part of Lamaze "natural childbirth" training, in which women are encouraged to substitute "pressure" for pain;

• imaginative transfer of context: reframing the pain in some other context so as to interrupt the flow of negative thinking and facilitate the generation of coping strategies;

• external attention-diversion: focusing on external aspects of the environment, such as counting ceiling tiles (Barber and Cooper, 1972);

• internal attention-diversion: focusing attention on other self-generated thoughts, such as doing complex mathematical operations; and

• dissociation from pain: thinking that a painful bodily part, e.g. an arm, belongs to someone else.

The first, second, and sixth of these strategies were found by Tan (1982) to be the most helpful. We note that many of these strategies are sometimes embedded in hypnotic inductions.

All of these techniques for diverting attention from painful stimulation are consistent with cognitive research, which shows a limited supply of attentional resources: attention to one channel of input blocks the processing of input on other channels (Kahneman, 1973).

Stress Inoculation Training   "Stress inoculation training" refers to the kinds of strategies just described (Turk et al., 1983). The approach basically entails three interrelated steps: educating a person about the nature of pain; describing in detail the techniques available for coping with pain; and encouraging practice in and application of techniques that make sense to the patient. (The other usage of the term refers to training techniques, as in sports, whereby a person is presented with a challenge beyond the level that is likely to be encountered in game conditions, such as setting a pitching machine to hurl a baseball at 110 miles per hour.)

Biofeedback Biofeedback refers in general to the use of sophisticated instrumentation that provides a person immediate information on minute changes in such functions as muscle activity, heart rate, and blood pressure. This knowledge can be used by the person to control such somatic and autonomic activity to some extent.

Some fairly controlled studies (reviewed by Chapman, 1986) show that biofeedback from tension of muscles in the forehead is significantly better than no treatment or a placebo in reducing subjective ratings of chronic headache pain. There is no evidence, however, that biofeedback is superior to relaxation training alone in reducing acute pain; its effectiveness is most likely mediated by reducing anxiety (Gatchel et al., 1989), perhaps by enhancing sense of control.

Hypnosis The history of anesthesia is closely connected with hypnosis, for hypnosis was used widely in the middle and late nineteenth century by physicians like Bernheim and Charcot to reduce pain. The introduction of ether and other anesthetic drugs diminished the use of hypnosis, although it has been enjoying a resurgence of interest in childbirth, dentistry, and in treating the pain brought on by a variety of assessment and medical procedures (Hilgard and Hilgard, 1975). Except for its relaxation components, it is doubtful that putting someone into a hypnotic trance by itself reduces pain. Rather it is the *suggestions* that are given that are operative, such as intimating that a limb has become numb or that it is not one's own, or that "strong sensations" will "not matter." It is believed that cognitive strategies of diversion or dissociation can be strengthened by encouraging their use under hypnosis. A limiting factor, of course, is that people vary widely on how susceptible they are to hypnosis.

TREATING CHRONIC PAIN

As we have just seen, treating acute pain is concerned primarily with reducing nociception and influencing psychological factors in the perception of nociception. With chronic pain, the focus is on decreasing suffering, whether pain related or not, and decreasing pain behaviors and disability. It should be emphasized at the outset that success in the management of chronic pain is often *not* associated with reduction in reports of the experience of pain; rather, with reduction in such things as medication usage and with increase in activity (Fordyce et al., 1973). The goal is far less on nociception and the experience of pain than it is on "working through the pain" and adopting a "no pain no gain" philosophy that encourages restoration of function. This emphasis on pain behaviors is important (Gatchel et al., 1989). The idea is to "tough it out." What often happens is that increased activity can reduce nociception, as with back sprains, for which increase in muscle tone can itself reduce nociception over time as well as reduce chances of recurrence of acute attacks.

The principal researcher in this area is William Fordyce at the University of Washington, and his program is of the "pure operant" variety that rewards the patient for gradually increasing general activity level and social interaction, decreasing the use of pain medication, and reducing reliance on all pain-related health care services.

Fordyce's group focuses on the modification of maladaptive learned contingencies. Over time pain behaviors get reinforced by attention, nurturance, rest, avoidance of responsibilities and other burdens, and the receipt of money for disability. At the same time, healthy behavior is not reinforced or is even punished, possibly by cut-off of benefits or by a family worried about the patient's efforts to "get going." Fordyce's basic approach is to reverse the contingencies. The results are very positive in enabling chronic pain patients to regain functions that have been compromised by pain and suffering (see, e.g., Fordyce, 1976). Other behavioral programs that add to the basic approach include relaxation training and group discussion and support.

Another approach to treating chronic pain is through *cognitive interventions*, such as reducing stress with the use of covert self-statements that serve to decatastrophize the pain (Turk, 1978; Ellis, 1962; and Meichenbaum and Cameron, 1983).

The old-fashioned method of "counter irritation" has been more formally developed into a method of intervention which is generally referred to as "stimulation-produced analgesia." Neurostimulatory techniques for pain control include central stimulation, spinal cord stimulation, and peripheral stimulation. Peripheral stimulation is an outgrowth of what previously was referred to as counter irritation. It now involves mechanical or electrical stimulation of the peripheral nerves in the form of acupuncture, transcutaneous electrical nerve stimulation (TENS), and intramuscular injection of a local anesthetic to alleviate pain, increase range of motion, and enhance exercise tolerance. These methods are often used for the management of chronic pain, and they are generally administered by physicians or physical medicine specialists rather than psychologists. To the extent that counter irritation is helpful by providing a distraction, psychologists have developed many interventions (e.g., guided imagery, cognitive distraction techniques, hypnotic suggestion) that utilize distraction to manage both acute and chronic pain.

In general, a patient needs to learn about pain, particularly the distinction among the four aspects of pain, and the utility of various approaches for dealing with each one, especially suffering and pain behavior, which are separate from the acute nociception-pain phases that do require and merit medical attention.

There is a wide variety of diseases and medical conditions for which accepted (pharmacologic or otherwise somatic) treatment does not provide complete relief. Examples of these are rheumatoid arthritis, pneumococcal pneumonia, and degenerative spinal disease. Furthermore, there are diseases, some of them progressive, for which there is no known treatment for the pain they cause. Examples include terminal cancers and central pain conditions such as thalamic pain syndrome. For these latter problems, integrating psychological and somatic interventions often constitutes the most promising approach.

CONCLUSIONS

There is encouraging evidence in the pain-control literature that people can be taught nonpharmacological ways to cope with physical pain. Many of the procedures known to be useful for reducing anxiety also favorably influence pain because alleviating stress is known to decrease a person's experience of pain.

Central to current understanding of pain is the role of cognitive factors, that is, a person's construals of nociceptive input can have a profound effect on whether and how severely he or she actually experiences pain. Of particular importance are perceived control and the meaning attached to a painful experience. Procedures that enhance a person's control or sense of control appear to reduce pain because of the often demonstrated reduction of anxiety associated with increased control.

For many individuals, information about what to expect from painful experiences, such as surgery, reduces the experience of pain. Distraction is an effective strategy for coping with pain. Relaxation training is also useful for controlling pain, perhaps due in part to distraction as well as to the reduction of worry and anxiety. Suggestions given under hypnosis to susceptible individuals can also help them cope with pain, for example, imagining that an affected limb is not really a part of them.

Chronic pain can be managed by identifying and controlling psychological perpetuating factors. In most cases this would involve combining a variety of pure behavior-learning approaches with other cognitive-behavioral and relaxation interventions to encourage a patient to increase activity level even if experiencing discomfort and pain.

REFERENCES

Anderson, K.O., and F.F. Masur
    1983   Psychological preparation for invasive medical and dental procedures. *Journal of Behavioral Medicine* 6:1-40.
Andrew, J.M.
    1970   Recovery from surgery with and without preparatory instruction, for three coping styles. *Journal of Personality and Social Psychology* 15:223-227.
Averill, J.R.
    1973   Personal control over aversive stimuli and its relationship to stress. *Psychological Bulletin* 80:286-303.
Bakan, D.
    1968   *Disease, Pain, and Sacrifice: Toward a Psychology of Suffering.* Chicago: University of Chicago Press.
Bandura, A.
    1977   Self-efficacy: toward a unifying theory of behavioral change. *Psychological Review* 84:191-215.
Barber, T.X., and B.J. Cooper
    1972   The effects on pain of experimentally induced and spontaneous distraction. *Psychological Reports* 31:647-651.
Barnett, J.
    1986   The Comparative Effectiveness of the Millon Behavioral Health Inventory and the Minnesota Multiphasic Personality Inventory as Predictors of Treatment Outcome in a Rehabilitation Program for Chronic Low Back Pain. Unpublished Ph.D. dissertation, University of Texas Health Sciences Center, Dallas.
Beecher, H.K.
    1956   Relationship of significance of wound to the pain experienced. *Journal of the American Medical Association* 161:1609-1613.
Blitz, B., and A.J. Dinnerstein
    1971   Role of attentional focus in pain perception: manipulation of response to noxious stimulation by instructions. *Journal of Abnormal Psychology* 77:42-45.
Byrne, D.
    1964   Repression-sensitization as a dimension of personality. In B.A. Maher, ed., *Progress in Experimental Personality Research*, Vol. 1. New York: Academic Press.
Chapman, S.L.
    1986   A review and clinical perspective on the use of EMG and thermal biofeedback for chronic headaches. *Pain* 27:1-43.
Cohen, F., and R.S. Lazarus
    1973   Active coping processes, coping dispositions, and recovery from surgery. *Psychosomatic Medicine* 35:375-389.
Craig, K.D., and S.M. Weiss
    1975   Vicarious influences on pain threshold determinations. *Journal of Personality and Social Psychology* 19:53-59.
Darke, L.
    1990   Psychological Factors in the Management of Pain. Unpublished manuscript, Pain Management Center, University of California, Los Angeles.

Druckman, D., and J. Swets, eds.
1988 *Enhancing Human Performance: Issues, Theories, and Techniques.* Committee on Techniques for the Enhancement of Human Performance, Commission on Behavioral and Social Sciences and Education, National Research Council. Washington, D.C.: National Academy Press.

Egbert, L.D, G.E. Battit, and H. Turndorf
1963 The value of the preoperative visit by an anesthetist. *Journal of the American Medical Association* 185:553-556.

Egbert, L.D., G.E. Battit, C.E. Welch, and M.K. Bartlett
1964 Reduction in postoperative pain by encouragement and instruction of patients. *New England Journal of Medicine* 270:825-827.

Ellis, A.
1962 *Reason and Emotion in Psychotherapy.* New York: Lyle Stuart.

Flaherty, G.G., and J.J. Fitzpatrick
1978 Relaxation techniques to increase comfort levels of postoperative patients: a preliminary study. *Nursing Research* 27(6):352-355.

Fordyce, W.E.
1976 *Behavioral Methods for Chronic Pain and Illness.* St. Louis: C.V. Mosby.
1978 Learning processes in pain. In R.A. Sternbach, ed., *The Psychology of Pain.* New York: Raven Press.
1988 Pain and suffering: a reappraisal. *American Psychologist* 48:276-283.

Fordyce, W.E., R. Fowler, J. Lehmann, and B. DeLateur
1973 Operant conditioning in the treatment of chronic pain. *Archives of Physical Medicine and Rehabilitation* 54:399-408.

Gal, R., and R.S. Lazarus
1975 The role of activity in anticipating and confronting stressful situations. *Journal of Human Stress* 1:4-20.

Gatchel, R.J., A. Baum, and D.S. Krantz
1989 *An Introduction to Health Psychology*, 2nd ed. New York: Random House.

Geer, J.H., G.C. Davison, and R. Gatchel
1970 Reduction of stress in humans through nonveridical perceived control of aversive situations. *Journal of Personality and Social Psychology* 16:731-738.

Gendlin, E.T.
1962 *Experiencing and the Creation of Meaning: A Philosophical and Psychological Approach to the Subject.* New York: Free Press of Glencoe.

Glass, D.C., J.E. Singer, H.S. Leonard, D.S. Krantz, S. Cohen, and H. Cummings
1973 Perceived control of aversive stimulation and the reduction of stress responses. *Journal of Personality* 41:577-595.

Halpern, C.
1978 Substitution-detoxification and its role in the management of chronic benign pain. *Journal of Clinical Psychiatry* 43:10-15.

Hilgard, E.R., and J.R. Hilgard
1975 *Hypnosis in the Relief of Pain.* Los Altos, Calif.: William Kaufmann.

Horan, J.J., F.C. Layng, and C.H. Pursell
1976 Preliminary study of the effects of "in vivo" emotive imagery on dental discomfort. *Perceptual and Motor Skills* 42:105-106.

Janis, I.L.
1958 *Psychological Stress: Psychoanalytic and Behavioral Studies of Surgical Patients.* New York: Wiley.

Johnson, J.E.
1983 Psychological interventions and coping with surgery. In A. Baum, S.E. Taylor, and J.E. Singer, eds., *Handbook of Psychology and Health*, Vol. 4. Hillsdale, N.J.: Erlbaum.

Kahneman, D.

1973 *Attention and Effort*. Englewood Cliffs, N.J.: Prentice-Hall.

Kelly, J.T.

1986 Chronic pain and trauma. *Advances in Psychosomatic Medicine* 16:141-152.

Lazarus, R.S.

1966 *Psychological Stress and the Coping Process*. New York: McGraw-Hill.

Levine, J.D., N.C. Gordon, and H.L. Fields

1978 The mechanism of placebo analgesia. *Lancet* 23:654-657.

Loeser, J.D.

1980 Perspectives on pain. Pp. 313-316 in *Proceedings of the First World Conference on Clinical Pharmacology and Therapeutics*. London: Macmillan.

Meichenbaum, D., and R. Cameron

1983 Cognitive behavior modification: current issues. In G.T. Wilson and C.M. Franks, eds., *Contemporary Behavior Therapy: Conceptual and Empirical Foundations*. New York: Guilford Press.

Melzack, R., and P.D. Wall

1965 Pain mechanisms: a new theory. *Science* 150:971-979.

Peck, C.

1986 Psychological factors in acute pain management. In M.J. Cousin and G.D. Phillips, eds., *Acute Pain Management*. New York: Churchill Livingstone.

Shipley, R.H., J.H. Butt, B. Horwitz, and J.E. Farbry

1978 Preparation for stressful medical procedure: effect of amount of stimulus preexposure and coping style. *Journal of Consulting and Clinical Psychology* 46:499-507.

Shipley, R.H., J.H. Butt, and E.A. Horwitz

1979 Preparation to reexperience a stressful medical examination: effect of repetitious videotape exposure and coping style. *Journal of Consulting and Clinical Psychology* 47:485-491.

Sternbach, R.A.

1966 *Principles of Psychophysiology*. New York: Academic Press.

1974 *Pain Patients: Traits and Treatment*. New York: Academic Press.

Stevens, R.J., and F. Heide

1977 Analgesic characteristics of prepared childbirth techniques: attention focusing and systematic relaxation. *Journal of Psychosomatic Research* 21:429-434.

Stone, C.I., D.A. Demchick-Stone, and J.J. Horan

1977 Coping with pain: a component analysis of Lamaze and cognitive-behavioral procedures. *Journal of Psychosomatic Research* 21:451-457.

Tan, S.Y.

1982 Cognitive and behavioral methods of pain control: a selective review. *Pain* 12:201-203.

Turk, D.C.

1978 Cognitive behavioral techniques in the management of pain. In J.P. Foreyt and D.P. Rathjen, eds., *Cognitive Behavioral Therapy: Research and Application*. New York: Plenum.

Turk, D.C., D.H. Meichenbaum, and M. Genest

1983 *Pain and Behavioral Medicine: A Cognitive Behavioral Perspective*. New York: Guilford Press.

Turk, D.C., J.T. Wack, and R.D. Kerns

1985 An empirical examination of the "pain behavior" construct. *Journal of Behavioral Medicine* 8:119-130.

White, P.F.

1986 Patient-controlled analgesia: a new approach to the management of postoperative pain. *Seminars in Anesthesia* 4:255-266.

Wilson, J.F.
    1981 Behavioral preparation for surgery: benefit or harm? *Journal of Behavioral Medicine* 4:79-102.
Wolpe, J.
    1958 *Psychotherapy by Reciprocal Inhibition*. Stanford, Calif.: Stanford University Press.

9

Hiding and Detecting Deception

This chapter considers two broad questions: Can a deceiver be detected under conditions in which he or she is generally unaware of being suspected? Can a deceiver avoid being detected under those conditions? These questions largely rule out the use of polygraph tests, "truth" serums, and other invasive techniques for detecting deception, and no attempt is made to review the large literature on those techniques. (Interested readers are referred to reviews of the literature and discussions of the complex issues surrounding the use of invasive lie-detection techniques; see, especially, Ben-Shakhar et al., 1982; Lykken, 1981, 1985; Raskin, 1987.)

The possibilities for detecting deception under noninvasive conditions depend either on the content of the supplied information or on nonverbal behaviors inadvertently "leaked" by the subject. The content of the supplied information may be suspect because it is inconsistent with other information supplied by the subject or because it is inconsistent with information from other sources. The nonverbal information may also be suspect because of divergences from expressions or postures seen in other situations or because of known deception clues observed by the detector. In this chapter we deal primarily with deception clues that can be detected from nonverbal behavior.

The key assumption underlying the hope for detecting deception from nonverbal behavior is that a person, when knowingly lying or deceiving, enters a psychological state that differs from the state he or she is in when telling the truth. These psychological states, the deceptive and the honest, are further assumed to affect both verbal and nonverbal channels of communication. These channels, in turn, can be monitored by a detector's unaided perceptual processes. When one or more channels provide cues that "betray" the person's deceptions, researchers claim that leakage has occurred.

Within this framework, several possibilities arise. The simplest is that deception leaks in predictable ways for all people regardless of differences in experience or culture: the predictability would derive from a fixed set of communication cues, such as body movements, rather than facial expressions. More complicated are the possibilities that a variety of behavioral patterns are diagnostic, depending on a person's experience, training, and cultural background or the particular circumstances under which he or she is being observed. Moreover, it is possible that individuals are conscious about such cues and can manage the expressions or movements being monitored by an observer.

This chapter reviews ongoing research programs that focus on those issues: what has been learned from laboratory studies on deception and what needs to be learned through further experimental research. (The next chapter is more conceptual, reviewing various taxonomies and frameworks designed to broaden the concept of deception.) We also discuss the issue of cultural and other subpopulation differences in the interpretation and execution of deception in the context of generality of findings obtained in laboratory studies with American subjects.

PHYSICAL INDICATORS AND PSYCHOLOGICAL STATES

Although the problem of inferring specific psychological states from specific observed behaviors is quite complex, there is little doubt about the existence of linkages between internal states and external behaviors. A large research literature on nonverbal behaviors associated with emotions and intentions has made apparent the value of using such behaviors as windows on underlying psychological states.[1] The focus of this section is more specialized: to draw on relevant parts of the large literature on nonverbal behaviors for insights and suggestions for research on nonverbal indicators of deception.

The Laboratory Paradigm

Most of the contemporary experimental research on deception involves the communication of false verbal statements made with intent to deceive. Researchers are interested in the cues sent by deceivers and the cues used by receivers to detect deception; the cues consist, for the most part, of nonverbal behaviors coded systematically from replays of videotaped simulated performances (speeches, interviews), usually enacted by college students. This situation represents a particular type of lie captured by Knapp and Comadena's definition (1979:271) as "the conscious alteration of information a person believes to be true in order to significantly change another's perceptions from what the deceiver thought they would be without the alteration." It is less relevant to other forms of deception (as discussed in the next chapter).

The experiments have examined deception from the standpoint of a sender, who is perpetrating a lie or being honest, and from the standpoint of an observer, who attempts to detect whether a particular communication is deceptive or truthful. Experiments concerned primarily with senders ask subjects to convey false (or true) information, usually in response to questions from an interviewer who may be evaluating candidates for a job, interrogating suspects about a crime, or asking about issues in world affairs or local politics.

One series of studies asked subjects to take the role of the Soviet ambassador to the United States. In that role, subjects were interviewed for 15 minutes (in a "Meet the Press" format) about three then-current events: the Soviet invasion of Afghanistan, Soviet military activities in Cuba, and Soviet troops in Europe. Three experimental conditions consisted of misrepresenting actual Soviet policy (deception), avoiding direct answers to the questions being asked (evasion), and conveying actual Soviet policy as communicated to you (honesty). Other types of scenarios used in these experiments include car sales, making speeches about academic topics, conveying feelings about hospital scenes, and interactions stylized in the form of candid-camera situations. In all of these experiments, subjects' nonverbal behaviors are coded in each of several channels of communication: facial expressions, body movements, visual behavior, paralanguage (verbal utterances other than the content of the message). The coded behaviors are analyzed for differences by condition, which is usually a comparison of deceitful and honest communications.

Experiments concerned primarily with observers ask subjects to rate taped enactments of senders in a previous experiment or actors whose scripts were prepared by the experimenter. For example, in one experiment, observers were asked to rate the sales pitches made by salespersons with experience on incentive pay plans and automobile customers with experience in bargaining for trade-in allowances. In another experiment, observers rated the descriptions of student nurses' feelings about a film that was intended to arouse either positive or negative reactions; nurses in the deception condition were asked to conceal their actual feelings aroused by the negative film. In all of these experiments, observers report their perceptions of the communicators' deceptiveness, usually on a numerical scale that discriminates degrees of deceptiveness or honesty. Observers are also asked to indicate the extent to which they are confident in making these judgments. A variety of other impressions of communicators have been assessed in experiments, including, for example, liking for the product, anxiety, confidence, suspicion, aggressiveness, and comfort. The ratings of deception are analyzed for accuracy and related to expressed confidence. They are also correlated with particular nonverbal channels or behaviors used in the enactment and with the other impressions rated by the observer. The results obtained from both types of experiments are reviewed in the following sections, focusing first on the nonverbal behaviors displayed by subjects and then on the accuracy of observers who attempt to detect the deception portrayed by others.

Leakage

The relevance of nonverbal behaviors as clues to deception derives from the assumption that these behaviors, in particular, will leak information that a person is trying to hide. The rationale for this assumption is provided by Ekman and Friesen (1969) in terms of the variables of *automaticity* and *controllability*. These variables refer to the relationship between emotions and behavior. According to Ekman (1981:271): "When emotion is aroused certain changes occur in the face, body, and voice which can be considered automatic." Such automatic links present a problem for deceivers who attempt to control their nonverbal behavior during deception: they must override these links in order to avoid leakage. Some nonverbal cues are more likely to be controlled than others. Words and facial expressions have been found to be easier to control than body and tone of voice cues (Ekman, 1981; Zuckerman et al., 1981). Thus, deceivers should be most successful when using words, next most successful when using facial expressions, and least successful when using body movements and tone of voice cues. Indeed, according to the DePaulo et al. (1985) review of the evidence on detection, both body cues and tone of voice cues were found to be more revealing than facial cues. Less clear, however, are the results on verbal cues: these cues were found to be informative and revealing (see DePaulo et al., 1985, for an explanation).

Nonverbal cues that reveal deception to observers should also distinguish between the actual enactments of deceivers and truth tellers. In their early experiment on leakage, Ekman and Friesen's (1969) deceivers claimed that they attempted to disguise the face more than the body while perpetrating the deception. The discriminating cues provided by the body included decreasing use of hand illustrators (movements used for emphasis), increased use of self-adapters (movements directed toward one part of the body by another), and more postural position shifts for deceivers. More illustrator movements also were used by the deceivers (compared to truth tellers) in Mehrabian's (1972) study, while increased self-adapters and postural shifts were also found for the deceiving subjects in the McClintock and Hunt (1975) interview study. Further confirmative evidence was obtained by the Druckman et al. (1982) finding of coordinated body movements for deceivers: rocking, head-shaking, trunk swivels, and nodding movements varied together. That study also found more fidgeting with objects for deceivers and more leg movements for evaders (indirect deception). Two studies reported differences in vocal cues: Mehrabian (1971) showed more speech errors as deviations from baseline data; DePaulo et al. (1980) found tone of voice differences between deceivers and truth tellers. Taken together, these findings suggest where to look for clues to deceptive intentions. They do not, however, provide evidence for the specific role played by psychological states or emotions.

The concept of leakage is based on a model that construes psychological states or emotions as variables that mediate the relationship between nonverbal behaviors and intentions (see Druckman et al., 1982: Figure 1.1). While demonstrating the importance of these intervening variables, the results reported by Druckman et al. (1982) also illustrate the complexity of the relationships. Subjects (interviewees playing the role of the Soviet ambassador to the United States) in each of three experimental conditions (honesty, evasion, and deception) indicated their feelings on a postinterview questionnaire consisting of 26 bipolar adjective scales. The ratings were analyzed for condition differences and for correlations with each of 25 nonverbal behaviors coded for all subjects. Three types of states seemed to capture the diverse relationships obtained among these variables: involvement, stress, and confidence. Honest and evasive subjects displayed behaviors whose meaning indicated involvement. Evasive and deceptive subjects displayed behaviors that correlated with feelings of stress or tension. Subjects in all three conditions showed behaviors related to feelings of confidence or effectiveness. This evidence suggests which emotions reflect primarily honesty (feelings of involvement), direct and indirect deception (stress), and role-playing, which is characteristic of all three conditions (confidence). Interestingly, evasive subjects showed relations between nonverbal behaviors and two emotions, one found primarily for honest subjects (involvement), the other found primarily for deceivers (stress). This result is consistent with the definitions of evaders as being neither completely honest nor completely deceptive.

The results also identified a subset of nonverbal behaviors that indicate either high or low involvement, stress, or confidence: for example, looking at versus looking away from the interviewer as an indicator of high or low involvement for honest subjects or as an indicator of stress for evaders, shoulder shrugs versus trunk swivels as an indicator of high and low stress experienced by deceivers (see Druckman et al., 1982:Table 4.10). Supporting the concept of leakage, these findings highlight the role played by emotions or feelings in the process of making inferences from nonverbal behaviors to intentions. However, they also make evident some of the difficulties involved in the task of diagnosing deception or other intentions. In some cases, different nonverbal behaviors have similar meanings for different intentions, that is, they are functionally equivalent behaviors. In other cases, different nonverbal behaviors reflect different feelings for the same intention, as well as for different intentions. The challenge for researchers is to isolate the unique relationships between particular nonverbal behaviors and underlying feelings for particular intentions. These would be cues that diagnosticians could use with confidence; they have not yet been identified.

Motivated Liars

There seems to be a relationship between motivation to deceive and success at deceiving (DePaulo et al., 1985). The question asked is whether highly motivated deceivers are easier or harder to detect than their less well-motivated counterparts, that is, when the stakes for successful deception are either high or low. This question has implications for differences between professionals (higher stakes) and the amateurs used in most laboratory experiments (lower stakes). Results obtained from two experiments (summarized in DePaulo et al., 1985) are quite intriguing. When motivation to lie was high (e.g., deceivers were being monitored by a panel of their peers), nonverbal cues were more revealing than verbal clues; when motivation was low (e.g., deceivers were to play a "little" game), verbal cues were more revealing. The highly motivated deceivers were accurately detected by observers more often than the less highly motivated deceivers if the observers could see the nonverbal behaviors. When judges only had access to verbal statements, the highly motivated deceivers were quite successful (and more successful than their less motivated counterparts) in their deception. According to DePaulo et al. (1985:334): "the harder senders try to get away with their lies, the less successful they will be (when their nonverbal behaviors are showing)."

An explanation for these findings is that when emotionality is high, as it would be for high-stakes' performances, nonverbal leaks are more likely to occur. The highly motivated deceivers in the experiments of DePaulo and her colleagues showed more behavioral inhibition and rigidity, as well as more negativity, than the deceivers who were less motivated. The motivated deceivers may think that they are using a safe strategy by not moving, which they equate with not revealing, but this strategy backfired for reasons understandable in terms of the concept of leakage. Based on an hydraulic model analogy, attempts to control one channel of communication (e.g., facial expressions) leads to excessive activity in another channel (e.g., body movements). A more direct test of this hypothesis would be a comparison of conditions in which subjects are told to control their faces or their bodies while deceiving; more body activity in the former condition and more facial activity in the latter (in comparison with a baseline control condition) would support this hypothesis. This experiment has been done, and analyses are in progress.[2]

An implication of this research is that people are betrayed by their nonverbal behaviors in situations in which they are most motivated *not* to be detected. This implication is especially relevant for the challenges confronting professional deceivers (such as spies). From the standpoint of detectors, it would seem appropriate to monitor the unattended channels, that is, either those channels under less control by the deceiver or those that he or she believes are not being observed. For nonprofessionals, whether or not the challenge for successful deception is high, nonverbal deception cues are likely to be derived from different emotions: insecurity and concern about the managed impressions being conveyed (due in part to a lack of practice), guilt or anxiety about a morally dubious act, tension caused by the complexity inherent in a deceptive performance. The nonverbal behaviors that derive from these feelings may well differ from those that are the result of leakage. However, deceptive contexts vary considerably on a number of dimensions, and these dimensions of the situation affect both the displays shown by senders and impressions made by observers.

Faulty Detection

It is clear from the research on detecting deception that people have trouble distinguishing between lies and truthful statements. For samples of college students, there is a discernible bias in favor of judging messages as truthful when the frequency of lies and truth is about 50-50 (DePaulo et al., 1985). People who are professional lie detectors, on the other hand, evince a "deception bias," that is, they judge most (truthful and deceptive) messages as being deceptive (O'Sullivan et al., 1988); also see Kraut and Poe's (1980) study of customs inspectors, Hendershot and Hess' (1982) study of police detectives, and the Druckman et al. (1982) study of oil company executives. Both types of samples usually do no better than chance in accurately detecting deception: college students judge actual truthfulness more accurately than actual deception, while professionals are somewhat more accurate at judging actual deception than actual truthfulness. Despite the poor accuracy, however, both college students and experts indicate high confidence in their judgments (Druckman et al., 1982), and confidence may actually increase with experience (DePaulo et al., 1985). Of interest, then, is the question of why it is so difficult to detect deception.

The weak correspondence between actual and perceived deception cues suggests that the folk wisdom about how deceivers are supposed to act (e.g., less gaze, smile less, postural shifts, longer response time) are not diagnostic of deception. They are, however, widely held cultural stereotypes, and they are easier to predict than the actual cues that are likely to be more sensitive to context (DePaulo et al., 1985; O'Sullivan et al., 1988). Recent results reported by Bond et al. (1990) suggest that the stereotypes may be cross-cultural: their American and Jordanian subjects used similar nonverbal cues in making judgments of deception, which were inaccurate, evincing what is known as a "demeanor bias" (judgments based on the target's apparent honesty or dishonesty rather than the perceiver's detection skills). Modeling indicates that the dimensions used by judges of deception were the well-known impressions of appearing apprehensive and undependable, often looking away from the camera, fidgeting with objects, and a relatively poor sense of humor (Druckman et al., 1982). Yet, these impressions were misleading. The connection between observed behavior and impressions, on the one hand, and between impressions of emotions and intentions on the other were inaccurate.

One proposed explanation for these results is that detectors in the experiments rarely get feedback about whether the sender was actually lying or telling the truth. Without feedback, detectors cannot correct their judgments and the cues used in making these decisions. Another proposed explanation is that detectors are often insufficiently suspicious about the possibility that deception might be occurring; without being alert to the possibility, detectors are unlikely to search for diagnostic cues. Neither of these explanations is supported by research, however. Feedback does not serve to revise detectors' theories; rather, they tend to select "evidence" that supports their initial judgment and, in fact, increased their confidence in the (inaccurate) judgments (DePaulo et al., 1985). Similarly, increased suspiciousness does not improve accuracy although it may serve to decrease confidence in judgments. Other proposed explanations for the difficulty of detecting deception (O'Sullivan et al., 1988) include: the task of detecting strangers (used in most studies) is more difficult than detecting friends; detectors confuse the distinction between negative and positive emotions with lying versus telling the truth; some types of lies are easier to detect than others; and some liars may be better at lying than others. Each of these explanations is an empirical issue that can eventually be resolved by research; until then, it should be possible on the basis of what is known to improve accuracy even for detecting the lies of strangers in fleeting situations, for uncovering subtle lies, and for recognizing skilled liars.

IMPROVING DETECTION

Training

Detecting another person's intentions is a learned skill. As with other skills, it has been shown to improve with age and training. A number of studies (summarized in DePaulo et al., 1985) have shown that during adolescence, perceivers become increasingly sensitive to issues of sincerity and deceit (e.g., Flavell, 1977). The studies also indicate that children do progressively better as they get older at distinguishing between direct deception, on the one hand, and exaggerations, omissions, or slight distortions on the other.

Sensitivity to nonverbal deception clues contribute to detection accuracy. Such sensitivity may be related to the nature of one's job experience. A recent experiment assessed the detection accuracy of 509 professionals from agencies and occupations in which lie detection is part of the job: the Central Intelligence Agency, the Federal Bureau of Investigation, the National Security Agency, police, and judges (Ekman and O'Sullivan, 1991). Their results show that accuracy was not related to occupation and actually *decreased* with age and experience for some occupational groups. Closer examination of the accurate detectors revealed, however, that the critical variable may be job function. People in jobs in which they must interact with others on a regular basis were better detectors than those in administrative positions; the former tended to be younger than the latter due at least in part to promotions of relatively older workers to administrative positions. In addition to job tasks, frequent social interaction helps people detect deceivers. Knowing what to look for—in the sense of distinguishing critical from noncritical cues—and how to process those cues helps more.

Improvement can be accelerated further by training that is designed specifically to take advantage of relevant information. Lie-detection success improves when subjects are prompted to pay special attention to tone of voice cues (DePaulo et al., 1982; see also Zuckerman et al., 1985). Success also improved for subjects who are given a technical briefing intended to separate the nonverbal signals from the nonverbal "noise" (Druckman et al., 1982). In addition to specific nonverbal cues, subjects have been shown to do better when they pay attention to behaviors that are related to deceptiveness, such as ambivalence or tension (DePaulo et al., 1982).

It is clear that specialized training can make a difference. Less clear, however, are the specific dimensions of training likely to have the strongest impact. Three of the dimensions suggested are whether to focus on particular behaviors or psychological states (see above), to examine the difference between judging friends versus strangers (see O'Sullivan et al., 1988), and to compare different groups of detectors who vary in terms of their motivation and experience (see O'Sullivan et al., 1988). With regard to the difference between cues shown by deceiving friends and strangers, Buller and Aune (1987) found that friends attempt to control their arousal and negative affect cues more than strangers, although other cues were leaked by friends perhaps as a result of the masking.

The judgment heuristics used by observers are also interesting. An evaluation of alternative detection strategies indicate that providing observers with an information-processing approach to detection improves accuracy considerably. Referred to as "inference training," the strategy consists of an organized method for processing information about several critical cues (see Druckman et al., 1982:Figure 5.1). Significant gains in accuracy were found for subjects who were trained to distinguish between relevant and irrelevant cues (a technical briefing) and presented a strategy for processing the relevant cues. Judgments about another's intentions are based on both available information (observed cues) and the way the information is processed (judgment heuristic). An inappropriate strategy can lead to the wrong judgment, despite accurate information about the relevant cues.[3]

The gains obtained for inference training are consistent with research findings from cognitive social psychology (see, e.g., Nisbett and Ross, 1980). By taking account of combination rules and sequencing of behaviors, a processing strategy captures the concept of "display package," that is, the way that nonverbal behaviors are displayed for particular emotions or intentions. To be useful, however, the strategy must process known deception cues. The research uncovered the relevant cues in a first stage, followed by training detectors to use them in arriving at decisions about actors whose displays were based on the earlier findings. This requirement poses a dilemma for detection in situations in which the cues are unknown. The detector must either rely on the possibility of universal cues or suspend judgment until he or she has had more experience with the suspected deceiver. But it is unlikely that there are universal cues (see discussion below on context), and suspending judgment may not be viable under certain circumstances, e.g., a fleeting interaction with a suspected terrorist. Although there are no obvious nostrums to guide a detector in these situations, there may be useful ways to approach the problem (see next section on the role of analytical methodologies).

Further progress on the problem of detecting deception may depend on advances in methodology. One promising avenue is to apply the sophisticated approaches developed in other fields in which systematic diagnostic efforts have been made. Recent work in radiology provides a good example of decision aids that can determine the maximal accuracy provided by the cues. The aids address the general question: What are the relative weights of the possibly diagnostic clues (when their scale of values are merged to determine a probability of deception) that will maximize detection accuracy in each of the relevant deception contexts (see, e.g., Swets et al., 1991; Getty et al., 1988; Swets, 1988). Answering this question would go a long way toward a technique for training detectors.

Using Analytical Methodologies

The knowledge base for understanding the physical indicators of deception consists almost entirely of laboratory studies (reviewed above). A concern is whether, and to what extent, the results of those studies have relevance for other settings. Commenting on differences between the conditions of laboratory research and less formal observations outside the laboratory, Doob (1975) distinguishes between "professional" and "lay" observers. Professionals systematically decode nonverbal behaviors, channel by channel, from replays of videotaped performances (usually enacted by college students). Lay observers gain impressions of psychological states from a large number of relatively fleeting expressions, body movements, or vocalizations seen in particular social or cultural settings. Based on these different sources of information and approaches, Doob suggests two possibilities: experimental results do not aid the task of deciphering clues in the real world, and lay observers cannot use a professional's systematic approach for inferring intentions from behavior (see Doob's [1975:115-135] discussion of nonverbal symbols).

Doob's grim outlook for applying laboratory results and deriving accurate inferences from informal observations is only one interpretation of the problem. Another interpretation provides a more optimistic outlook in three ways. First, experimental results can highlight what to look for in broader terms than specific nonverbal behaviors (e.g., abrupt changes, leaks), and some findings have widespread generality (e.g., micromomentary facial expressions for emotions, sources of detection inaccuracies). Second, the approach of systematic observation with notation or coding rules, used in laboratory studies, can also be used for making informed observations outside a laboratory. Third, a lay observer has the *advantage* of viewing behavior within its context or cultural setting, helping to improve interpretations.

A lay observer can benefit from the laboratory-based research on deception clues. The research serves to direct an observer's attention to particular themes: for example, incongruities or inconsistencies between verbal and nonverbal behaviors for indicators of stress or irritability, tone-of-voice deviations from baseline observations for possible deception, and an increased intensity of behaviors in a variety of channels for commitment to policies. These themes call attention to relationships, particular nonverbal channels, or to the amount of feelings (see Rozelle et al., 1986, for an elaboration of these themes). Also, paying attention to qualities related to deception, such as ambivalence, indifference, and tension, has been shown to increase detection accuracy (DePaulo et al., 1982). Actual cues to deception reflect feelings of being less confident, more insecure, more self-conscious (due perhaps to a lack of practice at deceiving), and guilt since the act is morally dubious in most societies. This is useful information, even though it is based on averages across many subjects in different experimental situations. Intuitions about these and related qualities may improve lay observers' detection accuracy.

Laboratory research has contributed techniques for analysis that are also useful in field settings. Notation systems for coding nonverbal behaviors enable an analyst, who must respond to time-sensitive requests, to identify a subset of behaviors for on-the-spot commentary. A government or corporate analyst is frequently asked to provide interpretations without the benefits of penetrating analysis, extensive video footage, or hindsight, and coding systems are especially useful under these conditions. They provide an analyst with a structure for focusing attention on relevant details: for example, behaviors that change quickly (micro-momentary expressions) or obviously (incongruities), and those that occur within the time frame of a statement (leaks). These are the kinds of observations that can be used for making inferences from limited data. They may also be useful for an analyst who has access to more data (extended videotape coverage) and is given more time to develop interpretations. Under these conditions, it is possible to perform systematic analyses that include charting trends over time, making comparisons, and developing profiles. Each of these tasks is aided by a coding system that encompasses a range of situations, purposes of appearances (speech, interview, casual interactions), and verbal statements, as well as types of displayed nonverbal behaviors (channels and specific movements or expressions). By categorizing videotapes in this manner, it becomes feasible to test hypotheses about relationships, for example, between situations and observed behaviors. Analyzed over time, these relationships would highlight the influence of context (as varied situations) on nonverbal behavior.

Unlike laboratory researchers, field analysts (and lay observers) can develop interpretations based on observations of "subjects" in real world contexts. In essence, he or she can follow a subject, and, by so doing, record nonverbal behavior displays that occur under a variety of circumstances. These comparisons contribute to the development of profiles of coordinated movements that may change over time and situations. The coordinated movements can also be depicted in animated graphic displays (see Badler and Smoliar, 1979, for examples). Such displays illuminate "postural" or expression differences in the same people over time and also among people.[4] When associated with specific events and context, the displays lead to the question: How are the feelings and intentions that are evoked by different situations represented in body movements? When compared with displays shown by people in other cultural settings, the coded observations raise the question: What are the contributions of culture to observed nonverbal behaviors?

CONTEXT AND CULTURE

There is no reason to expect that a particular set of nonverbal behaviors is associated with every type of deceiver and every type of deceit. As noted by DePaulo et al. (1985:343):

Deceptive contexts vary considerably in the emotions, motivations, and expectations that they engender in the deceivers, and they also impose different cognitive-processing demands. As these and other important dimensions of deceptive contexts vary so, too, may the specific behaviors that distinguish lies from truths.

In other words, the critical physical clues to deception are likely to be situation and culture specific. Behaviors observed in one setting are likely to generalize only to other similar settings. A more complete understanding of the nonverbal indicators of intentions would result from frameworks that match behaviors to situations, that is, research-based taxonomies of situations and behaviors. Without such a framework, it is difficult to know the extent to which findings obtained from experiments with college students or amateurs apply also to people in occupations in which deception is assumed to be practiced and that people would like to detect (see, e.g., Doob, 1975). Referred to as a context-relevant approach to research (Druckman et al., 1982; Mahoney and Druckman, 1975), these observations are captured also by Ekman's (1978) concept of display rules.

Display Rules

Defined originally with regard to facial expressions, display rules are culturally learned "rules" for managing expressions. They serve to modify expressions in keeping with the demands of the social situation and may also reflect the cognitive processing that precedes the observed expression. Whether display rules are the primary determinant of observed nonverbal behaviors is an empirical issue that is captured in terms of the debate between universal and culturally specific bases for expressions. This debate has been the basis for a large number of cross-cultural experiments on facial expressions by Ekman and his colleagues. While not resolving the debate clearly in favor of the one or other explanation, their interpretation of the findings suggests that while the distinctive appearance of the face may be universal—that is, unique muscle movements are made for each primary emotion—the particular expression that appears in certain circumstances varies with culture (see below). However, these experiments have not investigated the role of culture in other channels of nonverbal expression. Nor did they focus specifically on cues to deception.

Culture and Facial Expressions

In spite of the fact that most literature on nonverbal behavior notes the importance of context and agrees that expressions of senders and theories of detectors are conditioned by rather specific environments, there is very little evidence that demonstrates such relationships. The number of cross-cultural studies is small, and there are practically no studies on cultural similarities and differences in deceiving or detecting deception. One issue, however, has received considerable attention by Ekman and his collaborators, namely, the debate between universal and culturally specific facial expressions.

Channel-by-channel reviews of nonverbal behavior studies indicate uneven attention to cultural factors (Harper et al., 1978; Druckman et al., 1982). The reported studies on kinesics (body language) have been largely descriptive, consisting of naturalistic observations and informal commentary (e.g., Argyle, 1975). One study of cultural differences in gazing behavior is probably the most extensive to date on that topic (Watson, 1970): Arabs, Latins, and Southern Europeans focused their gaze on the eyes of their partner, while Asians, Indian-Pakistanis, and Northern Europeans showed peripheral gaze or no gaze at all. Several cross-cultural studies on proxemics (the use of space) support Hall's (1966) observation that behaviors related to space are quite sensitive to cultural variation: for example, Watson and Graves (1966) found expected differences between Arabs and Americans in their space behavior and body orientations (see also Sommer, 1959; Little, 1968; Shuter, 1976; Baxter, 1970). In addition, studies have shown cultural differences in touching behavior (Watson and Graves, 1966; Jourard, 1966; Shuter, 1976).

The issue of universal nonverbal expressions versus culturally determined expressions has been probed in a series of studies on facial expressions. Defining the issue in terms of "relative importance," Ekman developed an approach that allows for both universal and culturally specific sources for expressions of emotion (see, e.g., Ekman and O'Sullivan, 1988). According to this "theory," eliciting events vary from culture to culture but the particular facial muscle movements triggered when a given emotion is elicited are universal. (Blends of emotions may be subject to more cultural variability than the primary emotions.) That is, although the underlying physiology for the primary emotions may be universal, the actual expression elicited is subject to cultural and situation-determined display rules. Display rules serve to control an expression or to modify or mask certain expressions that would be socially inappropriate or would reveal deception. Evidence relevant to this theory is presented in a series of experiments reported by Ekman and his colleagues.

One series of experiments explored the extent to which respondents from different cultures agreed on the facial configuration signifying contempt as opposed to anger or disgust (Ekman and Friesen, 1986; Ekman and Heider, 1988). They found that the expression is widely recognized as contempt (75 percent agreement across cultures) just as the "anger expression" was seen as signifying anger (74 percent agreement) and the "disgust picture" showed disgust (73 percent agreement). Less clear, however, is the explanation for such universality: agreement could be the result of either species-specific learning or biological evolution. If the result of learning, the expressions would be characteristic only of humans; if the result of evolution, they should also be observed in other species, such as primates. A resolution of this issue depends on demonstrations of cross-species similarities in the underlying physiology. Such a demonstration has not yet been presented.

In a particularly ambitious cross-cultural study (Ekman et al., 1987), respondents from ten cultures were asked to identify facial expressions as indicators of one or more of six emotions—happiness, surprise, sadness, fear, disgust, anger. Three pictures were selected for each of the six emotions. High levels of agreement were found for judgments of the strongest emotion, the second strongest emotion, and the relative strength of two different expressions of the same emotion in each set of pictures. The majority of the observers in every culture judge the emotions as predicted. The authors claim that these results are strong support for the view of universal facial expressions (although not for the species-specific learning versus evolutionary explanations of such agreement). However, several aspects of their research design may have biased the results in favor of high agreement: their procedures serve to take the expressions out of a social context, eliminate simultaneous speech and body cues, freeze the expression in a photograph, force special attention to it, and ask for judgments from detached uninvolved observers. Further studies are needed to observe how facial expressions change in different social contexts. Following Doob's (1975) advice, these studies should embed the expression in textual material in order to capture the content as well as the tone of the emotion. Of interest, then, is the question: Would similar levels of agreement be obtained for expressions viewed as part of a cultural context?

The issue of universality versus cultural specificity has not been addressed systematically in relation to other nonverbal channels. However, there is indication of considerable variation in the display of emblems— physical acts that can fully take the place of words. Ekman et al. (1984) report regional, national, and intranational (urban versus rural) variation among respondents in their survey of emblems and indicate that a geographical dictionary of emblems would be a useful compilation for researchers as well as travelers. Such work would raise a question of interest: Does the source of emblems differ from facial expressions with regard to the issue of universality versus cultural specificity?

Finally, in terms of the central theme of this chapter, we located only two teams of investigators who have been recently exploring cultural influences on deceptive enactments. Comparing Chinese experimental liars with truth tellers, Cody et al. (1989) report some similarities and some differences to findings reported in earlier studies with American subjects (see also Yi Chao, 1987). Like their American counterparts, Chinese liars found lying to be a more difficult challenge than telling the truth: they experienced difficulties in communicating detailed and thorough answers to the questions that required effort. (See DePaulo et al., 1985, for a review of the research with American subjects.) Overall, however, few nonverbal behavioral cues distinguished the Chinese liars from truth tellers: no differences were found in either arousal or visual cues, although some discrimination was found in the auditory channel. These findings may be explained in part by culturally learned constraints against the display of negative feelings. Both the liars and truth tellers were brief in communicating negative feelings; they smiled frequently and suppressed body and hand movements. While speech errors were related to deceit, many other paralinguistic variables related more strongly to question difficulty.

The researchers suggest that future cross-cultural research assess the more subtle cues to arousal and anxiety that are more sensitive to cultural influences, such as types of smiling, symmetry of expressions, and tone of voice. Another study shows that vocal stress may be a sensitive indicator of emotions associated with deception, at least for the male Chinese subjects in their sample (O'Hair et al., 1989). One implication of these findings is that different display rules operate in different societies, resulting in culturally specific expressions, some of which are manifest as deception cues. The mode of expression of nonverbal behaviors in various channels differs even if the same type of behavior is displayed. When stated as an hypothesis, this issue provides a basis for further research that would elucidate the cultural dimensions of deception clues.

Bond and his colleagues (1990) videotaped Americans and Jordanians while telling lies and truths about persons they liked or disliked. Similarities and differences in nonverbal displays between the cultures indicate some support for both culturally specific expressions and for universal expressions. They found similarities between the cultures on such nonverbal behaviors as smiling, head movements, blinking, and hand gestures. Differences were found on eye contact, movements per minute, and filled pauses: Jordanians displayed more of each of these behaviors. However, only one behavior, filled pauses, distinguished between the liars and truth tellers among the Jordanian subjects only: Jordanians displayed more filled pauses when lying than when telling the truth. It is little wonder then that the detectors from both cultures were inaccurate: very few nonverbal behaviors could be used as reliable cues to deception.

CONCLUSIONS

Three kinds of conclusions are suggested by this review of research related to deception. The evidence underscores the relevance of nonverbal behaviors as indicators of emotions and intentions, although it raises additional issues that can only be resolved by further research. It also suggests some strategies that can be used to detect intentions in real-world environments.

It is clear that a number of nonverbal behaviors are associated with deception. Particularly revealing are body movements and tone of voice changes, although a number of other behaviors also indicate deception in certain situations. Nonverbal behaviors reflect feelings or emotions more directly than specific intentions to deceive. Emotions—psychological states—can be considered as intervening variables, relating to observed behaviors and to inferred intentions. Nonverbal expressions are influenced by culture and context, but some components of emotional expression may be universal and independent of cultural overlays.

Motivated liars are easier to detect than nonmotivated liars. When emotionality is high, as in the case of tasks with high stakes associated with outcomes, nonverbal behaviors can be especially revealing. The revealing behaviors are likely to be those in a liar's unattended channels, which are leaked as a result of behavioral inhibition or rigidity.

Detectors, both amateurs and experts, are generally inaccurate despite high levels of confidence in their judgments. Neither feedback nor enhanced suspiciousness seems to improve their accuracy, but training them and providing them with a plan for processing information can increase accuracy of detection. The increased accuracy is more likely to occur if the discriminating cues to deception are known, and processing strategies aid the process of weighing and combining cues for judgments. In the absence of known relevant cues, whether to rely on possible universal or situation-specific cues remains an unresolved research issue.

Many questions are raised by the tantalizing information on deception and nonverbal behaviors. What nonverbal behaviors are associated with forms of deception that are not considered to be direct lies? What are the specific connections between nonverbal behaviors, emotions, and intentions as these occur in different situations? What are the implications of conscious control of facial expressions or body movements? There is a need to develop a framework that enables an analyst to match behaviors to situations in order to specify more precisely the contextual basis for behavior. What are the effects of varying types of lies and types of liars on the accuracy of detection? What are the dimensions of detection accuracy? There is a need to develop analytical strategies that aid the task of inferring intentions from behavior when the discriminating cues are not known. Cross-cultural studies of nonverbal behaviors associated with deception are needed. Little is known about the culturally specific display rules for every channel of communication, not only those manifest in facial expressions. On this topic, the gap between scientific evidence and anecdotal reporting is especially large. Researchers could take advantage of the large number of foreign students currently attending United States universities as a source for cross-cultural comparisons.

In spite of the number and breadth of unanswered questions, laboratory research does suggest particular aspects of behavior that may reveal intentions, for example, relationships between incongruities in verbal and nonverbal behaviors and stress, deviations from baseline observations of tone-of-voice as an indicator of possible deception, and an increased overall intensity of behaviors for extent of commitment to policies. Techniques developed for laboratory research may also be useful. They provide a structured and systematic approach to analysis for detecting deception in a variety of situations. The techniques are especially useful to an analyst who has access to videotaped interactions or who can interact with a subject over long periods of time. It is important not to rely solely on the judgments of "experts" even if they claim to be highly confident in those judgments. Expert-based judgments should be verified with other data gathered and processed in a systematic manner.

It should be possible to learn to distinguish between the universal and culturally specific expressions of emotions. The primary emotions may evoke similar expressions from one culture to another, and combinations of emotions seem to be subject to display rules, with which detectors can become familiar.

Leakage cues are likely to be evident in a highly motivated liar. A professional may be more likely to show signs of deception in unattended channels than an experimental subject, who operates in an environment in which the stakes for getting caught are relatively low.

NOTES

1. Comprehensive reviews of this evidence can be found in a number of sources. Harper et al. (1978) provide an ambitious summary of the literature organized by channel of communication, that is, paralanguage, facial expression, kinesics or body language, visual behavior, and proxemics or the study of space. An edited volume by Siegman and Feldstein (1978) reviews the evidence on specialized topics by the key researchers in those fields, for example, Dittmann on the role of bodily communication, Ekman on facial expression, Exline on visual interaction, Hess on pupillary behavior, and Patterson on the role of space. Druckman et al. (1982) present a channel-by-channel review of studies organized in terms of the functions of information processing and impression management; the same authors provided a more recent review appearing in Hargie's (1986) *Handbook of Communication Skills*. Influential frameworks for conceptualizing the diverse functions served by nonverbal behavior are those devised by Ekman and Friesen (1969), Birdwhistle (1970), Dittmann (1972), Mehrabian (1972), and Argyle (1975). To keep abreast of current developments in the field, readers can consult recent issues of the *Journal of Nonverbal Behavior*.

2. Results obtained from a preliminary analysis are instructive. Subjects participated in a main interview and a postinterview session; in the later, they were told to "fool the interviewer by controlling their facial expressions." In both segments, the same issue was discussed. Fifteen nonverbal behaviors (facial expressions and body movements) were coded for both the main interview and the postinterview sessions. Contrary to the leakage hypothesis, the difference scores indicated *less* movement on most indicators in the postinterview session. Following the experimenter's instructions, subjects spent considerably *more* time looking at the interviewer and *less* time looking elsewhere during the postinterview session. They also showed *less* activity on other indicators, the only exceptions being head movements and frowns, where they showed somewhat *more* movement during the postinterview session. Although this finding contradicts the idea of leakage, it does suggest a deception clue for deceivers who consciously control their facial expressions. The clue is *less* overall animation, which has also

been found to discriminate among deceivers, evaders, and truth tellers (Druckman et al., 1982:137) and to distinguish between deceivers sensitive to detector's possible suspicions about their deception and those not sensitive to suspicions in the Buller et al. (1989) study. It also replicates the DePaulo et al. (1985) finding of behavioral inhibition for motivated liars discussed above. More definitive results await the analyses of data which have been obtained from a larger sample of subjects, some of whom were told to "control their face," while others were told to "control their body."

3. Another problem for detectors is posed by skillful deceivers. Skill at deceiving may be developed through on-the-job experience or by specific training programs. Studies by Ekman and Friesen (1974) and Alker (1976) suggest that experience in a profession (nursing, politics) may enhance a person's skill at deceiving. DePaulo et al. (1985) discuss training with regard to both effective and ineffective procedures. Appropriate training for would-be deceivers may be games where feedback is direct, unambiguous, and immediate. Inappropriate preparation may be repeated rehearsals of the future enactment. Careful planning may make a person appear less spontaneous and more tense, leading the observer to conclude that he or she is being deceptive. These suggestions apply more generally to the art of impression management, including those forms of impressions that are less morally dubious than deception.

4. The laboratory research addresses the question of what to look for and how to measure it. While contributing analytical strategies as discussed in this section, it would be facile to suggest that the findings from laboratory studies also contribute to the meaning of displays observed in other settings. The meaning of measured displays must be established in the setting of interest.

REFERENCES

Alker, H.A.
　　1976　Mystification and Deception in Presidential Press Conferences. Paper presented at the meeting of the American Psychological Association, Washington, D.C.
Argyle, M.
　　1975　*Bodily Communication.* New York: International Universities Press.
Badler, N.I., and S.W. Smoliar
　　1979　Digital representations of human movement. *Computing Surveys* 11:19-38.
Baxter, J.C.
　　1970　Interpersonal spacing in natural settings. *Sociometry* 33:444-456.
Ben-Shakhar, G., I. Lieblich, and M. Bar-Hillel
　　1982　An evaluation of polygraphers' judgments: a review from a decision theoretic perspective. *Journal of Applied Psychology* 67:701-713.
Birdwhistle, R.L.
　　1970　*Kinesics and Context.* Philadelphia, Pa.: University of Pennsylvania Press.
Bond, C.F., Jr., A. Omar, A. Mahmoud, and R.N. Bonser
　　1990　Lie detection across cultures. *Journal of Nonverbal Behavior* 14:189-204.
Buller, D.B., and R.K. Aune
　　1987　Nonverbal cues to deception among intimates, friends, and strangers. *Journal of Nonverbal Behavior* 11:269-290.
Buller, D.B., J. Comstock, R.K. Aune, and K.D. Strzyzewski
　　1989　The effect of probing on deceivers and truthtellers. *Journal of Nonverbal Behavior* 13:155-169.
Cody, M.J., W. Lee, and E. Yi Chao
　　1989　Telling lies: correlates of deception among Chinese. In J.P. Forgas and J.M. Innes, eds., *Recent Advances in Social Psychology: An International Perspective.* New York: Elsevier Science Publishers.

DePaulo, B.M., M. Zuckerman, and R. Rosenthal

1980 Detecting deception: modality effects. In L. Wheeler, ed., *Review of Personality and Social Psychology*, Vol. 1. Beverly Hills, Calif.: Sage Publications.

DePaulo, B.M., R. Rosenthal, C.R. Green, and J. Rosenkrantz

1982 Diagnosing deceptive and mixed messages from verbal and nonverbal clues. *Journal of Experimental Social Psychology* 18:433-446.

DePaulo, B.M., J.I. Stone, and G.D. Lassiter

1985 Deceiving and detecting deceit. In B.R. Schlenker, ed., *The Self and Social Life*. New York: McGraw-Hill.

Dittmann, A.T.

1972 *Interpersonal Messages of Emotion*. New York: Springer.

Doob, L.W.

1975 *Pathways to People*. New Haven, Conn.: Yale University Press.

Druckman, D., R.M. Rozelle, and J.C. Baxter

1982 *Nonverbal Communication: Survey, Theory, and Research*. Beverly Hills, Calif.: Sage Publications.

Ekman, P.

1978 Facial expression. In A.W. Siegman and S. Feldstein, eds., *Nonverbal Behavior and Communication*. Hillsdale, N.J.: Erlbaum.

1981 Mistakes when deceiving. *Annals of the New York Academy of Sciences* 364:269-278.

Ekman, P., and W.V. Friesen

1969 Nonverbal leakage and clues to deception. *Psychiatry* 32:88-106.

1974 Detecting deception from the body or face. *Journal of Personality and Social Psychology* 29:288-298.

1986 A new pan-cultural facial expression of emotion. *Motivation and Emotion* 10:159-168.

Ekman, P., and K.G. Heider

1988 The universality of a contempt expression: a replication. *Motivation and Emotion* 12:303-308.

Ekman, P., and M. O'Sullivan

1988 The role of context on interpreting facial expression: comment on Russell and Fehr (1987). *Journal of Experimental Psychology, General* 117:86-88.

1991 Who can catch a liar? Unpublished manuscript, Human Interaction Laboratory, University of California, San Francisco.

Ekman, P., W.V. Friesen, and J. Bear

1984 The international language of gestures. *Psychology Today* May:64-69.

Ekman, P., W.V. Friesen, M. O'Sullivan, A. Chan, I. Diacoyanni-Tarlatzis, K. Heider, R. Krause, W. Ayhrans LeCompte, T. Pitcairn, P.E. Ricci-Bitti, K. Scherer, M. Tomita, and A. Tzavards

1987 Universals and cultural differences in the judgments of facial expressions of emotion. *Journal of Personality and Social Psychology* 53:712-717.

Flavell, J.H.

1977 *Cognitive Development*. Englewood Cliffs, N.J.: Prentice-Hall.

Getty, D.J., R.M. Pickett, C.J. D'Orsi, and J.A. Swets

1988 Enhanced interpretation of diagnostic images. *Investigative Radiology* 23:240-252.

Hall, E.T.

1966 *The Hidden Dimension*. Garden City, N.Y.: Doubleday.

Hargie, O.

1986 *A Handbook of Communication Skills*. Dover, N.H.: Croom Helm, Ltd.

Harper, R.G., A.N. Wiens, and J.D. Metarazzo

1978 *Nonverbal Communication: The State of the Art*. New York: John Wiley.

Hendershot, J., and A.K. Hess
    1982 Detecting Deception: The Effects of Training and Socialization Levels on Verbal and Nonverbal Cue Utilization and Detection Accuracy. Unpublished manuscript, Department of Psychology, Auburn University.

Jourard, S.M.
    1966 An exploratory study of body-accessibility. *British Journal of Social and Clinical Psychology* 5:221-231.

Knapp, M.L., and M.E. Comadena
    1979 Telling it like it isn't: a review of theory and research on deceptive communications. *Human Communication Research* 5:270-285.

Kraut, R.E., and D. Poe
    1980 Behavioral roots of person perception: the deception judgments of customs inspectors and laymen. *Journal of Personality and Social Psychology* 39:784-798.

Little, K.B.
    1968 Cultural variations in social schemata. *Journal of Personality and Social Psychology* 7:63-72.

Lykken, D.T.
    1981 *A Tremor in the Blood: Uses and Abuses of the Lie Detector.* New York: McGraw-Hill.
    1985 The probity of the polygraph. In S.M. Kassin and L.S. Wrightsman, eds., *The Psychology of Evidence and Trial Procedure.* Beverly Hills, Calif.: Sage Publications.

Mahoney, R., and D. Druckman
    1975 Simulation, experimentation, and context: dimensions of design and inference. *Simulation and Games* 6:235-270.

McClintock, C.C., and R.G. Hunt
    1975 Nonverbal indicators of affect and deception. *Journal of Applied Social Psychology* 1:54-67.

Mehrabian, A.
    1971 Nonverbal betrayal of feeling. *Journal of Experimental Research in Personality* 5:64-73.
    1972 *Nonverbal Communication.* Chicago: Aldine.

Nisbett, R., and L. Ross
    1980 *Human Inference: Strategies and Shortcomings of Social Judgment.* Englewood Cliffs, N.J.: Prentice-Hall.

O'Hair, D., M.J. Cody, X. Wang, and E. Yi Chao
    1989 Vocal Stress and Deception Detection Among Chinese. Paper presented at the annual meetings of the Western Speech Communication Association, Spokane, Wash.

O'Sullivan, M., P. Ekman, and W.V. Friesen
    1988 The effect of comparisons on detecting deceit. *Journal of Nonverbal Behavior* 12:203-215.

Raskin, D.C.
    1987 Does science support polygraph testing? In A. Gale, ed., *The Polygraph Test: Lies, Truth, and Science.* Beverly Hills, Calif.: Sage Publications.

Rozelle, R.M., D. Druckman, and J.C. Baxter
    1986 Nonverbal communication. In O. Hargie, ed., *A Handbook of Communication Skills.* Dover, N.H.: Croom Helm, Ltd.

Shuter, P.
    1976 Proxemics and tactility in Latin America. *Journal of Communication* 26:46-52.

Siegman, A.W., and S. Feldstein, eds.
    1978 *Nonverbal Behavior and Communication.* Hillsdale, N.J.: Lawrence Erlbaum.

Sommer, R.
   1959   Studies in personal space. *Sociometry* 22:247-260.
Swets, J.A.
   1988   Measuring the accuracy of diagnostic systems. *Science* 240:1285-1293.
Swets, J.A., D.J. Getty, R.M. Dickett, C.J. D'Orsi, S.E. Seltzer, and B.J. McNeil
   1991   Enhancing and evaluating diagnostic accuracy. *Medical Decision Making* 11:9-18.
Watson, O.M.
   1970   *Proxemic Behavior: A Cross-Cultural Study.* The Hague, Netherlands: Mouton.
Watson, O.M., and T.D. Graves
   1966   Quantitative research in proxemic behavior. *American Anthropologist* 68:971-985.
Yi Chao, E.
   1987   Correlates of Deceit: A Cross-Cultural Examination. Unpublished doctoral dissertation, Department of Communication, University of Southern California.
Zuckerman, M., D.T. Larrance, N.H. Spiegel, and R. Klorman
   1981   Controlling nonverbal clues: facial expressions and tone of voice. *Journal of Experimental Social Psychology* 17:506-524.
Zuckerman, M., R. Koestner, and A.O. Alton
   1984   Learning to detect deception. *Journal of Personality and Social Psychology* 46:519-528.
Zuckerman, M., R. Koestner, and M.J. Colella
   1985   Learning to detect deception from three communication channels. *Journal of Nonverbal Behavior* 9:188-194.

10

A Broader Concept of Deception

Although laboratory studies of lying have produced interesting results, critics can point to many features that might limit their generality to "real world" deception. The lying is done by individuals who are not experienced at deception. Because the lying is done at the request of the experimenter, it may differ qualitatively from unsanctioned lying in social contexts. Laboratory lying does not, in itself, benefit the liar, nor does it do obvious harm to the target of the lie.

This chapter considers deception in a broader context. We begin with a review of attempts to provide a framework for understanding deception and lying. Some of those attempts were aimed at constructing theories of deception; others were aimed at understanding how ordinary individuals conceptualize deception. We focus on these latter approaches to determine whether, in principle, it is possible to detect if a given individual is being truthful or is trying to deceive. We then suggest additional research paradigms to supplement the standard one. The goal of this new paradigm is understand how different cultural and subcultural groups represent deception and its moral implications. As discussed in Chapter 9, an individual can be expected to "leak" deception cues when he or she has violated a cultural norm; thus, it is important to know what the cultural norms are and what constitutes a violation for that individual.

Morality is a concern because of its impact on leakage. In most situations, a person has to rely on verbal and nonverbal cues to judge if someone is lying or trying to deceive in other ways. As discussed in Chapter 9, these cues, in turn, are assumed to reflect an internal psychological state. Presumably, internal states that correspond to guilt can produce physiological and motor responses that may reveal the guilty state to a discerning detector. At least this is the basic premise that underlies the attempts to discover cues to deception.

TYPES OF DECEPTION

Lying in the real world covers more than lying studied in the laboratory: lying is often done for personal or ideological gain; it can harm the victim, and it is often carried out over a considerable span of time. More broadly, deception includes more than lying. In fact, deception can be carried out without explicit lying.

Deception can be defined broadly as the manipulation of appearances such that they convey a false reality. However, when one tries to list a variety of deceptions and their contexts, it becomes difficult to find a common set of features that characterizes all of them. At best, the various types of deception bear what Wittgenstein (1953) calls a family resemblance to one another. Deception includes both dissimulation (hiding or withholding information) and simulation (putting out wrong or misleading information). Both deception and lying can be accomplished by omission as well as by commission. Interestingly, folk theories of deception are more likely to attach moral significance to deceptions accomplished by commission than to those accomplished by omission.

The first psychologists to study deception looked upon conjuring or sleight-of-hand magic as the paradigm (Hyman, 1989). Certainly, conjuring is one of the few occupations in which success depends entirely on the ability to deceive. Although deception is the essence of conjuring, such deception differs from the deception of the confidence man or that of the spy. A conjuror engages in "sanctioned deception": he or she has an implicit contract with the audience that doing a good job means fooling the onlookers. A magician would not be a good magician if he or she failed to deceive the audience. A conjuror's "victims" know, even before the tricks have been done, that the magician intends to fool them.

Deception, unlike conjuring, generally depends for its success on keeping intended victims unaware that deception is taking place. And many deceptions, unlike magic tricks, are definitely not sanctioned by society. Although most lying and deceiving are considered immoral by almost all cultures, some forms are sanctioned, or at least tolerated, by social customs. In the United States, such tolerated untruths include "social lies" and "white lies." Jokes, fantasies, teasing, and fibbing are other examples of untruths that carry little or no social disapproval. These considerations suggest that one way deceptions vary is in the perceived harm that they can do to other people or society.

There are many examples of the varied types and contexts of deception. Many adolescent children have successfully "fooled" adults; some have gained notoriety as psychics or individuals around whom poltergeist phenomena occur. Both children and adults have succeeded in fooling doctors into giving them unneeded prescriptions and even unnecessary operations. Consumer and health fraud has always been a huge industry in civilized countries. Military and strategic deception have been practiced since countries or even tribes have existed. Feints and ploys are highly valued and important forms of deception in games and sports. Fraudulent psychics, gambling cheats, and impersonators are everywhere. Confidence games and swindles continually take their toll of seemingly willing victims. Forgery is a criminal case of deception. In recent years, more and more articles and books have been devoted to plagiarism and other deception in science (e.g., National Academy of Sciences, 1989). Self-deception has also recently been gaining much attention among philosophers, psychologists, and sociobiologists.

All these forms of deception are interesting and worthy of study, but the focus of this chapter is more limited: two individuals in face-to-face communication. Under these circumstances, the questions of hiding and detecting deception are about leakage and the extent to which one of the parties can detect whether the other is talking or acting deceptively. One focus is how to generalize the existing findings from laboratory research to more realistic settings and to wider contexts of deception.

Although the focus is on two individuals in face-to-face communication, it is important to remember that most important informational exchanges occur within a more complicated organizational setting in which structural and psychological factors interact and help to determine, in important ways, the consequences of the exchanges. These added complexities are briefly addressed.

THEORIES, TAXONOMIES, AND FRAMEWORKS

During the late 1800s and early 1900s several psychologists tried to develop a psychology of deception, using conjuring as the paradigm case for deception (Hyman, 1989). By discovering and classifying the principles that conjurors use to mystify audiences, the psychologists hoped to provide a general framework for understanding all deception. But, for the reasons noted above, conjuring is probably not the best paradigm for deceiving.

A few writers have tried to develop taxonomies as frameworks for a theory of deception: a good taxonomy helps focus on which studies are most likely to contribute to the development of an adequate theory. At first, any taxonomy has to be considered highly tentative; it is likely that as research is surveyed, some categories will be found to include no representatives and many studies will be difficult to fit into any category. More broadly, a good taxonomy cannot be evaluated in general terms because its usefulness depends on the purposes of its users.

Some theorists on deception have developed preliminary taxonomies that can be used as a basis for developing more comprehensive systems for future investigations. A major objective of the existing taxonomies is to develop a scientific theory of deception. Such a theory would consist of basic concepts, variables, and laws that would enable people to understand and explain deception. Just as the current theories of physics, chemistry, and biology deviate greatly from earlier intuitive notions about how the world "works," we can expect that a scientific theory of deception will probably have little in common with common sense ideas of deception.

The current attempts to develop a framework for understanding deception, in fact, do not depart very much from general intuitions about deception. In some cases this simply reflects the primitive state of theorizing about deception. The developers of the taxonomies have to begin with the concepts and data that exist in everyday terminology. Presumably, with more scientific investigation and further refinements, the taxonomies will begin to deviate more and more from everyday concepts and terminology.

A few attempts to develop a framework, however, deliberately adopt the stance of the layperson. Hopper and Bell (1984), for example, base their approach on what they refer to as "the linguistic turn." This approach seeks the basis for a taxonomy within the language usage of ordinary people. Others have as their focus the deliberate attempt to find out how people conceptualize deception and lying. Thus, we can identify two motivations for studying the folk psychology of deception: one is based on the hope that the folk psychology, with suitable refinements, can be transformed into a scientific psychology of deception; the other is to study the folk psychology as an end in itself. As will be pointed out, this latter motivation may have important implications for questions raised in this chapter.

A brief overview of some frameworks devised for the purpose of developing a scientific theory of deception is discussed below, followed by a look at taxonomies deliberately aimed at understanding how ordinary people conceive of deception.

Frameworks as Scientific Theories

Chisholm and Feehan (1977) provide an analysis of deception from a logical, philosophical viewpoint. They identify three dimensions for distinguishing among deceptions: omission-commission; positive-negative; intended-unintended. The combination of these dimensions provide eight different categories of deception.

Daniel and Herbig (1982) define deception as the deliberate misrepresentation of reality to gain a competitive advantage; thus, they differ from Chisholm and Feehan in that only intended misrepresentations would count as deceptions. They add a further restriction in that the misrepresentation has to be aimed at providing a "competitive advantage" to the deceiver. They divide deceptions into three categories: cover, lying, and deception. Cover refers to secret keeping and camouflage. Lying is subdivided into simple lying and lying with artifice. Lying is more active than cover in that it draws the target away from the truth. Artifice goes beyond straight lying in that it involves manipulating the context surrounding the lie. Deception is not the same as lying; lying focuses more on the actions of the liar, and deception deals with the effects on the receiver. Daniel and Herbig further classify deceptions as ambiguity-increasing and ambiguity-decreasing: the former deceives by confusing the target, the latter misleads by building up the attractiveness of one wrong alternative.

In a different approach, Heuer (1982) builds a taxonomy in terms of the underlying psychological biases that are assumed to result in deception. He lists various perceptual and cognitive biases that may help to develop a theory of deception and counterdeception. Heuer's approach points to the fact that one can attempt to base a taxonomy on an ordering of the various exemplars of deception or, instead, on an ordering of psychological and sociological constructs that may explain deception. Each approach has its merits. The ultimate goal is to develop a framework that can account for the effectiveness of deception. But one can argue that it might be wiser to begin the search with a taxonomy that is based on surface similarities and dissimilarities among exemplars of deception. Possibly, there might be some value in trying to start with both types of taxonomies.

One attempt to create a theory of deception includes the only taxonomy that has been put to a test. Whaley (1982) devised a taxonomy on the basis of systematic analysis of examples from war and conjuring. He also obtained inputs from diplomats, counterespionage officers, politicians, businessmen, con artists, charlatans, hoaxers, practical jokers, poker players, gambling cheats, football quarterbacks, fencers, actors, artists, and mystery story writers. The resulting framework was tested by classifying an exhaustive list of magic tricks. All deception for Whaley is a form of misperception. He divides misperceptions into other induced, self-induced, and illusions. Self-induced misperception is what we ordinarily refer to as self-deception. Other-induced misperception includes misrepresentation (unintentional misleading) and deception proper (deliberate misrepresentation).

Every deception, according to Whaley, is comprised of two parts: dissimulation (covert, hiding what is real) and simulation (overt, showing the false). Both dissimulation and simulation come in three forms: the three types of dissimulation are masking, repackaging, and dazzling; the three types of simulation are mimicking, inventing, and decoying. In decreasing order of effectiveness, these components of deception can be listed as masking, repackaging, dazzling, mimicking, inventing, and decoying. Nine categories of deception are obtained by combining the three kinds of dissimulation with the three kinds of simulation. Whaley claims that these nine types exhaustively classify all deceptions; he was able to classify every magic trick into one of these nine categories. Whether other researchers and independent judges can use his system to reliably classify the same magic tricks, as well as other deceptions, into these categories remains to be seen.

One schematic framework was developed for understanding deception in intelligence work (Epstein, 1989). The framework is attributed to the late J.J. Angleton, who was a senior officer, as well as a controversial person, in the Central Intelligence Agency. The basic idea is that of a deception circle that includes, as a minimum, a victim (target person or group), an inside person, and an outside person. The outside person is typically an enemy agent who pretends to have become an informant. He is the source of disinformation to the target group. For the disinformation to be effective, however, the enemy must know how it is being accepted and interpreted by the target group. The feedback comes to the enemy from the inside man (usually a "mole" or other enemy agent who has managed, over a period of years, to penetrate the innermost sanctums of the target group). With the appropriate feedback, the enemy can tailor and fine-tune the disinformation so that it is more consistent with what the target group believes or wants to believe. This deception circle, which also characterizes many other successful forms of deception, such as confidence games, provides a potent and almost irresistible way to plant disinformation. Although this model is relatively simple, it is important in making clear that the dynamics of successful deception typically involve organizational and social factors that go beyond the simple dyadic relationship of the informer and the "informed."

Frameworks Based on Folk Psychology

Philosophers and some psychologists debate the role that folk psychology—common beliefs—should play in a scientific psychology. One position is that folk psychology should play no role since many folk beliefs about human behavior have been wrong. Trying to build a scientific psychology on the basis of folk psychology, according to this position, would hamper progress by starting with vague, contradictory, and almost certainly wrong beliefs. People who advocate this position argue that the science of psychology should begin with those concepts and laws that have already been shown to be useful in biology, physiology, and neuroscience.

The contrary view maintains that any complete science of psychology must take into account people's beliefs about their own and others' mentality and behavior. This is the view accepted in this chapter. We believe that any attempt to understand and explain deception must somehow take account of how ordinary people conceptualize deception.

One obvious way in which a folk psychology of deception can matter is related to the leakage hypothesis, which assumes that people enter a particular psychological state when they believe they are violating a social norm. The experience or state of guilt is accompanied by hormonal and muscular changes that can potentially be detected by an observer. Perhaps the best use of this hypothesis is to predict or detect deception on the basis of beliefs and acts that constitute deceptions and transgressions for a given individual. What a person believes about lying and deception is part of that individual's folk psychology.

Two empirical studies have attempted to describe the way ordinary people conceptualize lying and deception. Although both studies were psychological investigations, the investigators were communication scientists (Hopper and Bell, 1984) and linguists (Coleman and Kay, 1981). Subsequently, another linguist carried out a provocative analysis of the Coleman and Kay study (Sweetser, 1987). These studies are important because they show that the paradigm laboratory experiment might be supplemented by approaches that better elicit leakage cues from members of various groups.

A Taxonomy in Psychological Space

One taxonomy of deception was devised by looking for systematic relationships among deception terms used by speakers of English (Hopper and Bell, 1984). By examining how their subjects classified 46 terms related to deception, the investigators inferred that folk theories of deception recognize six types: playings, fictions, lies, crimes, masks, and unlies. This taxonomy organizes the deception realm in terms of perceived similarities among the various concepts that refer to deception in some sense. The investigators suggest that their taxonomy is hierarchical. The six categories can be subsumed under two more general categories, benign fabrications and exploitative fabrications: benign fabrications include fictions and playings; exploitative fabrications include lies, crimes, masks, and unlies.

Hopper and Bell add further organization to their taxonomy by looking for attributes or dimensions along which they can order their categories with respect to one another. Their statistical analyses identify three such dimensions and hint at three additional ones. The dimension that accounts for most of the ordering among the deception terms is evaluation: it contrasts socially acceptable, harmless, and moral types of deception with socially unacceptable, harmful, and immoral deceptions. The two other dimensions that account for most of the ordering among their categories are detectability and premeditation. The three additional dimensions that may also play a role are directness, verbal-nonverbal, and prolonged.

The investigators had their subjects—180 undergraduates in an American university—each sort 46 words into categories that seemed to go together. The 46 words had been selected to represent a larger set of 120 deception terms. The assumption was that the more subjects who put the same two words in the same category, the more these two words were psychologically similar. After obtaining an index of similarity between every pair of words, the authors used multidimensional scaling to construct a psychological space for these terms.

Hopper and Bell had another group of subjects rate each of the deception words on ten bipolar adjective scales, such as good-bad, harmless-harmful, moral-immoral, direct-indirect. In our own analysis, we used these ratings with factor analytic procedures to generate a psychological space for the 46 terms. The resulting space was similar to the one that Hopper and Bell found using their clustering procedure. Our analysis indicated that two psychological dimensions were sufficient to account for the variations of the terms on the rating scales. Figure 1 shows 31 of the words plotted in this two-dimensional space. (We have omitted 15 of the terms from the graph because they overlapped with other terms and would have made the graph unintelligible.)

For our purposes, it is the principle illustrated by this figure that matters. We labeled one dimension "harmfulness": the terms that are high on this dimension (on the right-hand side) tended to be highly rated on scales such as bad, harmful, unacceptable, and immoral; the terms that are low on this dimension (on the left-hand side) were highly rated on the opposite scales, good, harmless, socially acceptable, and moral. The second dimension is labeled covertness: those items that are high on this dimension (at the top) were rated high on covert, indirect, and nonverbal; those at the opposite end of this dimension (at the bottom) were rated high on overt, direct, and verbal.

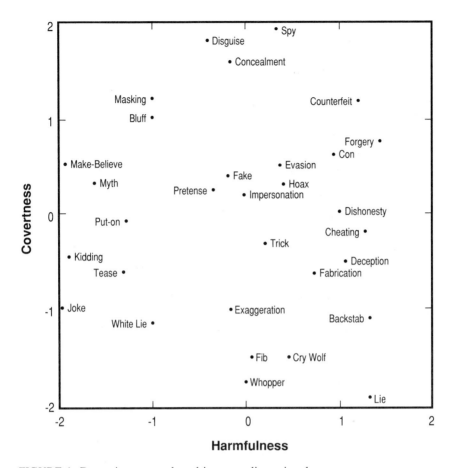

FIGURE 1 Deception terms plotted in a two-dimensional space.

Notice that the concept *lie* is located at the bottom right-hand corner of the figure. The subjects agreed in rating lying as harmful, socially unacceptable, and immoral, as well as being highly verbal and direct. *Deception* also is high on harmfulness but is relatively neutral on the covertness dimension. This suggests that the subjects recognize that some deceptions can be highly verbal, such as lying, but that they can also be nonverbal. Although *fib* and *whopper* are near *lie* on the covertness dimension, they are rated as relatively neutral on the harmfulness scale. A *white lie* is rated as only somewhat harmless and somewhat overt.

There are some possible limitations of these data. The variations among the terms are circumscribed by the limited number and range of rating scales used. Some important dimensions in the folk psychology of deception may have been left out. A more important limitation is that the role of context is omitted. *Disguise* is rated as neutral on harmfulness though covert, but a disguise used for a costume party is quite different from a disguise used to rob a bank. Perhaps the apparently neutral rating simply reflects that some respondents rated it as harmful and others rated it as neutral. Similarly, most jokes are harmless, but certain practical jokes can be quite cruel and harmful.

Despite these limitations, however, Hopper and Bell's data probably capture some important aspects about how undergraduates in our culture perceive deception. Presumably, if such subjects were telling a lie as a joke, they would display less leakage than if they were telling a lie about who wrote their term paper. We have illustrated this procedure in some detail because we believe that, with suitable refinements, it can be used to yield psychological spaces for different subgroups and cultures. We might expect that different groups would differ on which kinds of deception they placed at the socially acceptable and socially unacceptable ends of the harmfulness dimension. This could be useful information, for example, if leakage cues to deception mainly occur when an individual is deceiving in a way that *his or her culture* finds socially unacceptable.

A Prototype Theory

Another way to uncover the psychological space with respect to deception was illustrated by Coleman and Kay (1981). These authors carried out their empirical study of the word *lie* as an assault on the previously dominant checklist theories of meaning. The checklist view assumes that the meaning of a word consists of a set of features: any object that contains these features belongs to the category defined by that word. For example, *bachelor* refers to any object that is human, adult, male, unmarried. According to the checklist theory, any person who possesses all four of these defining features is a bachelor, and a person who lacks one or more of these features is not a bachelor. The classic theory of meaning asserts that the possession of these defining features is both necessary and sufficient for being a bachelor. Such a definition establishes what is called an equivalence class—every person who satisfies the definition is as much a bachelor as every other bachelor. Even before this classical theory began to be challenged in the 1970s, some scholars had pointed to problems with the classical definition. For example, is the Pope a bachelor? What about a widower?

The alternative view of meaning, which became popular during the 1970s, is known as the prototype theory. Prototype theories recognize the intuitive notion that some members of a category are better exemplars than others. Much of the early work supporting this theory had been done with colors (Rosch, 1975). Not all examples of the color red, say, are equal. People in different cultures agree that some examples are better reds than others. Additional experimental work dealing with directly perceptible objects such as plants, animals, utensils, and furniture supported the prototype theory. Coleman and Kay wanted to show that the prototype phenomenon can also be found in words referring to less concrete things, such as the speech-act word *lie*.

They first used standard linguistic analysis to devise a definition of a "good" (true) lie. A good lie is one for which the speaker (S) asserts some proposition (P) to addressee (A) such that:

(1) P is false (false in fact);
(2) S believes P to be false (believe false); and
(3) in uttering P, S intends to deceive A (intent to deceive).

In the checklist or classical theory these three properties would be necessary and sufficient for a statement to be a lie. The prototype theory asserts that a concept such as *lie* is a "fuzzy set" in which different members vary in their degree of goodness or closeness to the prototype. Statements that possess all three properties would be the best examples of a lie. Statements that possessed only two of the three defining properties might still be considered lies, but not very good examples. Statements that had only one of the properties would be considered even poorer examples of lies. Finally, statements that possessed none of these three properties would not be considered as lies.

Coleman and Kay (1981) conducted an empirical test of the theory by constructing brief stories to correspond with each of the eight possible combinations of possessing or not possessing the property. The story corresponding to the possession of all three properties was as follows (p. 31):

(1) Moe has eaten the cake Juliet was intending to serve to company. Juliet asks Moe, "Did you eat the cake?" Moe says, "No." Did Moe lie?

The story corresponding to the possession of none of three defining properties was (p. 31):

(2) Dick, John, and H.R. are playing golf. H.R. steps on Dick's ball. When Dick arrives and sees his ball mashed into the turf, he says, "John, did you step on my ball?" John replies, "No, H.R. did it." Did John lie?

As expected, all 67 of Coleman and Kay's American subject's agreed that (1) was a lie and that (2) was not a lie. What they were interested in was how these respondents would react to the other stories, which possessed either one or two of the defining characteristics. Story (3), for example, had two defining characteristics: false in fact and intent to deceive. It lacked the property that S believes P to be false. This story was as follows (p. 31):

(3) Pigfat believes he has to pass the candy store to get to the pool hall, but he is wrong about this because the candy store has moved. Pigfat's mother doesn't approve of pool. As he is going out the door intending to go to the pool hall, Pigfat's mother asks him where is going. He says, "I am going by the candy store." Did Pigfat lie?

Pigfat's statement was considered to be a lie by 58 percent of the judges; 37 percent judged it not to be a lie; and 5 percent could not make a decision.[1] In general, the results supported the prototype model. The more defining properties a story contained, the more likely it was to be judged a lie. The authors noted some minor departures from the ordering that their theory would have predicted. In part, these departures could be attributed to the fact that each story differed in content. Coleman and Kay also obtained comments from their subjects. In agreement with their theory, the comments referred to the three prototypical properties to justify why a statement was judged as a lie. But the subjects also referred to other properties, such as the reprehensibility of the acts and the motives of the person making the statement.

The authors discuss their reasons for not including some of these additional properties in the prototype for *lie*. They distinguish between prototypical and typical properties of a concept. Lies, in their view, are prototypically statements that the speaker believes to be false, intends the hearer to believe, and are, in fact, false. Lies are also typically reprehensible, but not prototypically so. They conclude (Coleman and Kay, 1981:38):

Although this is not the only plausible way to do so, we summarize our observations by saying that reprehensibleness, although characteristic of typical acts of lying, is not a prototypical property of such acts, and as such does not play a role in the semantic prototype (or in the meaning) of *lie*.

This distinction between prototypical and typical properties of a concept is controversial. We do not take a side in this controversy; we discuss the issue here because, regardless of whether reprehensibility is a prototypical or typical property of lying, it may matter for the leakage hypothesis. Only acts that are reprehensible or otherwise morally unacceptable to a given individual would be expected to lead to those states that generate nonverbal leakage. To gain an understanding of how different cultural groups construe various types of lying and deception, the Coleman and Kay approach should be extended by adding stories that also vary on such properties as perceived social acceptability, potential harmfulness, and the like.

A Linguistic Approach

Sweetser (1987) uses the data from Coleman and Kay's investigation to provide an alternative interpretation. Like Hopper and Bell, Sweetser wants to describe the folk theory or conception of lying; unlike Hopper and Bell, her method is linguistic rather than psychological. Sweetser notes the view of concepts as fuzzy sets rather than classical equivalence classes, but she argues for a different account.

She suggests that within folk psychology, the classical view may actually hold. She claims that the folk definition of lying holds for a prototypical, simplified model of the world. This prototypical world contains maxims such as: (1) be helpful; (2) correct information is helpful; (3) speakers only talk about information they have good reasons to know is correct; (4) listeners can correctly assume that speakers know what they are talking about. In this prototypical context, if the speaker's statement is false, then it is clearly a lie.

When subjects are not completely sure whether a speaker is lying, Sweetser argues that this is not because the specific act differs from the prototypical lie, but rather the act occurs in a context that differs from the prototypical one. A joke is a false statement deliberately uttered by the speaker. It is not clearly a lie, according to Sweetser, because the context in which the joke is made differs from the prototypical one. In the prototypical context for defining a lie, conveying true information is paramount. But in the context of a joke, playing is paramount, and conveying true information is irrelevant. Subjects are unsure about whether a joke is a lie because they are not sure that a lie can occur in a context in which the truth is irrelevant.

Sweetser's analysis of lying highlights the need to keep context in mind when devising a taxonomy of deception. Indeed, we believe that an adequate taxonomy of deception will include a taxonomy of the contexts in which each kind of deceptive act can occur.

Sweetser's analysis points to a further issue that may be important for a good taxonomy. She states that a speaker feels less immoral if he or she manages to deceive the target without directly lying. She suggests that deceivers feel less guilt about deceiving by implication rather than by deceiving by an explicitly false claim. (In contrast, she also suggests that a victim feels *more* resentment by having been deceived by implication than by a direct lie.) If Sweetser is correct, then it could be hypothesized that a deceiver is less likely to leak deceptive signals when engaging in indirect deception than in direct deception.

Implications for this hypothesis are derived from the Druckman et al. (1982) experiments reviewed above. These investigators found both similarities and differences in displayed nonverbal behaviors between subjects in an evasion (indirect deception) condition and those in a direct deception condition. Discriminant-analysis results showed that the evaders were more similar to deceivers than to honest subjects in overall displays. However, the evaders could be distinguished from deceivers in terms of particular nonverbal behaviors displayed during certain time periods and as deviations from baseline data: for example, deceivers made more speech errors (calculated as a deviation from a baseline period) than evaders. These findings suggest that evaders are not less likely to leak deceptive signals; rather, *different* cues may be leaked by indirect (evaders) and direct deceivers.

The cross-cultural question is intriguing. Several interesting suggestions are made in the anthropological, linguistic, and other related literatures. A first reading of the literatures provides a pessimistic answer to the possibility of finding universal indicators of deception. Some cultures seem to have notions of what constitutes lying and deception that differ markedly from American folklore. Even more disquieting is the claim that in some cultures lying and deceiving, in several contexts, are not only socially acceptable, but actually considered exemplary behavior when the fabrications succeed.

The reason these first impressions of cross-cultural differences are disheartening is because of the assumption that a deceiver will only leak his or her intentions when knowingly deceiving and violating a social taboo. Thus, one faces the task of finding out what is considered a socially unacceptable fabrication within various cultural groups. Once such contexts have been discovered, then interrogations could be arranged so as to put informants, for example, in a situation in which they would be violating a cultural taboo if they lied when presenting information to interrogators. Our reading of the literature indicates that if a socially unacceptable deception for a given informant has been identified, then circumstances can be created that will lead to leakage if the informant is willfully lying.

Socialization

Our focus has been on a folk psychology of deception because it seems to offer the best way to achieve a general theory of deception. The leakage hypothesis assumes that a given individual will display potentially detectable signs when he or she is in a certain psychological state. As we have noted, a key issue is the extent to which these diagnostic cues are universal—that is, to what extent they show the same pattern across cultures and situations—and the evidence to date suggests the possibility that there may be both universal and culturally specific aspects to leakage displays.

Presumably, the underlying psychological state that gives rise to leakage corresponds to what is ordinarily labeled guilt, shame, humiliation, disgrace, or dishonor—terms that refer to how people feel when they violate a social taboo. Everyone is raised within family and cultural settings that teach which acts are socially unacceptable. This socialization process is considered to impart a relatively permanent tendency to experience guilt or a similar state whenever a person commits, or even considers committing, social transgressions. Such tendencies may persevere even when an individual, as an adult, consciously rejects many of the values within which he or she was raised.

One assumption, then, is that for all cultures people will react with a guilty state when they believe they are violating a cultural norm. Knowing the folk psychology for various cultures becomes important if one wants to know what constitutes a cultural taboo for a given individual. That is why the techniques used by Hopper and Bell and by Coleman and Kay have been discussed in some detail. By properly refining and adapting their methods, information can be gathered on how individuals from various cultures and subcultures conceive of deception and lying. This information, in turn, might lead to determining what sorts of stories or actions constitute socially unacceptable behaviors. Such findings could then be used to create appropriate stimuli that may elicit leakage if the individual is, in fact, trying to deceive.

This model assumes people have been socialized. What about individuals who have not been socialized? In the past, psychologists and psychiatrists diagnosed some individuals as psychopaths or sociopaths. Whether such diagnostic categories are still useful or appropriate is debatable; the current tendency is to use the term "antisocial personality." Folklore and clinical observation suggest that antisocial people are able to lie and deceive successfully because they have undeveloped social consciences and no feelings of guilt. A few experiments have been carried out with such persons using the polygraph; all of them are controversial and the results are contradictory.[2] Whether antisocial people turn out to be better or worse than normal people at hiding and detecting deception, the practical consequences are not clear. It is doubtful, for example, that an intelligence agent would want to trust a person so diagnosed, even if such a person could successfully deceive the enemy.

INTERACTIVE SETTINGS

The discussion in this chapter (and in Chapter 9) deals with the simplest situation in which deception occurs, a face-to-face confrontation between two individuals, in part because this situation has been the context of most of the research. Another reason is that such a situation provides a starting point for considering extensions to more complicated and realistic interactions.

The typical dyadic situation is one in which the two individuals interact and each adapts his or her behavior in the light of what the other person says and does. In contrast, all the research on the leakage hypothesis has been conducted within a relatively static, noninteractive mode. Typically, the detector makes judgments in response to a videotaped presentation. The detector cannot continue and ask further questions, nor can the deceiver adjust his or her behavior on the basis of feedback from the detector. But this is just the context in which ordinary dyadic communication occurs.

It is possible that a detector can do better than the dismal performances so far reported if he or she is allowed to actually interact with the sender. However, the sender might actually do even better at hiding deception in an interactive mode, because the deceiver can use feedback from the victim to adjust both the content and mode of presentation so as to be more acceptable to the victim.

The Expression Game

Goffman's (1969) concept of an "expression game" depicts the dynamics of interaction between a detector and a sender. Accurate reading of expressions is made difficult by the paradox that "the best evidence for (the detector) is also the best evidence for the sender to tamper with" (Goffman, 1969:63). The detector's challenge is to determine the significance of a cue when he or she knows that the sender is managing his or her expressions. The detector must anticipate what the subject expects him or her to look for and then focus attention on other cues. The sender is challenged by the need to fool the detector when he or she knows that the detector is assessing his or her moves. The sender must anticipate the cues likely to be used by the observer and then control them. As Goffman (1969:58) notes: "uncovering moves must eventually be countered by counter-uncovering moves." Both the detector and sender are vulnerable. The objective for each is to minimize his or her vulnerability under difficult circumstances. This assessment dilemma renders the expression game a highly sophisticated art form.

The dynamics of the expression game pose an analytical problem. Both senders (encoders) and receivers (decoders) determine the outcome of the communication process. The problem is one of disentangling effects of senders and receivers. Accurate detection may be the result of encoding skill, decoding skill, or both. Consequently, an analyst does not know whether detection is due to style of presentation or astute observation. One solution is to control part of the interaction, either the sender's enactments or the observer's clues, as is done in most laboratory experiments. By so doing, however, one may lose the essential features of an interactive situation. This problem illustrates the difficulties in making the transition between laboratory and field settings.

The World of Intelligence Agencies

Theories of deception, such as those outlined in Epstein (1989), often assume deception works best when it can be tailored to the expectations and desires of the victim. Intelligence agencies attempt to do this tailoring by using feedback about which parts of the disinformation are being accepted and which parts are being rejected by the victim. One source of such feedback is provided by information gained in face-to-face communication between informant and interrogator. In the world of spying, however, the most effective form of feedback comes from an inside person (or mole) who has penetrated the target agency. The deception loop includes several layers of an organization. The disinformation (lying) from a presumed informer makes its way from the controlling agent up through the various layers of the bureaucracy. The inside person sees how this information is being accepted and interpreted and informs the enemy agency. The enemy agency, in turn, adjusts the disinformation being provided by the informant to better fit with the expectations and desires of the enemy.

As this example illustrates, deception can and often does involve several levels of organizational complexity. A complete understanding of how deception operates in most real-world situations often requires considerations at several levels of analysis such as the international scene, the relation between states, governmental structures, internal special interest groups, and the like (Handel, 1976; Mauer et al., 1985). Much of this complexity deals with how information is accepted and used or not. This, in turn, relates to the problem of detecting deception because it is possible that even when cues to deception should be obvious to an interrogator, the disinformation being provided may so fit in with preconceptions and desires of superiors that the interrogator subconsciously ignores all the signs to the contrary.

As many have pointed out, an interrogator (case officer) who controls an informant has much of his esteem and pride invested in this informant. A symbiotic relationship exists between a case officer and an informant. The informant requires the trust of the case officer so that the information being provided will be accepted. The case officer needs to believe that the informant is trustworthy because his or her reputation depends on controlling this important source of information. In fact, even when an informant is a plant, he or she will make sure to provide enough true information, along with disinformation, to ensure that the case officer is rewarded and promoted. In this way the case officer becomes even more dependent on the trustworthiness of the informant.

Once a case officer and his or her superiors have decided that an informant is trustworthy, the dynamics of the situation are tilted toward maintaining the belief in the reliability of the informant. Careers can be made, or broken, if the agency ultimately decides that an informant was a true defector or a plant. A variety of institutional and psychological factors come into play to maintain the belief, even in the face of subsequently strong information to the contrary, in the trustworthiness of the agent. Striking cases of such institutional self-deception have been documented by Epstein (1989), Handel (1976), Watzlawick (1976), and Whaley (1973).

Such institutional self-deception typically involves accepting or rejecting the *content* of information. At the level of face-to-face communication, we have been focusing on the nonverbal cues rather than the content of what is being communicated. The two bases for judging the credibility of information obviously interact. When the content of the information is consistent with the beliefs and desires of the receiver, then the tendency to accept the information as accurate is strong. As noted above, the relationship between suspicion and detection accuracy— how much a tendency to believe or disbelieve can override the ability to pick up deception cues—is important for research.

CONCLUSIONS

From the discussion in the chapter we draw four conclusions. The first conclusion is based on the assumption that leaked cues to deception occur when an individual's psychological state reflects the experience of guilt. However, the situations that produce guilt may vary with an individual's cultural background and experience. Therefore, detection of deception would be improved if one could anticipate the sorts of settings that constitute social transgression or a guilt-producing state for particular individuals.

The research on the folk psychology of deception and on the prototypical structure of lying are examples of methods for assessing perceptions of socially unacceptable deceptions within subcultural groups. With suitable refinements, those methods can be used to discover what stories and deceptive acts might induce leakage for particular individuals.

Once discovered, the stories could be varied systematically to determine whether leakage occurs (or is enhanced) when an individual deceives under conditions that violate his or her cultural norms. The analysis would compare the reactions of various cultural groups to the same set of stories, with different stories hypothesized to produce nonverbal leakage for different groups.

Our second conclusion about cultural differences has practical implications. An interrogator can arrange a situation that will violate a cultural taboo if deception occurs. One possible way of doing this is to use an interrogator of the same cultural background as that of the informant. If the folk psychology of the informant holds that deceiving is immoral only when the victim is a member of one's own culture, then this setting should produce leakage clues if the informant is, in fact, lying.

The third conclusion concerns extending and modifying the laboratory research paradigm as a technique for studying deception clues. In order to examine complex interactions between individuals operating in organizational contexts, it would be necessary to supplement classical laboratory experiments with modern quasi-experimental methods, careful surveys, and detailed case histories. Moving between experimental and field studies also entails the development of statistical procedures that enable an investigator to make the comparisons of interest.

The fourth conclusion is a recommendation for the use of videotapes for research and training. Ongoing face-to-face interactions pose a problem for detecting subtle deception clues. Videotaped exchanges between interrogators and informants can be replayed for details easily overlooked in the course of an ongoing conversation. Independent observers can analyze the interactions, providing judgments that may be free from the biases possessed by participants. Moreover, taped discussions can provide baseline data on cues emitted from a number of communication channels. Such information can serve as a basis for evaluating deviations from past behavior. They can also be used to train individuals to code nonverbal behavior for leakage clues.

NOTES

1. Coleman and Kay obtained confidence ratings along with the judgments of whether a statement was a lie. They were able to use these ratings to construct a more refined rating scale. For the sake of simplicity, only the simple judgments of lying are discussed here.

2. Robin-Ann Cogburn, a doctoral student at the University of Oregon, is currently conducting research with antisocial persons who are in the state prison system. She is using a variation of the classic laboratory paradigm to test the leakage hypothesis with them.

REFERENCES

Chisholm, R.M., and T.D. Feehan
  1977   The intent to deceive. *The Journal of Philosophy* 74:143-159.
Coleman, L., and P. Kay
  1981   Prototype semantics: the English verb *lie*. *Language* 57:(1)26-44.

Daniel, D.C., and K.L. Herbig

    1982 Propositions on military deception. In D.C. Daniel and K.L. Herbig, eds., *Strategic Military Deception*. New York: Pergamon Press.

Druckman, D., R.M. Rozelle, and J.C. Baxter

    1982 Nonverbal Communication: Survey, Theory, and Research. Beverly Hills, Calif.: Sage Publications.

Epstein, E.J.

    1989 *Deception: The Invisible War Between the KGB and the CIA*. New York: Simon and Schuster.

Goffman, E.

    1969 *Strategic Interaction*. Philadelphia, Pa.: University of Pennsylvania Press.

Handel, M.I.

    1976 *Perception, Deception, and Surprise: The Case of the Yom Kippur War*. Jerusalem Papers on Peace Problems, No. 19. Jerusalem, Israel: The Hebrew University.

Heuer, R.J.

    1982 Cognitive factors in deception and counterdeception. Pp. 31-69 in D.C. Daniel and K.L. Herbig, eds., *Strategic Military Deception*. New York: Pergamon Press.

Hopper, R., and R.A. Bell

    1984 Broadening the deception construct. *Quarterly Journal of Speech* 70:288-302.

Hyman, R.

    1989 The psychology of deception. *Annual Review of Psychology* 40:133-154.

Mauer, A.C., M.D. Tunstall, and J.M. Eagle, eds.

    1985 *Intelligence: Policy and Process*. Boulder, Colo.: Westview Press.

National Academy of Sciences

    1989 *On Being a Scientist*. Committee on the Conduct of Science. Washington, D.C.: National Academy Press.

Rosch, E.

    1975 Human categorization. Pp. 1-72 in N. Warren, ed., *Advances in Cross-Cultural Psychology*. London: Academic Press.

Sweetser, E.E.

    1987 The definition of lie: examination of folk models underlying a semantic prototype. In D. Holland and N. Quinn, eds., *Cultural Models in Language and Thought*. New York: Cambridge University Press.

Watzlawick, P.

    1976 *How Real is Real? Confusion—Disinformation—Communication*. New York: Random House.

Whaley, B.

    1973 *Codeword Barbarossa*. Cambridge, Mass.: MIT Press.

    1982 Toward a general theory of deception. *The Journal of Strategic Studies* 5:178-192.

Wittgenstein, L.

    1953 *Philosophical Investigations*. New York: Macmillan.

PART IV

Performing

I N THIS PART WE DISCUSS ISSUES concerning ways to optimize the performance of individuals and teams, particularly by interventions that take place just prior to or during actual performance. The committee's decision to divide this topic into two chapters was based on the view that what works for individual performers may not work for groups. This view is supported by results of numerous studies on group problem solving: for example, unlike individuals, groups must deal with coordination problems with respect to the pooling and processing of information and a division of tasks.

An increasingly popular topic for psychologists is research on performance in sports. The literature to date has contributed both to the further development of theories of performance under pressure and to understanding of performance in a variety of individual and team sports. Continuing the committee's work on effects of mental practice (Druckman and Swets, 1988:Chapter 5), the discussion in Chapter 11 summarizes the results of studies conducted since the earlier report appeared. A number of other practical implications are suggested by the research summarized in this chapter, which covers preperformance interventions, the use of preparation rituals, the use of physiological indicators to assist in determining effective performance, and the use of exercise. The rapid increase of knowledge in this field suggests a virtually unlimited potential for contributions to understanding and improving performance under pressure.

Shifting the focus from individual to group performance, Chapter 12 emphasizes the need to invest in long-term research on groups that perform in operational environments. This topic has received very little attention in the research and development community. Although the academic research to date has some implications for improving suboptimal group performance, it is limited by a failure to capture a number of critical dimensions present in actual group situations. By elucidating some of these dimensions, the chapter provides a framework for designing laboratory and field studies that are relevant to the types of situations found in a variety of military and industrial organizations. There is much to be learned about the way that groups perform; this chapter provides guidance on how to proceed.

11

Optimizing Individual Performance

One of the long-standing concerns of sports psychology has been an understanding of performance under pressure. Unlike the military, the "pressure" in a sport is not usually intended to put someone at risk of life and limb. Although fear of injury may create pressure in some sports, more frequently competitive pressure is associated with a threat to one's self-esteem.

Since the mid-1970s there has been interest among psychologists to use sports as a naturalistic laboratory in which to conduct research on performance under pressure. In this chapter we review the rather expansive sports literature in four areas: the relationship between the mental health model, mood, and motor performance; cognitive-behavioral interventions for sport and motor performance; preperformance routines (i.e., preparation rituals), sports performance and electrophysiological correlates associated with these routines; and the effect of exercise on reactivity to psychosocial stressors. In the last section, we turn to a different area of research, neuroscience, to consider broader issues of the brain and performance.

THE MENTAL HEALTH MODEL OF SPORTS PERFORMANCE

A recent mental health model of athletic performance (Morgan, 1985) posits that success in sports is negatively correlated with psychopathology: that is, anxious, depressed, hysterical, neurotic, introverted, withdrawn, confused, fatigued, or schizoid athletes do not perform as well in sports as athletes with more positive mental health profiles. Scientifically speaking, Morgan's model may not seem very provocative, but its common sense and intuitive appeal has advantages in its gaining acceptance among the public (see Morgan, 1980).

Morgan maintains that his model has an intermediate level of complexity: that is, that the model can specify relationships [e.g., $y = f(x)$]. Morgan implies that the flow of causality is from psychological states to success in sports, not the other way around. However, he does not provide evidence for this flow, and it could be argued that the flow is in the opposite direction: that self-protective mechanisms may operate for athletes believing that they will not make a team or place first, which subsequently affects psychological states.

Morgan (1985:71) further maintains that this type of model "also predicts specific responses will be dependent upon specific stimulus conditions." Although the model does not clearly spell out all of the stimulus conditions, its empirical basis suggests that it may be limited to certain types of sports. With few exceptions (LeUnes et al., 1986; Morgan, 1981), most of the evidence has come from sports that emphasize muscular or cardiorespiratory endurance—body building, cycling, karate, wrestling, speedskating, soccer, rowing, distance running, and swimming. The model has been applied to other types of performance tasks. (In considering the use of this model for military settings, it seems most appropriate for dynamic, large-muscle activities or cardiorespiratory endurance tasks that involve intense aerobic/anaerobic training over a period of months.)

The basic model is a between-subjects static model, consisting of predictions of desirable psychological states for optimal performance. It has also been extended to a within-subjects dynamic model consisting of monitoring athletes throughout different stimulus conditions associated with intense training. Morgan (1985) believes the evolving dynamic model will ultimately prove to be superior to the static model in understanding changes in athletic performance. We first present the static model to better understand its features, which are also incorporated into the dynamic model.

Static Model: The "Iceberg Profile"

Although Morgan's work is admittedly pretheoretical, the measuring instruments used to test the static model represent existing psychological theory applied to sports (e.g., Eysenck et al., 1982). Specifically, Morgan's research has primarily focused on several standard psychological instruments: the State-Trait Anxiety Inventory (STAI) (Spielberger et al., 1970); the Profile of Mood States (POMS) (McNair et al., 1971/ 1981); the Eysenck Personality Inventory (EPI) (Eysenck and Eysenck,

1968, which measures extroversion, neuroticism, and conformity; the Somatic Perception Questionnaire (SPQ) (Landy and Stern, 1971); and the Depression Adjective Checklist (DACL) (Lubin, 1967). The conformity measure (i.e., lie scale) of the EPI was used throughout Morgan's research to infer the validity of subjects' self-report responses. In some studies (Morgan, 1981; Morgan and Johnson, 1978), the Minnesota Multiphasic Personality Inventory (MMPI) was used in place of the other instruments.

To test the model, Morgan defined psychopathology as higher scores relative to college student norms on introversion, neuroticism, trait anxiety, tension, depression, anger, fatigue, and confusion, as well as on the MMPI clinical scales used to diagnose problems dealing with psychological adjustment. Thus, Morgan predicted that athletes displaying psychopathology—defined as one standard deviation above the 50th percentile on the scales—would have lower levels of performance compared with athletes displaying a more "positive mood profile."

In a review of seven of his own empirical studies testing the static mental health model with pre-elite and elite athletes, he found a consistent pattern, relative to college student norms (McNair et al., 1971/1981): higher than average vigor and extroversion scores (i.e., positive characteristics for performance) and lower than average scores on the scales indicative of potential psychopathology. For example, on the POMS inventory, which has become most associated with tests of Morgan's mental health model (see LeUnes et al., 1988, for an annotated bibliography), the positive mood profile has become known as the "iceberg profile." This term refers to the shape of the curve relative to 1967 college student norms when raw scores on the six scales are plotted on the POMS profile sheet; see Figure 2. Since vigor happened to appear on these scoring forms in a middle position among the other moods and since athletes typically score above the population average on vigor, the plot looked like an iceberg.[1]

In all this research, the measured relationship of mental health to performance has been somewhat indirect. In no case were actual performances compared with athletes' responses on psychological inventories at the time the inventories were completed. Instead, they were inferred from final placement in competitions (e.g., 1st or 2nd) whether they made or did not make a team, or from expert ratings of elite runners within a 2-year period (Morgan et al., 1987a). In most studies the time span between athletes' completing the psychological inventories and the performance outcome was less than a week. In other studies in which trait measures (e.g., MMPI) were used, this time span was either much longer (as much as 4 years), or the response set used for the POMS (i.e., "past week including today") did not necessarily include the time in

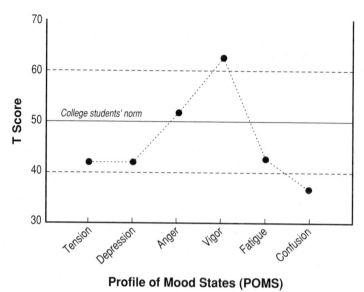

Profile of Mood States (POMS)

FIGURE 2   Comparison of profile of mood states of athletes and college student norms.

which the performances occurred (Morgan et al., 1987a). In spite of the rather crude performance measures, the findings have been remarkably consistent in showing that better athletes displayed a more positive mental health profile than athletes who were slightly worse (Morgan, 1985). The robust pattern generalized across several muscular and cardiorespiratory endurance-type sports and several samples of athletes. (Morgan also concluded that the findings were not likely due to response distortion since scores on the EPI lie scales were not correlated with any of the psychometric variables or performance.) The accuracy of the prediction was high but less than perfect. Using an a priori clinical analysis as the prediction basis, Morgan (1985) concluded that the accuracy of the prediction was between 70 and 80 percent and always exceeded base-rate or chance expectancies.[2] Although Morgan's model suggests a high degree of predictive accuracy, he maintains that this level of precision is not acceptable for selection purposes.

Considering that in Morgan's (1985) early research the mental health model was capable of making fine-grain differentiations with reasonable accuracy among high-level performers, an important question is whether the findings have held up in more contemporary research studies by other investigators. Although several of the studies cited in the annotated bibliography of LeUnes et al. (1988) claim to support Morgan's iceberg profile, many of these studies made no statistical comparisons to a control group. Instead, these studies simply plotted the means of a single group of athletes and contrasted them to the normative sample reported in the POMS test manual (McNair et al., 1971/1981). The unusually consistent findings relative to the test norms are likely due to an inappropriate comparison group; the norms were obtained from participants in psychological tests and students in psychology courses and "should be considered as very tentative" (McNair et al., 1971/1981:19). More recent studies of undergraduate college nonathletes (Boyle, 1987; Dyer and Crouch, 1987) demonstrate that the mean scores for tension, depression, and vigor have decreased over the past 20 years. This instability over time, which represents from 2-7 points on the various POMS subscales, and the current controversy surrounding the factor structure of the POMS (Boyle, 1987; Norcross et al., 1984; Reddon et al., 1985), suggests that the normative sample reported in the POMS manual is an inappropriate comparison group. Thus, studies of this type offer no convincing support for the iceberg profile and the mental health model.

A better test of the replicability of Morgan's findings for the mental health model are studies that provide comparison groups similar to those reported by Morgan (1985). We found 14 such studies that compared the POMS scores of two groups of athletes representing two levels of performance outcome (13 in LeUnes et al., 1988; Morgan et al., 1987b). Of the 148 total comparisons made with the six scales, only 27 (18 percent) were statistically significant and 24 (16 percent) in the predicted direction. The pattern predicted by the mental health model may have been present in these studies, but the power of the statistical tests may not have been sufficient to detect differences because of the small number of subjects. To examine this possibility, the directions of the 148 comparisons were examined relative to the predictions of the mental health model. As shown in Table 1, the percentage of supportive versus nonsupportive findings was calculated for each study. Compared to chance expectations of 50 percent supportive, these 14 studies yield an unimpressive overall average percentage of 53 percent supportive findings. As a whole, the findings from other investigators, as well as Morgan's studies (Morgan and Pollock, 1977; Morgan et al., 1987b), fail to clearly support the predictions of the mental health model.

In the face of these more recent findings, it is highly questionable that the POMS instrument, which is primarily used to test the mental health model, is sensitive enough to reliably differentiate among athletes who are already highly proficient. In addition to small samples and performance measures that have been indirect and often distally linked in time with psychological measures, the susceptibility of the POMS to distorting influences may also contribute to the lack of sensitivity in differentiating among athletes. For instance, Boyle (1987) has noted that

TABLE 1 Comparisons of the Outcomes and Directions of Performance Changes Predicted by the Mental Health Model

Study and Year	Sport	N^a	Total Comparisons	Comparisons in Predicted Direction	
				Number	Percent
Craighead et al., 1986	Basketball	61	6	2	33
Daiss et al., 1986	Football	60	4^b	1	25
DeMers, 1983	Diving	60	18	8	44
Dyer and Crouch, 1987	Running	40	12^c	8	66
Guttman et al., 1984	Skating	11	18	14	77
LeUnes and Nation, 1982	Football	180	18	14	77
Miller and Miller, 1985	Netball	20	6	3	50
Morgan and Pollack, 1977	Running	19	6^d	1	16
Morgan et al., 1987b	Running	27	6	0	0
Riddick, 1984	Swimming	79	18	9	50
Silva et al., 1981	Wrestling	15	6	4	67
Silva et al., 1985	Wrestling	86	6	6	100
Tharion et al., 1988	Running	34	6	3	50
Wilson et al., 1980	Running	30	18	18	100

[a]Number of athletes.

[b]Data not reported for two subscales.

[c]Comparisons between beginning runners and advanced runners at 3 hours and at 10 minutes prior to performance.

[d]Comparisons between world-class middle long distance runners and college middle distance runners.

social desirability and other response sets, inadequate self-insight, and item transparency affect POMS scores. Miller and Edgington (1984) have demonstrated the susceptibility of the POMS to response distortion or "faking good" when physical education students were led to believe the test results might influence team selection. The resulting extreme iceberg profile prompts considerable concern that the strong situational demands of team selection and placement in athletic competition may produce distorting influences that override instructions to subjects to answer the POMS as honestly as they can and that may be unique to the POMS and, thus, not detectable by the conformity scale of the EPI. Overall in fact, the static model has had limited success in predicting levels of athletic performance.

Dynamic Model: Measuring Overtraining

A more viable and methodologically sound approach of the mental health model may be to use measures of mood to monitor athletes across different conditions of situationally induced pressure brought about by manipulating the training stimulus. This section reviews studies examining this dynamic mental health model.

An interesting extension of the mental health model has been in the area of overtraining and staleness. Staleness is an undesirable or pathological condition that, in a sports context, often results when one is not able to fully recover from the acute fatigue caused by overtraining (Morgan et al., 1987a). (Overtraining should not be confused with overlearning, in which the physical demands of the task do not interfere with successful performance.) The most obvious symptoms of staleness include "physiological and psychomotor retardation, chronic fatigue, depressed appetite, weight loss, insomnia, decreased libido, muscle soreness and elevated depression and tension" (Morgan et al., 1987a:110).

In most endurance sports, coaches plan times during the year or season when they can increase the volume of training by altering the intensity (i.e., time at a fixed distance) or duration (i.e., constant pace but varied distance). Intensity and duration of training increases nearly fourfold during several weeks or months prior to important competitions. Most coaches believe that with the proper training stimulus, the process of overtraining can lead to enhanced athletic performance as long as the athlete is allowed sufficient time to recover from the acute fatigue brought on by the intense training. Often, however, the training stimulus is not appropriate, and athletes are unable to recuperate fully within 12-24 hours following an intense workout. As the intense training continues, chronic levels of fatigue develop and performance deteriorates.

The undesirable effects of overtraining are sometimes checked by monitoring resting heart rate, blood pressure, lactate, creatine kinase, cortisol, or catecholamine levels. If values on these measures deviate from normal, then the training stimulus can be cut back in a dose-response manner. Just as these physiological manifestations of overtraining can be monitored to prevent staleness, Morgan et al. (1987a) argue that staleness can also be prevented by systematically monitoring changes in mood. By examining mood states (e.g., with POMS) during training cycles consisting of light training, intense or overtraining, and tapering phases, staleness can be diagnosed early and prevented by reducing the training stimulus until the athlete once again displays a mood profile conducive to optimal performance (i.e., the iceberg profile). Without physiological or psychological markers to prevent staleness, the only known treatment is a dramatic reduction or change in training or, in extreme cases, complete rest by discontinuance of training.

With the exception of one study conducted with wrestlers,[3] most of the longitudinal studies by Morgan et al. (1987a) have been with collegiate swimmers. In these studies, varsity swimmers were given the

POMS scale at 1-month intervals from September (training load at approximately 3,000 yards/day) to the peak training load in January (11,000 yards/day) until just before the conference championship in February (peak training load was tapered to 5,000 yards/day). In this research, global mood disturbance was measured with the response set of "how you have been feeling during the past week including today." Global mood disturbance was calculated by summing the negative mood scales (anger, confusion, depression, fatigue, and tension), subtracting the "vigor" score from this total, and then adding a constant of 100 to prevent the occurrence of negative values.

During the 10 years that Morgan and his colleagues monitored mood scores on approximately 200 female and 200 male competitive swimmers, the greatest global mood disturbance typically occurred in late January when athletes were training twice a day to accomplish the peak training load. This increase in global mood disturbance usually resulted from a statistically significant increase in fatigue and a significant reduction in vigor. During this time about 5-10 percent of the swimmers experienced what was considered as staleness: the swimmers' performances had deteriorated, and they were unable to train at customary levels. They were referred to counseling psychology and outpatient psychiatric services, and approximately 80 percent of them "were judged to possess depression of clinical significance" (Morgan et al., 1987a:108).

Of the eight studies summarized by Morgan et al. (1987a), only one study controlled for nonathletic stressors—social, economic, and academic—in the life of college students. Throughout the semester (September through early December), 44 collegiate swimmers and 86 nonathletic college students (controls) completed the POMS bimonthly from week 3 to week 13 of the semester. As shown in Figure 3, the swimmers scored significantly lower than the controls at the beginning of the semester. However, as the training volume increased during the ensuing weeks (weeks 5 to 11), the swimmers experienced a significant global mood change; the controls did not change significantly at any point throughout the 13-week period. The swimmers had significantly higher mood disturbance than the controls during weeks 9 through 13. As the swimmers were not yet into the taper phase, there was no support for the findings of other studies (see Morgan et al., 1987a) that a return to normal mood levels occurs once the training stimulus was lowered.

In several of the research reports of the static and dynamic mental health models, Morgan has argued that psychobiological tests of the models would provide greater understanding than does a purely psychological approach. Illustrative of this is a recent psychobiological study (O'Connor et al., 1989) conducted with 14 female collegiate swimmers and 8 active college females who served as controls. As in other swim-

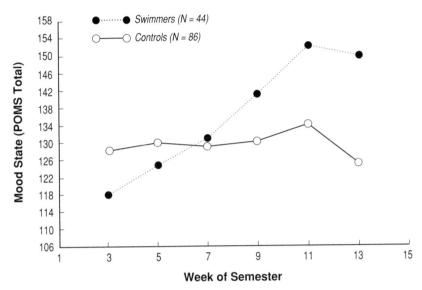

FIGURE 3   Moods of student athletes and nonathletes.

ming studies, the training volume of the swimmers increased from 2,000 yards/day in September (baseline) to a peak of 12,000 yards/day in January (overtraining), followed by a reduction in training to 4,500 yards/day by February (taper). The swimmers had more global mood disturbance in comparison with the controls during overtraining followed by a reduction in global mood disturbance after the taper period. The salivary cortisol levels of the controls did not change across time periods, while the swimmers had higher cortisol levels than controls during the baseline and overtraining periods. The swimmers had cortisol levels similar to the control subjects during the taper phase.[4]

In this study the team's coach (who was not given the mood and cortisol data) classified three swimmers as being stale because they had a performance decrement of 5-10 percent for 2 weeks or longer. For each of these women, the period of staleness coincided with the end of the overtraining period. Using a nonparametric test to examine the 3 stale and 11 normal swimmers, the results showed that the stale group had significantly higher global mood disturbance and salivary cortisol levels than the normal group. This finding is merely suggestive since the stale athletes may also have had more mood disturbance during the baseline period.

The results of this study (O'Connor et al., 1989) are consistent with other studies (Morgan et al., 1988) showing a convergence of physiological and psychometric measures of distress in swimmers during a period of increased training. The fact that tension remained elevated following the taper period may have been due to anxiety associated with an impending conference championship. The differences in salivary cortisol levels during the baseline are also problematic. This difference may have been due to limitations associated with only collecting one cortisol sample for each training phase and the time frame in relation to training in which these samples were obtained (O'Connor et al., 1989). Although no subjects in this study possessed negative affective states of clinical significance (i.e., one standard deviation of the population average of college females), three subjects had prolonged performance decrements that resulted in their being diagnosed as stale.

Global mood disturbance has recently been shown to be related to athletes' running economy (Williams and Krahenbuhl, in press) and mood state following a rapid 6 percent weight loss (Horswill et al., 1990). For example, it has been noted for some time that even in elite runners there is considerable day-to-day variability in ventilation measures, which exercise physiologists use to infer how economically one runs at a constant workload. Comparing the POMS to daily ventilation measures showed a surprisingly high association, $r = .80$. It appears that these within-subject comparisons of mood state over days or months can detect when athletes may feel undue pressure in their lives that can slightly (e.g., running economy, weight loss) or dramatically (e.g., staleness) affect their performance. The implications of the dynamic model are far-reaching.

Summary

There are a number of shortcomings in the studies testing the static and dynamic mental health models. These shortcomings include the use of a single-group design in several studies, which greatly limits their internal validity; most of these studies were cross-sectional, exploratory, descriptive, or retrospective in nature. Many of the studies only used comparisons to college norms established more than 20 years ago, and it is possible that these norms are not stable over time and are no longer still representative of college students today. Most of the studies had very small numbers of subjects, which greatly restricted the use of multivariate statistics for testing the predictions of the model and for determining the strength of the predicted relationships. The studies were limited in scope to endurance sports for which the training stimulus was easily quantifiable. Finally, there is meager physiological validation for the predictions of the mental health model.

In addition to these shortcomings, another major problem in the series of studies testing the static model has been in the quantification of performance. The performance measure employed represented an out-come, such as won or lost, made or didn't make the team; but an athlete might have performed very well relative to his or her past performance (e.g., personal best), but still failed to win. Yet Morgan would label the performance as unsuccessful. If, instead, the performance measure was actual swimming times and distances, a ratio scale of measurement could be developed to detect small group differences and enable future investigators to determine if athletes having the greatest performance decrements actually have more global mood disturbance.[5]

The results of studies using control groups to test the static model have produced inconsistent results. It may be too much to expect that a self-report measure of mood can be sensitive enough to reliably dis-criminate among levels of athletic proficiency, let alone predict which athletes will make a team or place first in a given contest. With the use of within-subjects designs with control groups (Morgan et al., 1987a:Study 7; O'Connor et al., 1989), the studies testing the dynamic mental health model have had more internal validity and have shown a greater degree of consistency in supporting the predictions of the model. The dynamic model also has the distinct advantage of being able to specify the situ-ational variables (e.g., training intensity) that lead to predictable mood changes characteristic of what is known as staleness.

COGNITIVE-BEHAVIORAL INTERVENTIONS

Sports psychologists have studied cognitive-behavioral interventions as a means of facilitating sports performance since the late 1970s. The general assumption is that cognitive-behavioral interventions can help performers achieve greater control of their precompetitive arousal states and maintain attentional focus on the task at hand. The studies reported in this section do not measure arousal/attentional processes directly; rather, they infer these processes from performance changes. Improve-ments in arousal and attention, which can be achieved by practice in cognitive-behavioral intervention techniques, is believed to result in higher levels of motor performance. As defined by Greenspan and Feltz (1989), "interventions" consist of actions, initiated by someone other than the performer, that focus on psychological skills in an attempt to improve performance.

For this review, the interventions typically reported in the sports psy-chology literature have been put into five categories: (1) relaxation with no attempt to alter cognitions (e.g., progressive muscle relaxation, autogenic training, biofeedback, and hypnotherapy); (2) imagery (in-cluding "mental practice"); (3) mental preparation strategies (e.g., asso-ciation-disassociation strategies and goal setting); (4) skill development strategies (e.g., modeling); and (5) cognitive restructuring-coping strategies (i.e., when a clear and deliberate attempt is made to alter cognitions) (see Greenspan and Feltz, 1989; Whelan et al., 1989). Before turning to recent reviews of cognitive-behavioral interventions in a sports performance context, we consider the motor performance literature on imagery and mental practice; this material represents an update on the topic in the committee's first report (Druckman and Swets, 1988:Chapter 5).

Mental Practice and Motor Performance

Although there are a few studies that show that mental practice can enhance retention (Annett, 1979), most of the research literature deals with mental practice and motor performance. According to Richardson (1967:95): "mental practice refers to the symbolic rehearsal of a physical activity in the absence of any gross muscular movements." Meta-analytic reviews show that, across many types of motor tasks, mental practice groups performed significantly better than control groups. This is the case whether one examines group differences at the posttest (effect size = 0.48; Feltz and Landers, 1983) or pretest-posttest change scores (effect size = 0.47; Feltz et al., 1988). The motor performance studies contained in these meta-analytic reviews usually have greater internal validity than the sports studies, but less external validity (see Campbell and Stanley, 1963). The motor performance studies are more often laboratory studies, in which subjects have been randomly assigned to treatment conditions. An even more important difference is that the motor performance tasks are typically novel tasks that control for the effect of prior experience and also minimize practice of the task during the intervention period.

Although those meta-analytic and narrative reviews (Richardson, 1967; Singer, 1972; Weinberg, 1982) have concluded that mental practice is better than no practice at all, a more interesting question is whether mental practice can be as good as or better than physical practice. To investigate this question, subjects in the mental practice, physical practice, and control groups (no practice) receive the same number of practice trials. In addition, many of the motor performance studies have included an additional condition of combined practice. In this case, the ratio of physical to mental practice has been 50:50 so that subjects receive half the number of trials of the 100 percent physical and half the number of trials of the 100 percent mental practice groups. Although some reviewers (Richardson, 1967; Singer, 1972; Weinberg, 1982) have suggested that mental practice or a combination of mental and physical practice can be as effective or more effective in improving performance than 100 percent physical practice, the meta-analytic review by Feltz et al. (1988) found otherwise. For pretest-posttest change scores, it showed effect sizes of 0.79 for physical practice, 0.62 for the 50:50 combined practice, 0.47 for mental practice, and 0.22 for no practice (control group).

In the committee's first report (Druckman and Swets, 1988:65), the possibility was raised that a combination of mental and physical practice might approach or exceed improvement of the 100 percent physical practice group if the ratio included a majority of physical practice trials, for example, 70:30. With tasks like pursuit rotor (a spinning disc with a quarter-sized target that a person tries to track and that records "time on target" [Oxendine, 1969]), standing broad jump and hand dynamometer (a device used to measure grip strength [Wills, 1966]), combined practice groups (75:25 and 50:50) have not been found to be significantly different from physical practice groups. However, the results of these studies are far from conclusive. Not only were these effects not found for other tasks examined in these studies—soccer kick, modified free-throw, and hand dynamometer—but these studies also lacked necessary control groups to clearly interpret the influence of physical and mental practice on motor performance.

A more complete test of the hypothesis that combinations of physical and mental practice can affect motor performance as much as physical practice alone was recently conducted (Hird et al., 1991). This study compared different ratios of physical to mental practice for performance on a cognitive task (peg board), which requires perceptual and symbolic task elements, and on a motor task (pursuit rotor). Subjects (36 males and 36 females) were randomly assigned to one of six groups: control (practice on a lateral balancing task); physical practice; mental practice; or one of three combined physical and mental practice groups, 75:25, 50:50, and 25:75. There were seven practice sessions, consisting of four trials per session for the peg board and eight trials per session for the pursuit rotor. The results showed that all treatment conditions significantly improved performance from pre- to posttest, except for the control group for the peg board task. Consistent with the Feltz and Landers (1983) meta-analysis, effect size calculations indicate that mental practice was more effective for the peg board than for the pursuit rotor. Also, effect sizes and significant linear trends for the posttest scores for both tasks show that as the relative proportion of physical practice increased, performance was enhanced (see Table 2). These findings indicate that reducing or replacing physical practice with mental practice would be counterproductive if performance enhancement was the only consideration. However, for conditions under which physical practice may be expensive, time consuming, fatiguing, or injurious, combined mental and physical practice or mental practice alone is clearly more effective than no practice.

TABLE 2 Comparative Effects of Physical and Mental Practice

Group	Hird et al. (1991)		Feltz and Landers (1983)	Feltz et al. (1988)
	Peg Board	Pursuit Rotor		
Physical Practice	2.05	1.52	—	0.79
75:25 Combined	1.54	1.32	—	—
50:50 Combined	1.36	1.10	—	0.62
25:75 Combined	1.07	0.95	—	—
Mental Practice	1.06	0.50	0.48	0.47
Control (no practice)	—	—	—	0.22

NOTE: All numbers are effect sizes.

Although physical practice was better than combined mental and physical practice and mental practice alone in these studies, in real-life settings mental practice is not always used as a replacement or trade-off for physical practice. Rather, mental practice is often used as a supplement to physical practice. There has been a paucity of motor performance research that has examined the performance effects that occur when varying amounts or types of mental practice are systematically added to a constant amount of physical practice. This question has been addressed in sports, when the regular training and competitive schedule of athletes is supplemented (although not systematically) with cognitive-behavioral techniques. These field experimental studies are presented in the next section.

Sports Performance

The generalizability of the motor performance findings has been questioned, primarily because athletes' participating in real-world sports tasks were not the central focus of the studies. Recently, the emphasis in sports psychology studies has been to broaden the scope to include a number of strategies that emphasize cognitions, thoughts, or mental activities as mediational processes and/or as the central change mechanisms (Whelan et al., 1989). Collectively these strategies have been called cognitive-behavioral interventions and include such "psychological skills" as imagery, relaxation, biofeedback, hypnotherapy, cognitive restructuring, systematic desensitization, self-monitoring, performance-contingent rewards, and goal-setting. At the same time, reviewers have narrowed their focus to the sports context. Thus, they selected for their reviews only those studies that used athletes who competed on a regular and organized basis, and in which performance (the dependent variable) was measured in a noncontrived competitive situation in the sport in which the athletes regularly competed.[6]   The overall results of these reviews provides strong support for a relationship between cognitive-behavioral interventions and an enhancement of sports performance. For instance, Whelan et al. (1989) found that the average effect size (0.62) represented more than one-half a standard deviation advantage in the performances of the athletes receiving cognitive-behavioral interventions compared with control groups who were denied this supplemental mental training. Likewise, Greenspan and Feltz (1989) observed the same facilitation of sports performance in 87 percent of the studies in their review.[7]

The effects of cognitive-behavioral techniques were robust with respect to four factors (Whalen et al., 1989): type of control group used (no treatment, attentional, placebo, etc.); team or individual sport; open or closed skills;[8] and performance measured in competition or practice conditions. Effect sizes were higher (0.62) in studies using appropriate motivational control groups to infer causality. In addition, in the studies of athletes' performing in conditions of competitive pressure (competing directly with others), training in cognitive-behavioral techniques significantly enhanced performance (effect size of 0.31, $p < .05$); this effect size, however, was less than half of what it was when no competition was present (0.75, $p < .01$). The type of outcome measure was also an important moderating variable. Studies that used objectively determined performance, physiological, or self-report measures all showed significant effect sizes (> 0.49, $p < .05$). In contrast, when the outcome measure was based on the ratings of judges or trained observers, the effect size was not statistically significant (0.29, $p > .05$).

The type of skill and the skill level of the performer were also rated by Whelan et al. (1989). Significant effect sizes were found for tasks primarily involving accuracy, endurance, and strength; significant effect sizes were not found for tasks that emphasized balance or speed. In terms of skill level, the effect sizes were significant for both novice and proficient performers. However, with so few intervention studies being conducted with elite athletes (usually defined as national team, Olympic, or professional level), no meta-analytic information on the effectiveness of interventions could be provided for this level of competitor.

The issue of whether cognitive-behavioral interventions actually work with elite level athletes was the topic of discussion on the 1988 pre-Olympic games telecast on the ABC television program *Nightline*. William P. Morgan, a prominent sports psychologist from the University of Wisconsin at Madison, mentioned that there is no scientific evidence that the intervention techniques used with athletes actually improve performance. Since the topic of the *Nightline* program dealt with the psychological preparation of Olympic athletes, it later became clear that Morgan's remarks were being addressed to the dearth of intervention studies on elite athletes. But of four studies with elite athletes, 75 percent show positive effects of cognitive-behavioral interventions on sports performance. For example, semiprofessional baseball players improved batting efficiency average as a result of performance that was contingent on monetary rewards (Heward, 1978) and an Olympic pommel-horse athlete, who received stress-inoculation training, improved performance in a number of meets more than other gymnasts (Mace et al., 1987).

In studies with comparison groups, the results are mixed. For instance, Mumford and Hall (1985) found that sectional and national level figure skaters given four 50-minute sessions of various kinds of imagery were not rated any differently by judges than figure skaters who watched films related to, but not of, skating figures. In another study involving elite athletes, Kim (1989) obtained the complete cooperation of Korean sports administrators to randomly assign Olympic rifle shooters to treatment conditions. The 48 subjects (aged 18-30) were assigned in equal numbers to four groups: a relaxation/imagery group, a meditation/imagery group, a combined relaxation/imagery/meditation group, and a no-treatment control group. The subjects in the first two groups listened to either a relaxation/imagery or a meditation/imagery audio-cassette tape in a private room two times a day over a 6-week period for a total of 13 hours of treatment. Subjects in the combined group listened to the meditation/imagery tape for 3 weeks and then listened to the relaxation/imagery tape for 3 weeks. The subjects in the control group listened to a tape that contained classical music without any instruction.

The results of Kim's (1989) study showed no pretest differences among groups, but there were significant pretest-posttest differences for anxiety and performance. Although no differences were found for the relaxation/imagery and control groups, the meditation/imagery and combined meditation/relaxation/imagery groups showed both significant posttest reductions in self-reported anxiety and better shooting performance. Analysis of posttest scores only revealed a significant difference among groups for shooting performance ($p < .05$), and Scheffe post hoc tests showed this was due to the combined group performing better than the control group.[9] Kim (1989) concluded that his findings support Suinn's (1983) and Smith's (1980) contention that combining treatment components is an effective clinical technique for enhancing performance.

These studies suggest that the effects of interventions used with elite athletes may be more beneficial if multiple component treatments are used. This finding is consistent with Greenspan and Feltz's (1989) review: where using a multiple component treatment (e.g., relaxation combined with imagery or modeling), three of the five studies (Hall and Erffmeyer, 1983; Lee and Hewitt, 1987; Weinberg et al., 1981) showed better performance in competitive conditions than studies using a single component treatment (e.g., only imagery). In comparison to Mumford and Hall's (1985) findings, Kim's results are consistent with Whelan et al.'s (1989) observations that greater intervention effects are found with tasks that are more objectively scored than those by judges' ratings. Moreover, they are in accord with the general progressive relaxation literature (reviewed by Borkovec and Sides, 1979), in which more treatment sessions were shown to produce changes in physiological measures of arousal than fewer sessions.

There are also data from some single-subject design studies in which the interventions were remedial in nature (reviewed by Greenspan and Feltz, 1989). Six cognitive restructuring studies involved an athlete or coach seeking help for an anxiety or concentration problem, and the author of the study then evaluated the problem, developed an intervention, applied it, and then assessed it (Hamilton and Fremouw, 1985; Heward, 1978; Heyman, 1987; Kirschenbaum and Bale, 1980:Study 2; Komaki and Barnett, 1977; Meyers et al., 1982).[10] Five of the studies showed significant improvements in performance. This success rate was higher than the control-group studies reviewed by Greenspan and Feltz (1989). These findings are also consistent with the general clinical literature that shows patients who are given progressive muscle relaxation by a therapist have stronger effects than nonpatients. In addition, subjects receiving instructions directly from a therapist showed a greater relaxation response than did subjects receiving standardized taped instructions with no opportunity to control their training progress (Borkovec and Sides, 1979). Thus, the reviews of the sports literature generally support Borkovec and Sides' (1979:119) conclusion:

The likelihood of producing significant physiological reductions via progressive relaxation appears to be greater when multi-session, subject-controlled training is conducted with subjects for whom physiological activity contributes to a presenting, clinical problem.

At first glance the reviews of the sports literature appear to show rather consistent findings; however, Greenspan and Feltz (1989) also acknowledge several cautions in interpreting this literature. Most of this literature is based on collegiate samples, with very few studies examining cognitive-behavioral interventions with elite or young athletes. According to Greenspan and Feltz (1989), future research needs to emphasize: the use of appropriate single-subject or treatment group designs sufficient to infer causality; comparison of different interventions; the development of more treatment manuals so that future research can become more standardized; assessment of nontargeted areas (e.g., cognitive changes) in addition to the targeted performance components; and follow-up assessments to determine the long-term effects of different psychological interventions on athletes performing in competitive situations.

Furthermore, although the meta-analyses of mental practice and cognitive-behavioral interventions in general have consistently shown that these techniques can enhance motor performance and sports skills, there are individual studies that have not shown positive effects. Since the 1989 reviews of Greenspan and Feltz and Whelan et al., there have been studies showing enhanced performance (Feltz and Riessinger, 1990; Kendall et al., 1990) and studies showing no effects of cognitive-behavioral interventions (Lawrence et al., 1990; McCullagh et al., 1990a, 1990b; Morrison and Walker, 1990). Some of the studies showing nonsignificant effects have been conducted in military settings; all of them are directly relevant to issues raised in the committee's first book (Druckman and Swets, 1988). In the next two sections, we compare these studies with previous reviews on cognitive-behavioral techniques in order to gain insight into why some studies show positive effects and others do not. This comparison is divided into the two primary types of cognitive-behavioral technique used, modeling and imagery or mental practice.

Modeling

Although there is an extensive amount of research on modeling of social skills, modeling or observational learning of motor or sports skills has not received prolonged and systematic study. A recent review (McCullagh et al., 1989) proposed an integrative model that attempts to consolidate several aspects of various motor behavior disciplines—motor learning and control, sports psychology, motor development, etc. It is clear from this review that there are many factors associated with the observer, the observer's perception of the action, the demonstration, rehearsal strategies, behavioral responses, and feedback that are influential in how modeling can affect skill acquisition and performance. In general, studies examining attentional, retentional, and motivational aspects of modeling have shown enhanced performance of people who are exposed in comparison with control groups that are not exposed to such demonstrations. This section covers research that examined modeling through the use of commercially available videotapes (theoretical and practical issues dealing with modeling are presented in Chapter 4).

In two studies supported by the United States Tennis Association, McCullagh et al. (1990b) examined the effectiveness of using Sybervision sports training videotapes as a learning tool for the tennis serve. College students with limited tennis playing experience were compared in a pretest-posttest design on their form and accuracy in the tennis serve. In the first experiment, there were the following four groups: a Sybervision tape of Stan Smith (12 subjects), physical practice of 20 serves per session (13 subjects), Sybervision plus physical practice (10 subjects), and physical activity instruction unrelated to tennis (i.e., motivational control, 9 subjects). As recommended in the Sybervision instructions, the treatment of seven sessions extended over 4 weeks. In addition to assigning points (0 to 5) for accuracy of the serve, the subjects' performances were filmed and later evaluated by two experienced tennis instructors for their form in executing the proper stance, grip, toss, backswing, and point of contact and follow-through; with 0-5 points for each of these technical elements, the form scores for each of the 10 pretest and 10 posttest serves ranged from 0 to 25. The results showed only that all groups made a significant improvement in form scores from pretest to posttest. There were no effects for accuracy, and neither measure showed differences among the groups.

With the small sample size used in this study, there may not have been sufficient statistical power to detect differential improvement made by the treatment groups. Unfortunately, McCullagh et al. (1990b) did not give information on the relative strength of the performance gains. Although the interaction was not statistically significant, inspection of the effect sizes for each group revealed that the combined group of Sybervision and physical practice had the largest effect size (0.42), followed by Sybervision only (0.30), control (0.17) and physical practice (0.13).

A second study by McCullagh et al. (1990a) attempted to add additional components to the Sybervision tennis serving demonstrations to see if this would facilitate the performance (accuracy and form) as well as subjects' ability to recognize errors in another player's serves. Following the pretest of 10 serves, the 46 subjects were randomly assigned to either the Sybervision only group, Sybervision plus physical practice group (20 serves per session), Sybervision plus mental rehearsal group (Sybervision audiotape at end of each session accompanied by imagery), and Sybervision plus verbal cues (videotape with audiotape overlay of brief verbal cues directing subject's attention to racquet position, weight shifts, form and height of ball toss, fluid motion, backswing, point of contact, and follow-through). The results revealed that all groups significantly increased in form but decreased in accuracy from pretest to posttest. These results were attributed to the emphasis in the Sybervision instructions on Stan Smith's form. This emphasis may have carried over to the posttest and resulted in subjects' concentrating on form to the detriment of accuracy. (No meaningful information was derived from the error recognition data since, with the measure used, even the judges had trouble identifying errors.) Finally, no one group had significantly better form than any other group, although the effect sizes for the Sybervision plus imagery group (1.48) and Sybervision plus verbal cues group (1.30) were considerably higher than the Sybervision only group (0.66) and the Sybervision plus physical practice group (0.64). Compared to the earlier study (McCullagh et al., 1990b), the larger effect sizes for the Sybervision group were likely due to subjects' in the second study (McCullagh et al., 1990a) seeing the videotape twice as many times within the same time and number of sessions.

Two modeling studies—one of diving and one of basketball foul shooting (cited in Whelan et al., 1989)—showed statistically significant group effects (Feltz et al., 1979; Hall and Erffmeyer, 1983). These studies did not examine Sybervision, but both contained a videotape of a model that was combined with other treatments: for example, relaxation/imagery, focus on sensory cues, physical practice, informational feedback, or repetition of important steps (cues) in the model's demonstration. These conditions yielded a 20 percent improvement in number of correct dives (Feltz et al., 1979) and a 9 percent improvement in basketball foul shooting (Hall and Erffmeyer, 1983).

The subjects in Hall and Erffmeyer's (1983) study were highly experienced female basketball players. This study also had more pretest and posttest performance trials (100 each) than the Sybervision studies. These factors may have helped to produce more stable performance scores. In addition, due to greater experience on the task, the subjects may have been able to gain more information from the model. In a study of bowling, Rothstein and Arnold (1976) concluded that experienced subjects benefited more from videotapes of bowlers than did novice performers. This finding suggests that having a background in the sport may be an important prerequisite for deriving knowledge from a videotape of an expert model.

An important differentiating factor in the Feltz et al. (1979) study of diving, but not in the McCullagh et al. studies of tennis serving, was the provision of informational feedback following each trial. Feedback on the correctness of the subject's performance, combined with having the subjects verbally repeat the steps in the dive that the model demonstrated, may have been important in the videotape group's achievement of a 20 percent increase in correct dives. McCullagh et al. (1990b:16) recognized the importance of knowledge of results or knowledge of performance and suggested that the Sybervision program would "never really be effective unless it is supplemented with personalized instruction."

The potency of providing feedback for motor skill acquisition is well recognized. In sports, simple as well as complex techniques that provide feedback about one's own performance are becoming increasingly more popular. For example, at Vic Braden's Tennis Academy feedback techniques include wall markings to provide information on the consistency of the ball toss for the tennis serve and slow motion films of performers' tennis techniques. With the use of computer technology, subjects can also be provided with knowledge of outcomes (e.g., with the laser rifle system at the U.S. Olympic Training Center or the shooting system at Ft. Benning) or sophisticated knowledge of technique (Peak Performance or SelSpot Systems). For example, subjects can be given, in real time, kinematic information about their movement such as force/time curves (Howell, 1956), position/time graphs (Hatze, 1976), or kinematic feedback (Newell et al., 1983, 1985). Although there is now a wealth of biomechanical technology to quantify movement and present this information in more sophisticated ways, the implementation of this technology in providing systematic feedback to facilitate learning of physical skills is in its infancy. The basic problem that needs to be addressed is "what information feedback to use and how to use it to optimize learning for beginners and to help advanced performers make corrections in their well-learned techniques" (Christina, 1987:35). More research needs to be conducted to determine, for real-world tasks, the ways in which task conditions should be structured and feedback given (i.e., by type, amount, scheduling, etc.) to those learning new skills or effecting changes in well-learned skills.

Imagery and Mental Practice in Military Settings

Although the sports and motor performance literature has generally shown that imagery and mental practice are effective in enhancing performance, there are some recent applications to military settings that have failed to find this relationship. One study examined various measures of soldering performance in groups that were either trained in imagery rehearsal, relaxation, or received no training (control) (Lawrence et al., 1990). Another study examined tank gunnery performance for subjects in a no-treatment control group and a mental practice group (Morrison and Walker, 1990). A close examination of these studies revealed several limitations in the design and methodological procedures. Those limitations render these studies virtually useless in determining if these cognitive-behavioral techniques are effective in military settings, but they are instructive in identifying methodological procedures that may mask imagery and mental practice effects in operational military environments.

Unlike most of the motor performance laboratory studies on mental practice, in which subjects are randomly assigned to experimental and control conditions, the military studies used intact groups. The use of intact groups raises a risk that variables other than the one of interest (i.e., independent variable) may affect the dependent performance measures, and this may have been a problem in these military studies. The disparities among or between groups could be due to any number of factors associated with the characteristics of the groups. For instance, in the Lawrence et al. (1990) study, there was more variability among the three intact groups in each treatment condition than there was between the mental rehearsal, relaxation, and control groups. Likewise, in the Morrison and Walker (1990) study, there was a substantial difference between the mental practice and control groups at the pretest.[11] These problems are not uncommon when intact groups are used. The mental practice group happened to have higher general technical (GT) scores (i.e., word knowledge, paragraph comprehension, and arithmetic reasoning) than the control subjects. This led the researchers to suggest that this may have influenced the significantly higher pretest tank gunnery scores of the mental practice group.

There are other methodological problems in the military studies. The study by Lawrence et al. (1990) used judges' ratings which have been shown to be associated with the weakest sports performance effects (Whelan et al. 1989). In addition, subjects in this study may not have been sufficiently motivated since their soldering performances were voluntary and were not being graded.

Methodological problems could have masked the effects of mental practice on tank gunnery performance in the Morrison and Walker (1990) study. A mental rehearsal briefing given before, instead of after, the pretest could have affected the superior pretest performance of the mental practice group. In addition, while waiting their turn, control subjects watched their partners perform on the simulator; thus, modeling effects for control subjects, combined with the possible use of mental practice, may have offset the mental practice effects for the experimental subjects. Morrison and Walker were aware of these potential confounding variables, but dismissed them as unavoidable in operational military conditions. Like many psychological variables, the small to moderate performance effects produced by cognitive-behavioral interventions are unlikely to be evident when operational routines place major methodological restrictions on the study. These problems are also present in sports settings, but as the Kim (1989) study has shown, they can be overcome. By gaining the cooperation of coaches or sports administrators, some routine procedures may be changed in order to permit a study to detect group differences in performance. Once the effect has been scientifically demonstrated under altered operational conditions, it can then be decided whether the effect is beneficial enough to suggest incorporation into the operational routine.

Summary

The sports psychology literature convincingly shows that cognitive-behavioral techniques can produce small to moderate improvements in various types of motor performance. Most of the studies illustrating these effects have used novice or proficient performers, and there are a few studies that have even shown these effects in elite athletes. Although few individual studies have been designed to examine variables that may moderate these small to moderate improvements, the narrative and meta-analytic reviews suggest that the performance gains accruing from cognitive-behavioral interventions and their measurement can be enhanced if they include: multiple components, imagery, relaxation, feedback, modeling, cognitive restructuring, etc.; direct administration of the treatment rather than indirect administration by audiotape, particularly in the case of progressive muscle relaxation; the use of many sessions, particularly for tasks with more motor and fewer cognitive components; and behavioral, self-report, or physiological performance measures rather than judges' ratings. In addition, the interventions show stronger results for subjects who have problems with precompetitive anxiety or concentration. Even if some of these factors are not present, cognitive-behavioral interventions can still improve performance. However, the effects may be less or they may take longer to achieve. In operational environments in which intact groups are typically used and strict adherence to methodological procedures are often not possible, the effectiveness of cognitive-behavioral interventions may be difficult to discern. Recently, investigators have attempted to tie cognitive-behavioral techniques more closely to actual sports performance by building these techniques into the preperformance routines of the athletes. The popular and scientific literature dealing with the use of cognitive-behavioral techniques in the preperformance routines of athletes are presented in the next section.

PREPERFORMANCE ROUTINES, SPORTS PERFORMANCE, AND PHYSIOLOGICAL MEASURES

One recent concern among sports psychologists is that cognitive-behavioral techniques taught to athletes in noncompetitive settings may not generalize to performance in settings characterized by intense competitive pressure. The basic premise in this type of research is that the few seconds preceding the execution of a motor skill are critical for successful performance (Gould et al., 1980; Mahoney and Avener, 1977; Suinn, 1977). Whether athletes have good mental control the day before or an hour before competition may have little to do with the control they exhibit immediately prior to performance. By training athletes to incorporate cognitive-behavioral techniques at the time of actual performance, it is believed that their levels of concentration will be enhanced and thus their performance will be improved. The varied literature on preperformance routines is presented in this section in two parts: performance effects of preperformance routines and electrophysiological correlates associated with these routines.

Preperformance Routines and Sports Performance

Structured preperformance routines have typically been used by experienced performers executing skill activities when the environment is static (e.g., tennis serve, golf putt, archery, gun shooting). According to Crews and Boutcher (1986b:291), a preperformance routine consists of "a set pattern of cue thoughts, actions, and images consistently carried out before performance of the skill." They suggest that athletes have learned a preperformance routine "to divert attention away from negative, irrelevant information, to stop attention focusing on a well-learned skill (e.g., disruption of automatic processing), and to establish the appropriate physical and mental state for the ensuing task" (Crews and Boutcher, 1986b:291). If athletes do not have a well-established preperformance routine, they say one should be developed for them. Before it is developed, an athlete should have some proficiency in a variety of cognitive-behavioral techniques.

An example of a commercially available preperformance routine is Loehr's (1989) mental toughness training program. To improve a person's tennis games, this videotape teaches tennis players a series of steps to be followed during the time between points. As director of sports science for the U.S. Tennis Association and consultant to the Nick Bolletieri Tennis Academy, Loehr has observed the between-point behaviors of numerous expert tennis players and has interviewed them about their between-point cognitions. He has concluded that there is a four-part pattern exhibited by the top players that reveals more about their mental toughness than can be ascertained during point play. Loehr believes that his unique player development system will produce a more confident, mentally tough athlete—the "challenge attitude"[12] who will perform at a high level more consistently.

The mental toughness training program has four stages: positive physical response, relaxation response, preparation response, and rituals response. The positive physical response stage begins immediately following the scoring of a point and lasts 3-5 seconds. According to Loehr, mentally tough athletes maintain their composure and display a strong, fighting, positive physical image. They may clap for opponents, clinch their fists for a good shot, or simply walk away from a mistake. They typically place the racquet in their opposite hand, carried by the throat at the balance point, as they walk briskly back to the baseline. Their eyes are forward and down and the shoulders are back.

The second stage, the relaxation response, lasts 6-15 seconds, depending on the stress associated with the previous point and the amount of preparation needed for the next point. During this stage, a player's eyes are directed toward the racquet strings and the physical image they present continues to be strong and competitive. The high energy walk back to the baseline continues as athletes walk back and forth until breathing and heart rate stabilize. It is also common for expert tennis players to relax the arms and hands, do stretches, or take deep breaths during this stage.

The third stage is the preparation response, which begins as players move toward the baseline to serve or receive the serve, and also lasts about 6-15 seconds. Players typically lift and direct their eyes to the opposite side of the court and make a strong statement with their bodies: for example, "I will win this point." Following this there may be a momentary pause while the players covertly go over the score and their intentions for the next point.

The last stage is the ritual response, which lasts 5-8 seconds and begins as soon as a player steps to the baseline. The purpose of this stage is to adjust arousal levels and deepen concentration. The two components characterizing this stage are bouncing the ball two or more times and pausing after the last bounce to help slow the service motion under the pressure of competition. When returning a serve, players' rituals typically consist of stimulation of the feet or making a physical gesture (such as jumping up and down on their toes or swaying back and forth). During this stage, top tennis players only think about the serve (if they are serving) or the return (if they are returning the serve). They do not think about technical aspects of tennis, such as the grip, strokes, or stance: this type of cognitive elaboration in the moments prior to response execution is believed to interfere with athletes' ability to play instinctively and automatically.

Although this is a preset routine, Loehr suggests that after it is taught, athletes can individualize the content making up the various stages of the preperformance routine. The observations that led to Loehr's model of the between-point behavioral and mental routines of expert tennis players was not experimental research. Although Loehr's preperformance routine has been used, there are no scientific studies that have examined its effectiveness. The crucial question is whether those using structured preperformance routines perform better than those who do not use them. Fortunately, there is an emerging sports science literature that has addressed this question.

Observational analyses of professional golfers also reveal the use of well-defined, consistent routines for both putts and full swings (Crews and Boutcher, 1986a). The cognitive-behavioral strategies incorporate such mental functions as choosing a target, visualizing the flight of the ball to the target, kinesthetically feeling a perfect shot, and using cue words. Juxtaposed with the mental routine, the preshot routine incorporates taking a practice swing that simulates the desired swing, aligning the feet in relation to the target, "waggling" the club, and glancing at the hole.

Using cognitive and behavioral elements like these, Crews and Boutcher (1986b) assigned 15 golfers from a beginning golf class to an experimental, preshot routine group and 15 to a control group (no preshot routine). Following an 8-week preshot routine training program, Crews and Boutcher found that the performance of the preshot routine group improved only for the better male golfers, and they concluded that preshot routine training improved performance when physical skills were well learned. In another study of 12 collegiate golfers (Boutcher and Crews, 1987), both males and females improved the consistency of the preshot routine behaviors following a 6-week training period, but only the females improved in task performance.

Preshot routines have also been effective in improving basketball free-throw shooting performance (Lobmeyer and Wasserman, 1986) and novel motor task performance (Singer et al., 1989). Following a preshot training program, subjects improved 7 percent in performance when using their preshot routine than when not using the routine (Lobmeyer and Wasserman, 1986). In a laboratory environment, ten subjects were taught a five-step learning strategy that sequentially consisted of readying, imaging, focusing, executing, and evaluating. Following four practice trials, subjects in the "learning strategy group" performed significantly faster—and not at the expense of greater number of errors—than did a control group and the group that previewed the location of the six targets.

Preperformance routines have generally been effective in improving motor or sports performance of beginning level performers, but their effects have yet to be demonstrated in elite performers. Although the introduction of a preshot routine resulted in a more consistent preperformance routine and led golfers to report that the intervention had a positive effect on their concentration, Cohn et al. (1990) failed to find immediate improvements in performance for three subjects. This study, however, used very few observations (2-8 rounds of nine-hole play) following the introduction of the preshot routine. With elite performers, it is possible that much more practice in using a preshot routine is necessary to improve par-level golf performance.

Interview data from athletes and the general assumptions of investigators support the idea that a preperformance routine increases a performer's concentration and facilitates performance. Although athletes given training in a preperformance routine report better concentration, retrospective reports of cognitive processes are known to be unreliable (Nisbett and Wilson, 1977); retrospective reports are often based on implicit, a priori assumptions of the cause of subsequent behavior. Furthermore, athletes' inability to describe their preperformance state is consistent with descriptions of the cognitive state associated with "peak performance" as being characterized by (Gallwey, 1981): body/brain integration; allowing things to happen rather than trying to force a particular performance outcome; total absorption in the activity while maintaining unconscious awareness of process cues (relevant feelings, balance and weight distribution, etc.); lack of recall due to the mind being "blank" immediately prior to the response; and obvious difficulty in putting the cognitive and behavioral actions of the preperformance period into words. Trying to obtain self-reports during the preperformance routine is counterproductive since it will interfere with the desired state of automatic processing in the moments before response execution. Thus, several investigators have examined electrophysiological indicators of attention while athletes are in a preperformance routine prior to the performance of a discrete, closed skill that involves minimal movement. This literature, which has dealt with measures of heart rate and electroencephalographic (EEG) activity, is reviewed in the next section.

Physiological Correlates of Preparation to Perform

The experimental psychology literature offers several research techniques with which to measure attention (e.g., a dual-task paradigm to divide attention, readiness potentials, and averaged evoked potential of the EEG). Although these techniques have been used with shooters (Landers et al., 1985; Rose and Christina, 1990), the manipulations involved disrupt performance on self-paced tasks (and sports) and thus decrease the ecological validity. An alternate approach has been to use continuous psychophysiological measures (previously used in laboratory studies of attention) to examine the performance of archers, shooters, and golfers (Hatfield and Landers, 1987; Landers, 1985). Although several psychophysiological measures have been used in this research, the ones that have produced the most consistent results during athletes' preperformance routines in the sports of archery, rifle shooting, and golf putting have been measures of cardiac deceleration and spontaneous EEG activity.

Cardiac Deceleration

Stimuli of various types produce a pattern of beat-by-beat cardiac acceleration or deceleration in the 3-5 seconds prior to a response. The direction and magnitude of change has been related to performance and is suggested to be an indicator of an individual's attentive state. This cardiac pattern prior to initiating a response has been subject to varying explanations (see Coles, 1984; Graham, 1979; Jennings et al., 1978; Kahneman, 1973; Lacey et al., 1963; Obrist et al., 1970; van der Molen et al., 1985).

Lacey's intake-rejection hypothesis (Lacey, 1967; Lacey et al., 1963) is one hypothesis that attempts to explain the cardiac pattern that occurs prior to a response. According to this hypothesis, as a person focuses on the external environment and attempts to take in external stimuli, the heart decelerates; then, as the person focuses internally and rejects external stimuli, the heart accelerates. Tasks requiring internal cognitive elaboration of a problem-solving sort (e.g., mental arithmetic, reversed spelling, sentence structure) produce cardiac acceleration (Lacey et al., 1963). Cardiac deceleration has typically been found in a motor response paradigm, a reaction-time (RT) task (Lacey and Lacey, 1964, 1966, 1970). Using a 4-second RT foreperiod, Lacey and Lacey found a pattern of deceleration three or four beats prior to the stimulus; this pattern terminated with the onset of the stimulus light.[13] Performance on the RT task was associated with greater cardiac deceleration, although the correlations were low (Lacey and Lacey, 1964, 1966, 1970).

The intake-rejection hypothesis has been criticized for being too general. Several investigators have suggested that task specificity might be responsible for disagreements in interpreting cardiac patterning associated with information processing (Bohlin and Kjellberg, 1979; Carroll and Anastasiades, 1978; Coles, 1984; Elliott, 1972; Graham, 1979; Hahn, 1973; Jennings et al., 1978). The original work by Lacey et al. (1963) stated that cardiac deceleration was an indication of the intention to note and detect external events. In examining the nature of the tasks, it is apparent that there are actually two components occurring simultaneously that comprise the intake-rejection hypothesis. One is the intake of the external stimuli (warning and imperative stimulus) created in the foreperiod of the RT task and the rejection of the external environment to solve the problems in the math task. The second component is the type of cognitive task used to create the intake-rejection situation. In 1963, Lacey et al. referred to the RT task as one that increases sensory awareness, while the math task increases cognitive elaboration and processing within the brain. The name of the hypothesis stresses the intake and rejection component; however, it is possible that it is the processing component required that determines cardiac pattern.

Other investigators have questioned that cardiac deceleration is simply an indication to note and detect external events. The Laceys (1974), for example, suggested that anticipatory deceleration may also be associated with intention to respond. Coles (1984) has argued that these two intentions are confounded and that cardiac deceleration primarily reflects motor readiness, not anticipatory sensory input. Contrary to Coles (1984), Graham (1979) believes that stimulus input is reflected by cardiac deceleration and preparation for output produces cardiac acceleration.

Regardless of whether cardiac deceleration is indicative of intake of sensory information, preparation for output, or sensory awareness, it is hypothesized that experienced athletes with a consistent preperformance routine have better attentional skills and would thus show a pattern of cardiac deceleration prior to performance. Several studies have investigated the relationship between cardiac deceleration and attention in the few seconds before response execution in sports (with minimal potential for movement artifact in the cardiac measure). For example, Stern (1976) used the sequence of "get set," 5 seconds, "go" commands and found that subjects preparing for either a sprint up a flight of stairs or a bicycle sprint showed a phasic cardiac change of acceleration until 1 second before the "go" signal and then showed a deceleration from 1 second to the "go" command. Hatfield et al. (1987) found a trend for cardiac deceleration in elite rifle marksmen in the 2.5 seconds prior to the execution of the shot. Among highly skilled golfers, significant cardiac decelerations of 4-11 beats per minute have been found within 3-7 seconds of a putt (Boutcher and Zinsser, 1990; Crews, 1989; Molander and Backman, 1989). Only Salazar et al. (1990) reported cardiac acceleration in elite archers immediately prior to arrow release. This may have been due to the physical demands of overcoming the 31-50 pound bowstring tension. When archers have used lower bowstring tensions (20-25 pounds) (Landers et al., 1991a) or shot at shorter distances (Schmid, 1989), cardiac deceleration has been clearly evident.

There is also evidence in these cross-sectional studies that cardiac acceleration is associated with poorer performance (Molander and Backman, 1989) with novice performers (Schmid, 1989) and that greater degrees of cardiac deceleration are associated with better performance (Boutcher and Zinsser, 1990; Crews, 1989). Schmid (1989) found that "subconscious shooters" had greater cardiac deceleration than "cognitive shoot-ers."[14] The degree to which cardiac deceleration differences noted be-tween novice and experienced performers are associated with learning the task has been investigated in archers. The archers experienced a 62 percent increase in performance over a 12-week period in which they had received 27 sessions of archery training (35 hours total) from the 1988 Olympic coach of the U.S. National Archery Team (Landers et al., 1991a).[15]   In contrast to studies conducted with laboratory RT tasks (Hahn, 1973) or sports tasks with novice performers (Stern, 1976), the studies investigating sports tasks with experienced athletes have gener-ally shown greater deceleration.

Hemispheric Asymmetries in the Brain

In addition to examining cardiac deceleration during athletes' preperformance routines, Hatfield et al. (1984, 1987) also investigated associated time-locked EEG asymmetries between the hemispheres of the brain. The use of EEG measures was prompted by their promotion as a more direct measure of attentional states (Gale and Edwards, 1983; Obrist, 1981), their success in differentiating varying states of attentional focus (Davidson et al., 1976; Ray and Cole, 1985; Ray and Kimmel, 1979), and their stability and reliability over time (Gasser et al., 1985; Wheeler et al., 1989). The use of this measure was partly based on Walker and Sandman's findings (1979, 1982) that cardiovascular changes differentially influence the left and right sides of the brain. More re-cently, Sandman and Walker (1985) have pointed out that cardiovascu-lar influences on the activity in the right and left hemispheres may vary from moment to moment and that the ability of an organism to detect and react to the environment may be intimately linked to hemispheric asymmetry. Although cardiovascular changes have been shown to be related to hemispheric changes (Walker and Sandman, 1979, 1982; Sandman and Walker, 1985) and hemispheric asymmetries have been predictive of performance accuracy (Gevins et al., 1987, 1989), these studies have neither investigated experienced athletes during their preperformance routines nor have they used spontaneous EEG measures.

By using skilled individuals to reduce response variability in EEGs (O'Connor, 1981), Hatfield et al. (1984, 1987) examined spontaneous EEGs during the preparatory period within 7.5 seconds prior to the trigger pull by elite rifle shooters. They found that left temporal (T3) and left occipital (O1) EEG alpha activity (8-12 Hz) significantly in-creased during that period. This suggests that the activation level in the left hemisphere was declining. Further examination of the relationship between heart rate and EEG revealed that, within 2.5 seconds prior to the shot, cardiac deceleration was associated with increased alpha activity in the left hemisphere while right alpha remained constant. Hatfield et al. interpreted these findings as indicative of cognitive changes (reducing the covert verbalizations of the left hemisphere and increasing the visual-spatial processes dominant in the right hemisphere), which allow dominance of the right hemisphere at the time of the shot.

In subsequent EEG studies with archers and golfers, second-to-second changes in EEGs prior to the response and multiple EEG bands have been examined. During the preparatory period (3-5 seconds), which is characterized by intense concentration, experienced athletes have shown greater increases in left hemisphere alpha activity than in right hemisphere activity (Crews, 1989; Landers et al., 1991a; Salazar et al., 1990). The asymmetry was greatest at 1 second before the response (shot or putt) and was not evident earlier (up to 5 seconds) or immediately following the response (Wang and Landers, 1987). This effect was independent of minor bodily movements (e.g., eye blinks) (Crews, 1989; Landers et al., 1991a; Salazar et al., 1990). Furthermore, Salazar et al. (1990) have shown that even when the physical exertion of drawing a 40-50 pound bow was controlled, the hemispheric differences were still evident.

Although left hemispheric activity increases more than right hemispheric activity (particularly in the alpha range), better performance has been found to be associated with a moderate increase in left hemisphere EEG activity at the time of the shot or putt (Crews, 1989; Landers et al., 1991a; Salazar et al., 1990). Comparisons of best and worst shots revealed no significant right hemisphere spectral power differences, but there were significant left hemisphere differences (Landers et al., 1991a; Salazar et al., 1990). (The muscular forces and handedness were the same for best and worst shots, so the differences in EEG activity could not be attributed to muscular contaminants.) Although reliable EEG asymmetries have been observed in highly experienced performers, the above-mentioned studies do not provide information on whether these EEG patterns are developed through training in the skill. Recent studies by Landers et al. (1991a) and Landers et al. (1991b) suggest that these EEG patterns are trainable. For example, in rank beginners, the EEG asymmetries were not evident 2 weeks into training, but were evident at a time (14th week) when archery performance had improved 62 percent (Landers et al., 1991a). In Landers et al.'s study (1991b), the moderate increase in left hemispheric EEG activity immediately before the motor response was used as a model of "correct performance" in a biofeedback training study. A group of 24 pre-elite archers were randomly assigned in equal numbers to three groups: a correct feedback group (i.e., greater left hemisphere low-frequency activity), an incorrect feedback group (i.e., greater right hemisphere low-frequency activity), and a no feed-back control group. The pretest and posttest consisted of 27 shots with EEG data collected for the left and right temporal hemispheres. Analyses indicated that the correct feedback group significantly improved performance, while the incorrect feedback group showed a significant performance decrement from pretest to posttest. The control group showed no significant pretest-posttest differences in performance. EEG analyses showed differences that were consistent with the training given to the incorrect, but not the correct, feedback group. Overall, these training studies demonstrate that the EEG patterns observed during athletes' preperformance routines become more similar to the patterns observed in elite athletes with increased training or specific EEG feedback known to be associated with better performance.

Summary

The studies examining preperformance routines show that they are used by better performers, and people trained in the use of these routines generally show better performance. Preperformance routines teach athletes to habitually use cognitive-behavioral techniques at strategic times in their sports performances. Most of the sports studies have been conducted in practice settings, and more research is needed to compare the benefits of preperformance routines in practice with their benefits in competitive settings. The consistent patterns in EEG hemispheric asymmetries and cardiac deceleration during the latter stages of the preperformance routine suggest that they are learned responses that are indicative of better attentional focus and that result in overall better performance. These psychophysiological measures can assist in determining the efficiency of preperformance routines.

From questionnaire responses of best and worst performers (Crews and Landers, 1991), it appears that those patterns may be indexing a state of automatic processing: best performers are focused on overall bodily awareness and relevant external cues (e.g., hole or target); worst performers, who failed to consistently display the asymmetric EEG pattern, were more often focused on what might be called cognitive elaboration of specific cues (e.g., backswing, club head, etc.). Crews and Landers (1991) have noted that by increasing total awareness, the best golfers were perhaps adopting a "let it happen," automatic approach, while the worst performers were perhaps trying to "make it happen" and cognitively control the putt (Gallwey, 1981). Further research is necessary to substantiate the value of a preperformance routine in fostering a state of automatic processing.

EXERCISE AND STRESS

The relationship between aerobic fitness and psychological well-being is an area within the field of exercise and sports psychology that has received considerable attention in the last 5 years. Research interest among exercise scientists on such topics as depression, anxiety, sleep, and reactivity to psychosocial stressors has intensified with the recognition that the life-styles of millions of Americans are disrupted due to anxiety and depression (Dishman, 1982; Morgan, 1979) and that primary care physicians routinely prescribe exercise for these and other emotional disorders (Ryan, 1983). Recent meta-analytic reviews have shown that aerobic exercise can have a small but reliable effect in reducing state (acute) and trait (chronic) anxiety (Petruzzello et al., 1991), increasing slow wave (i.e., stages 3 & 4) and total sleep time (Kubitz et al., 1991), and decreasing depression (North et al., 1990). Although these reviews fail to show that exercise is psychologically more beneficial than the more conventional psychological techniques—relaxation, imagery, group therapy, cognitive restructuring, etc.—it is known that carefully prescribed exercise can have additional health benefits (weight loss, enhanced cardiorespiratory efficiency and muscle tone, reduced risk of heart attack, etc.), and this may help to promote adherence to a psychological intervention program involving exercise.

Related to the topic of performance under pressure is whether or not exercise contributes to the reduction of psychosocial stress. As of 1987, Crews and Landers had identified 34 studies that had attempted to determine if the magnitude of the psychosocial stress response was lower among exercisers, or if recovery from psychosocial stress was more rapid among exercisers. Since 1987, there have been approximately 20 additional studies on this topic. Typically, these studies have included four laboratory stressors: (1) cognitive performance tasks, such as solving timed arithmetic problems; (2) passive response tasks, such as viewing films of industrial accidents or medical operations; (3) active physical performance tasks, such as exercise; and (4) passive physical performance tasks, such as holding an immersed limb in ice water (Crews and Landers, 1987). Although these stressor tasks are quite different from operational tasks which create stress reactions—such as those in everyday life or those in more pressured settings such as in the military—they do produce sizable elevations in heart rate and therefore may be relevant for other settings. For example, Crews and Landers (1987) calculated heart-rate response above initial values and found that the 34 studies could be categorized into high (> 30 beats/minute) or low (< 30 beats/minute) stress response. Other measures of stress less frequently examined in these studies included systolic and diastolic blood pressure, skin response, hormonal, muscle activity, and psychological self-report.

For the 1,449 subjects, the meta-analytic results showed an overall effect size of 0.48 (Crews and Landers, 1987). This result indicates that, regardless of the type of physiological or psychological measure used, aerobically fit subjects had a reduced stress response. (The magnitude of the effect represented nearly a one-half standard deviation gain in stress reactivity relative to control conditions.) The underlying assumption of this laboratory paradigm is that reduced physiological response to stress or faster physiological recovery results in less total time spent in stress at perhaps a lower level of stress. In other words, "exercise either acts as a coping strategy or serves as an 'inoculator' to more effectively respond to the intrusion of psychosocial stress" (Crews and Landers, 1987:S118).

The moderator variables examined in the Crews and Landers meta-analysis included: study and subject characteristics, such as published or unpublished studies, acute or chronic exercise, and male or female subjects; methodological characteristics, such as initial or baseline values of stress, whether statistically controlled, and correlational versus training designs; and stressor characteristics, such as low or high stress response, stress reactivity versus recovery from stress, and types of stress measures. A meta-analytic procedure (described by Hedges and Olkin, 1985) was used to determine if the measures were homogeneous across studies. The chi-square test did not reject the hypothesis of homogeneity of effect sizes: that is, the effect-sizes were not related to specific moderating variables, and so no further breakdown into moderating variables was warranted (Hedges and Olkin, 1985). Thus, the results suggest that all of the studies could be represented by the mean effect size, 0.48.[16]

Although some investigators (Abbott and Peters, 1989) have argued that the Crews and Landers' (1987) meta-analytic review has precluded conducting further studies in this area, Blumenthal (1989) has pointed out that there is a need for more experimental (i.e., training) studies. There is also a need for more studies that examine: whether anaerobic exercise produces the same buffer to psychosocial stressors as is found with aerobic exercise, and whether individuals experiencing more long-term, chronic levels of high stress (e.g., air traffic controllers) derive psychological benefits from exercise training (Crews and Landers, 1987).

Many authors have suggested various mechanisms to explain the effects of exercise on the psychosocial stress response. Earlier explanations focused on physical activity rather than aerobic exercise. For example, Gal and Lazarus (1975) suggested that physical activity can reduce stress reactions in four ways: (1) heightening feelings of control and mastery; (2) serving as a defense mechanism to help people forget about their distress so as to decrease anxiety; (3) providing an attention diversion; and (4) producing a means of energy discharge allowing for reasonably rapid body mobilization or arousal. Recently, other investigators (Light, 1982; Shulhan et al., 1986) have focused more on mechanisms that are directly tied to changes in aerobic fitness, such as changes in the release of endogenous opiates, baroreceptor function, release of insulin, sensitivity to beta-adrenergic stimulation, and stimulation of brain metabolism or levels of serotonin. As emphasized by Crews and Landers (1987), more research that examines these underlying mechanisms is necessary to determine how these changes in fitness actually reduce stress response or time spent in stress. In military settings, with the exception of orthostatic intolerance for those undergoing high "g" forces (e.g., fighter pilots) (Bedford and Tipton, 1987; Raven et al., 1984), aerobic conditioning may help alleviate psychological reactions in most operational conditions. As physical training is compatible with military training, it should not be too difficult to design studies in military settings to explore both the psychological and physiological effects of aerobic exercise.

In summary, several research studies have shown that aerobic exercise can help people to cope better with psychosocial stressors. The measures of coping ability used in the studies included physiological and psychological measures of reactivity to the laboratory stressor and of recovery to baseline levels following termination of the stressor. These effects are of a moderate size and are consistent across many studies, but the mechanisms for the effects are unknown.

BROADER VIEWS: NEUROSCIENCE AND PEAK PERFORMANCE

The foregoing review evaluates the research on techniques that may enhance the preparation to perform. It is also important to monitor research for potential breakthroughs in theory and methodology that may provide general guidelines for evaluating proposed techniques and their potential applications. Particularly in this "Decade of the Brain," it is instructive to ask whether advances in understanding of the human brain and how it controls behavior have aided in the search for methods that could potentially enhance human performance. In this section, we review these advances and discuss which lines of scientific inquiry are likely to provide a better understanding of human performance. In addition, ecological studies of individuals who achieve extraordinary high performance are reviewed in order to determine the validity of an "ideal performance state model."

One conclusion that is supported by considerable empirical data is that significant behavioral and performance enhancements can be achieved under certain conditions. While this conclusion may seem obvious to most readers, it should be remembered that behavioral constructs earlier in this century maintained that many behavioral properties were "fixed" entities, resulting from static physiological features. More recently, neurobiological studies revealed that enriched and impoverished environments have differential effects on numerous aspects of cortical structure (e.g., Diamond et al., 1987). Animals raised in enriched environments have an enlarged cortex and manifest performance superiorities (e.g., in maze running). Parallel behavioral research has identified some of the growth-promoting family, training, and other environmental conditions that may enhance performance (e.g., Bloom, 1985). Both the neurobiological and behavioral lines of research strongly support the idea that the innate characteristics of individuals are less important in performance than the encouragement, nurturance, education, and training they receive. The implications of these studies are unequivocal in their suggestion that, given the proper conditions, most individuals are capable of remarkable performance excellence. The challenge for researchers, as well as for institutions such as the Army, is to define the training techniques and environmental characteristics that enhance human performance.

Models of the Brain

In the previous section, and more extensively in the committee's first book (Druckman and Swets, 1988), we delineate some of the serious shortcomings in attempts to understand sports performance in the context of any simplified, metaphysical model of the brain. Sports performance is a quintessential problem in complex motor, cognitive, affective, and attentional processes, and it depends on functions that are widely distributed throughout both cerebral hemispheres. Studies that characterize the cognitive, attentional, or motor components of sports as "left hemisphere abilities" or "right hemisphere abilities" are fatally flawed. Not only is it inherently insupportable to characterize sports abilities by brain hemisphere, it is also methodologically and logically flawed to narrowly localize these complex processes.

Recent neuroscientific studies using imaging techniques have revealed that even simple motor processes, such as unilateral ballistic finger movements, have complex neuroanatomical and neurophysiological correlates (Roland et al., 1982; Druckman and Lacy, 1989); using a regional cerebral blood flow technique, the researchers found bilateral increases in blood flow during unilateral ballistic finger movements in the supplementary motor cortex, premotor cortex, parietal opercula, paracentral cortex, putamen, caudate, and thalamus. Using position emission tomography, regional cerebral blood flow, and other oxygen and glucose metabolic imaging methods, numerous studies show that even heavily overlearned tasks, such as handwriting, result in bilateral metabolic increases in many subcortical regions, especially in the striatum (Mazziotta and Phelps, 1984). When one considers the cognitive and other mental components of sports techniques, the picture is even more complicated. Mental imagery alone is known to increase oxidative metabolic values in 25 separate cortical areas (Roland et al., 1987).

When researchers attempt to localize mental or motor tasks in brain areas, the reliability of their results should be carefully considered. These studies must be considered preliminary in the context of the poor test-retest reliability, the biological variability between subjects, and the notoriously poor geographical resolution (i.e., the discrimination of one brain subregion from another) of these methods (Pahl, 1990). Any study attempting to localize a specific mental event that uses methods with a resolution of more than 5-7 millimeters is limited in its reliability. And experiments that use many subjects and average across subjects and trials may not provide any useful information since the geographical variability in certain localizable functions (such as language) is already so large that some information is probably lost of averaging across subjects.

Nevertheless, we encourage the use of novel neuroimaging techniques in the study of human performance. The application of techniques that are especially reliable in geographical resolution (e.g., positron emission tomography) in combination with techniques that are especially reliable in temporal resolution (e.g., endogenous evoked potentials) may be important in future human performance research. Careful application of the most sensitive techniques for the particular skill and purpose being considered will lead to the better understanding of brain-behavior relationships (Chollet et al., 1991; Druckman and Lacey, 1989).

"Ideal Performance State"

Psychological science has long been intrigued with mental states associated with an individual's "peak performance." The "virtues" or qualities that enhance human performance were major themes of Aristotle's *Nicomachean Ethics*, written more than 23 centuries ago. The empirical study of peak performances in modern times began less than two decades ago, however, with the work of Maslow (1971) and other existential psychologists. Using idiographic methods, Maslow characterized those performances—"peak experiences"—both by the character traits of the individuals who possessed the virtues or qualities of the self-actualizing personality and by the states these individuals recalled during their best moments. The concept of peak performance in sports was popularized in the self-help work of Garfield (1978).

The focus of a large portion of psychological research—as demonstrated in the review above—has been on the role of behavioral states and how they influence performance. Indeed, nearly all the commercial efforts in this domain suggest that achievement of these states is possible ("anyone can do it") and, thus, that such issues as character traits do not affect the attitudinal states. In fact, however, ideal performance state may not be easy to achieve: current clinical research suggest complex correlational relationships between high performance character traits and peak performance attitudes (Pirozzolo, 1991); at the same time, it is also likely that these traits and states are learnable (Loehr, 1989; Bandura, 1982) through a variety of "training" experiences.

In the rest of this section we review research that used mainly idiographic methods to characterize the behavioral state variously known as the flow state (Csikszentmihalyi, 1990), the peak experience state (Maslow, 1971), the ideal performance state, the zone, etc. Most of the empirical data collected for analysis in these studies come from naturalistic studies of everyday work and play. It is noteworthy, however, that these experiences and studies do not appear to differ from life-or-death alternatives experienced in the military: that is, intense battlefield experiences also seem to be associated with the same behavioral states (Csikszentmihalyi, 1990). Clinical experience with Vietnam veterans in Veterans Administration hospitals are consistent with other data suggesting that flow experiences occur with surprising frequency and intensity. Csikszentmihalyi (1990:69) states that war experiences can be "more exhilarating than anything encountered in civilian life."

As an early worker in the field, Maslow conducted hundreds of structured interviews that resulted in descriptions of common features of peak experiences: a temporary distortion of time perception; an overwhelming feeling of peacefulness, relaxation, wonder, and happiness; a total loss of fear and other negative emotions, including immature defensive strategies; and a complete absorption in the task at hand. These phenomenological observations were rooted in mysticism, but they nevertheless contributed to the study of metamotivational states, which are defined as higher needs for creativity and challenge.

Cross-national, cross-cultural, and other studies of the ideal performance state have documented an extraordinary concurrence in behavioral descriptions of the flow state (Csikszentmihalyi, 1990; Massimini and Inghilleri, 1987). Subjects report many, if not all, of the following affective, attentional, and cognitive states: a clearly focused "mind's eye" of task requirements; an unself-conscious absorption in the task at hand; an uncommon intrinsic motivation, which is an absence of goal states in which the subject is performing for external rewards, trophies, financial rewards, or even social approval; a strong sense of purpose (appropriate striving); a total commitment of the "project" in which the subject controls the contents of his or her consciousness and allows no room for distraction; a feeling of exercising control; a stretching of talents to match environmental challenges; a time transformational experience, which is most often characterized by time being slowed down but also can include a sense of accelerated temporal distortion; a sense of order in cognitive and motor set schemata; no wasted psychic or physical energy (or entropy); and the use of "higher" coping strategies ("transformational") rather than emotion-focused or regressive coping strategies.

A promising method for studying mental characteristics of high performance behavior is the experience sampling method (ESM), developed by Csikszentmihalyi and colleagues (e.g., Csikszentmihalyi and Larson, 1987). The ESM is a naturalistic method for assessing temporal and contextual fluctuations in mood and performance. It has been used in healthy normal people as well as clinical populations and in Western and non-Western countries, and it has shown good validity and reliability (Larson and Csikszentmihalyi, 1983; Massimini et al., 1987; Csikszentmihalyi, 1990). Subjects in studies employing the ESM are signaled by means of an electronic pager worn on the wrist which is activated several times a day at random intervals. When they are signaled, subjects stop and describe their thoughts and emotions. The ESM is a highly reliable technique for measuring the mood of the moment; it does not suffer from reconstructive memorial and affective biases. The experience of flow can be linked to what the subject is thinking and feeling at that moment; motivational or goal states; contextual variables, such as the people he or she is with at the time; and the "work" he or she is doing at the moment. The ESM has the limitation of terminating the unself-conscious flow state when it exists, however, since the subject must evaluate the contents of his or her consciousness. The ESM has been recently used in efforts to increase awareness of the contextual and psychological variables that promote peak performance (Pirozzolo, 1991; Pirozzolo and Csikszentmihalyi, 1991), although larger scale studies are clearly needed before firm conclusions can be drawn about the utility of the ESM and its efficacy in behavior change.

This kind of intervention technique clearly depends on a mental health model of sports performance. As intuitively appealing as the mental health model is, it is not without serious deficiencies, some of which are detailed above. Most important are the countless case examples of individuals who have succeeded in spite of hostile internal and external psychological environments, such as in the examples of Bettelheim (1960) and Frankl (1963), whose works focused on the severe psychological and physical adversities in concentration camps. Similarly, John Bunyan's *Pilgrim's Progress* was written in the humiliating environment of a prison (Maddi, 1965). The lives of Jesus Christ, Seneca, Galileo, Mill, Van Gogh, Dante, Freud, and Toulouse-Latrec, among numerous others, were characterized by physical pain, depression, and a variety of other indignities and suboptimal circumstances. A recent biography documents that one of the greatest baseball players of all time, Lou Gehrig, was riddled with self-doubt and low confidence and lived in a hostile family environment (Robinson, 1990).

Another possible explanation for the failure of the mental health model to predict performance is inattention to complex subject factors, including but not limited to subject self-schema. A recent study suggests that elated and depressed subjects respond differentially to positive and negative feedback (Anshel, 1988). Other neuroendocrinologic and neuropsychological factors undoubtedly play a role in this complex relationship between mood and performance. Future research should control for such potential artifacts, including the growing agreement of neuroscientists on the role of dietary factors on mood and performance (e.g., Deijen et al., 1989; Wurtman, 1982).

Two of the most popular interventions used by sports psychologists that require further research are the cognitive-behavioral technique of teaching preshot and preperformance preparatory routines and the use of psychological tests as motivational devices. As discussed above, there is no doubt that preperformance preparatory strategies exert influences on sports performance, but the nature and cause of the effects are by no means completely understood. The mechanisms of action that have been proposed include outcome or performance expectancies; improved sense of self-efficacy; improved attention control; reduction of unfocused arousal (off-target, entropic, physiologic efforts); more efficient cognitive strategies; and diminution of potentially destructive self-monitoring behaviors. A recent review argues that expectancy has a robust effect on motor performance (Neiss, 1990). Preperformance strategies and expectancies may control the path of cognitive events such that subjects rehearse overlearned motor sequences, channeling their attention and energies into an on-target, challenged approach to the task at hand, which, in turn, may interfere with off-target, unfocused-aroused perceptions of threat that inevitably leads to choking under pressure.

The additional considerations raised in this section suggest themes largely overlooked by contemporary research on human performance.

They contribute to the development of a broader framework to guide the research.

CONCLUSIONS

Mental Health and Athletic Success The mental health model has produced inconsistent results in differentiating successful athletes from less successful athletes in terms of individual mood scales. However, measures of global mood have been effective in identifying when individual athletes are experiencing a psychologically unhealthy, overtrained state. Thus, the use of global mood measures may be useful for monitoring the potential psychopathology associated with intense physical training.

Physical Versus Mental Practice If the goal is to maximize performance in the shortest possible amount of time, physical practice is superior to mental practice. However, if nonphysical practice time is available or if a person cannot physically practice, then the small effects due to mental practice can be useful for facilitating performance and for better retention.

Cognitive-Behavioral Interventions The overall effects of cognitive-behavioral interventions are small to moderate. These effects will be enhanced if treatments emphasize: multiple components, (relaxation, modeling, imagery, cognitive restructuring, etc.); direct administration of the treatment by an investigator, rather than an audiotape); many sessions; people who have problems with precompetitive anxiety or concentration; and tasks that are objectively scored.

Preperformance Preparation In closed skills (the environment is unchanging), an individually designed preperformance routine, "preparation ritual" with multiple components has been shown to facilitate performance. In closed skill sports that involve aiming (e.g., rifle shooting), better performers have a greater cardiac deceleration within 3.5 seconds of executing a motor response. In addition, better performances are associated with a moderate increase (above baseline rates) alpha activity in the left hemisphere of the brain and little or no change in activity in the right hemisphere. However, too great an increase in left hemispheric alpha activity is associated with worse shots. Electrophysiological patterns like heart-rate deceleration and EEG asymmetries that are related to performance can be used during the preparatory period (i.e., 3-5 seconds before response execution) to assist in determining the efficacy of preperformance routines.

Exercise and Stress   Aerobic exercise is related to reduced physiological and psychological response and quicker recovery from psychosocial stressors.

Neuroscience and Peak Performance   Further understanding of the bases for performance is likely to come from ongoing research in neuroscience and on "peak performance." Recent neuroscientific studies using imaging techniques have shown that even simple motor processes have complex neurophysiological correlates. Research on high performance behavior has made progress in identifying the affective, attentional, and cognitive states associated with such behavior.

NOTES

1. The iceberg profile does not convey a relationship in a true scientific sense; it is more an artifact resulting from connecting unrelated points with lines rather than representing mean values with a bar graph.

2. The 70-80 percent prediction accuracy may be inflated since in at least one study (Study 4) 7 of the 16 athletes did not have profiles that were "sufficiently remarkable to permit application of the clinical prediction model" (Morgan, 1985:74). Thus, they were eliminated and the prediction analysis was only carried out on the remaining nine athletes, and all nine predictions (100 percent) proved to be correct (Morgan, 1985). It is unclear why the seven athletes were "sufficiently remarkable" in this study. In other studies, it appears that all were included in the clinical prediction analysis, even though approximately 10 percent of the nonhospitalized population would have mental health problems of clinical significance (Morgan et al., 1987b).

3. The study of 40 members of the University of Wisconsin wrestling team did not show significant changes in their mood states over a 5-month period. Although 10 percent of the wrestlers developed mood disturbance, the failure of the group data to show significant changes in mood disturbance as a function of training stimulus may be due to the greater difficulty in calculating peak work loads in wrestling in comparison with swimming.

4. The only phase in which salivary cortisol was correlated with depressed mood was in the overtraining phase ($r = .50$; $p < .05$).

5. To provide a common metric and thereby equate times for various swimming distances, T scores can be calculated in much the same way as in the decathlon competition in track and field.

6. Most of the studies covered in these reviews were published between 1970 and 1989. The narrative review by Greenspan and Feltz (1989) dealt with 19 published articles (23 interventions) and the Whelan et al. (1989) meta-analytic review contained 49 published articles (121 comparisons across 333 outcome measures). The differences in the numbers of studies is because Whelan et al. included studies with a greater variety of interventions (e.g., goal setting, modeling, association/disassociation strategies, and hypnotherapy). In neither review were there unpublished studies (e.g., dissertations, government reports, papers presented at meetings). This led Greenspan and Feltz (1989) and Whelan et al. (1989) to suggest the possibility of a "file drawer" problem or publication bias. For example, either researchers obtaining nonsignificant results are not submitting their research for publication or journal reviewers are less likely to publish articles showing nonsignificant results than those showing significant results. This is certainly possible since Feltz and Landers' (1983) review of the motor performance literature showed that the effect size for unpublished studies was significantly smaller (0.32) than the effect size for published studies (0.74).

7. Although these findings could be overestimated without unpublished studies, the likelihood of unpublished studies substantially reducing an effect size of 0.62 is not great. According to Orwin's (1983) fail-safe formula, it would take nearly 120 studies showing very small effect sizes (e.g., 0.20) to reduce this moderate effect size to a small one. Since previous reviewers (Greenspan and Feltz, 1989) could not find many unpublished studies, it does not appear that missing studies would greatly influence the strength of this relationship. Thus, the effects appear to be real and are very robust in that they generalize across studies using very diverse interventions, research designs, subject characteristics, and sports.

8. "Open" skills, like those in basketball, football, and soccer, involve constantly changing environmental conditions such as blocking and faking. "Closed" skills, like those in bowling, archery, and free-throw shooting in basketball, involve stable environmental conditions.

9. Using the data in Kim's (1989) Table 1, we calculated pretest-posttest effect sizes for each group with the same formula used by Feltz et al. (1988). This secondary analysis revealed that the combined relaxation/meditation/imagery group was more effective in reducing anxiety (ES = 0.93) and improving performance (ES = 0.80) than the meditation/imagery group (ESs = 0.48 and 0.24, respectively), the relaxation/imagery group (ESs = 0.30 and -0.14, respectively), and the control group (ESs = -0.04 and 0.04, respectively).

10. These studies used an appropriate A-B-A-B single-subject design.

11. Although the mental practice group performed at an initially higher level than the control subjects, they made smaller pretest-posttest gains than did the control subjects. For example, the effect sizes for the pretest-posttest gains for the mental practice and control groups were 0.35 and 0.75, respectively, for firing rate; 0.76 and 1.26 for hit probability; and 0.66 and 1.04 for hit rate.

12. A challenge attitude is described by Loehr (1989) as involving 100 percent effort without fear. A player with this attitude feels free and aggressive and won't give up or become angry. Although a person can substantially improve the amount of time he or she displays a challenge attitude, one can never really master it.

13. As in the Lacey and Lacey (1980) laboratory research, cardiac deceleration patterns observed in sports are unrelated to sinus arrhythmia since decelerations have occurred with a variety of respiratory patterns (Boutcher and Zinsser, 1990; Crews, 1989).

14. In addition to a greater amount of cardiac deceleration prior to a shot, Schmid (1989) noted that elite archers exhibited a postshot delay in cardiac acceleration.

15. A planned comparison t test between epoch 1 (0.5 second before arrow release) and epoch 5 (2.5 seconds before arrow release) during the pre- and posttest revealed that cardiac deceleration was significant only during the posttest. The means for the posttest were 85.1 beats per minute at epoch 1 and 91.5 beats per minute at epoch 5. The heart rates for pre- and posttest at epoch 1 were not significantly different.

16. There is debate as to whether the Hedges and Olkin (1985) meta-analytic procedures are appropriate for studies like Crews and Landers (1987) in which a whole population of studies is considered. Hedges and Olkin's analysis of variance (ANOVA) analogue involves statistical assumptions of a sample derived from a population. When dealing with the entire population, the rather stringent procedures of the ANOVA analogue may not be necessary or even recommended. For example, they may conceal real differences between moderator variables. In the case of the Crews and Landers (1987) meta-analysis, subsequent investigation may reveal that effect sizes are greater for published studies that use chronic exercise and that use random assignment.

REFERENCES

Abbott, A.V., and R.K. Peters
   1989   Letter to the editor. *Psychosomatic Medicine* 51:218-219.

Annett, J.
1979 Memory for skill. Pp. 233-247 in M.M. Gruneberg and P.E. Morris, eds., *Applied Problems in Memory*. New York: Academic Press.

Anshel, M.H.
1988 The effect of mood and pleasant versus unpleasant information feedback on performing a motor skill. *Journal of General Psychology* 115:117-129.

Bandura, A.
1982 Self-efficacy mechanism in human agency. *American Psychologist* 37:122-147.

Bedford, T.G., and C.M. Tipton
1987 Exercise training and arterial baroreflex. *Journal of Applied Physiology* 63:1926-1932.

Bettelheim, B.
1960 *The Informed Heart*. New York: Free Press.

Bloom, B.
1985 *Developing Talent in Young People*. New York: Ballentine Books.

Blumenthal, J.A.
1989 Letter to the editor: response to Abbott and Peters. *Psychosomatic Medicine* 51:219-221.

Bohlin, G., and A. Kjellberg
1979 Orienting activity in two stimulus paradigms as reflected in heart rate. Pp. 169-197 in H.D. Kimmel, E.H. van Olst, and E.F. Orlebeke, eds., *The Orienting Reflex in Humans*. Hillsdale, N.J.: Erlbaum.

Borkovec, T.D., and J.K. Sides
1979 Critical procedural variables related to the physiological effects of progressive relaxation: a review. *Behavioral Research and Therapy* 17:119-125.

Boutcher, S.H., and D.J. Crews
1987 The effect of a preshot attentional routine on a well-learned skill. *International Journal of Sport Psychology* 18:30-39.

Boutcher, S.H., and N.W. Zinsser
1990 Cardiac deceleration of elite and beginning golfers during putting. *Journal of Sport and Exercise Psychology* 12:37-47.

Boyle, G.P.
1987 A cross-validation of the factor structure of the profile of mood states: were the factors correctly identified in the first instance? *Psychological Reports* 60:343-354.

Campbell, D.T., and J.C. Stanley
1963 *Experimental and Quasi-Experimental Designs for Research*. Chicago: Rand McNally.

Carroll, D., and P. Anastasiades
1978 The behavioral significance of heart rate: the Laceys' hypothesis. *Biological Psychology* 7:249-275.

Chollet, F., V. DiPiero, R. Wise, D. Brooks, R. Dolan, and R. Frackowiak
1991 The functional anatomy of recovery after stroke in humans: a study with positron emission tomography. *Annals of Neurology* 29:63-71.

Christina, R.W.
1987 Motor learning: future lines of research. *The Academy Papers* 20:26-41.

Cohn, P.J., R.J. Rotella, and J.W. Lloyd
1990 Effects of a cognitive-behavioral intervention on the preshot routine and performance in golf. *The Sport Psychologist* 4:33-47.

Coles, M.G.H.
1984 Heart rate and attention: the intake-rejection hypothesis and beyond. Pp. 276-294 in M.G.H. Coles, J.R. Jennings, and J.A. Stern, eds., *Psychophysiological Perspectives: Festschrift for Beatrice and John Lacey*. Stroudburg, Pa.: Hutchinson and Ross.

Craighead, D.J., G. Privette, F. Vallianos, and D. Byrkit
  1986 Personality characteristics of basketball players, starters and non-starters. *International Journal of Sport Psychology* 17:110-119.
Crews, D.J.
  1989 The Influence of Attentive States on Golf Putting as Indicated by Cardiac and Electrocortical Activity. Unpublished doctoral dissertation, Arizona State University.
Crews, D.J., and S.H. Boutcher
  1986a An exploratory observational analysis of professional golfers during competition. *Journal of Sport Behavior* 9:51-58.
  1986b Effects of structured preshot behaviors on beginning golf performance. *Perceptual and Motor Skills* 62:291-294.
Crews, D.J., and D.M. Landers
  1987 A meta-analytic review of aerobic fitness and reactivity to psychosocial stressors. *Medicine and Science in Sport and Exercise* 19(5):114-120.
  1991 Cardiac Pattern as an Indicator of Attention: A Test of Two Hypotheses. Unpublished manuscript, Department of Exercise Science and Physical Education, Arizona State University, Tempe.
Csikszentmihalyi, M.
  1990 *Flow: The Psychology of Optimal Experience.* New York: Harper and Row.
Csikszentmihalyi, M., and R. Larson
  1987 Validity and reliability of the Experience Sampling Method. *Journal of Nervous and Mental Disease* 175:526-536.
Daiss, S., A. LeUnes, and J. Nation
  1986 Mood and locus of control of a sample of college and professional football players. *Perceptual and Motor Skills* 63:733-734.
Davidson, R.J., G.E. Schwartz, and L. Rothman
  1976 Attentional style and self-regulation of mode specific attention: an EEG study. *Journal of Abnormal Psychology* 85:611-621.
Deijen, J., M. Heemstra, and J. Orlebeke
  1989 Dietary effects on mood and performance. *Journal of Psychiatric Research* 23:275-283.
DeMers, G.E.
  1983 Emotional states of high-caliber divers. *Swimming Technique* May-July:33-35.
Diamond, M., E. Greer, A. York, D. Lewis, T. Barton, and J. Lin
  1987 Rat cortical morphology following crowded-enriched living conditions. *Experimental Neurology* 96:241-247.
Dishman, R.K.
  1982 Contemporary sport psychology. *Exercise and Sport Sciences Reviews* 10:120-143.
Druckman, D., and J. Lacey, eds.
  1989 *Brain and Cognition: Some New Technologies.* Committee on New Techniques in Cognitive Psychophysiology, Commission on Behavioral and Social Sciences and Education, National Research Council. Washington, D.C.: National Academy Press.
Druckman, D., and J.A. Swets, eds.
  1988 *Enhancing Human Performance: Issues, Theories, and Techniques.* Committee on Techniques for the Enhancement of Human Performance, Commission on Behavioral and Social Sciences and Education, National Research Council. Washington, D.C.: National Academy Press.
Dyer, J.B., III, and J.G. Crouch
  1987 Effects of running on moods: a time series study. *Perceptual and Motor Skills* 64:783-789.

Elliott, R.

1972   The significance of heart rate for behavior: a critique of Lacey's hypothesis. *Journal of Personality and Social Psychology* 22:398-409.

Eysenck, H.J., and S.B.G. Eysenck

1968   *Manual for the Eysenck Personality Inventory*. San Diego, Calif.: Educational and Industrial Testing Service.

Eysenck, H.J., D.K.B. Nias, and D.N. Cox

1982   Sport and personality. *Advances in Behavior Research and Therapy* 4(2):1-56.

Feltz, D.L., and D.M. Landers

1983   The effects of mental practice on motor skill learning and performance: a meta-analysis. *Journal of Sport Psychology* 5:25-57.

Feltz, D.L., and C.A. Riessinger

1990   Effects of in vivo emotive imagery and performance feedback on self-efficacy and muscular endurance. *Journal of Sport and Exercise Psychology* 12:132-143.

Feltz, D.L., D.M. Landers, and U. Raeder

1979   Enhancing self-efficacy in high-avoidance motor tasks: a comparison of modeling techniques. *Journal of Sport Psychology* 1:112-122.

Feltz, D.L., D.M. Landers, and B.J. Becker

1988   A revised meta-analysis of the mental practice literature on motor skill learning. Pp. 1-65 in D. Druckman and J.A. Swets, eds., *Enhancing Human Performance: Issues, Theories and Techniques. Background Papers*. Committee on Techniques for the Enhancement of Human Performance, Commission on Behavioral and Social Sciences and Education, National Research Council. Washington, D.C.: National Academy Press.

Frankl, V.

1963   *From Death Camp to Existentialism*. Boston: Beacon Press.

Gal, R., and R.S. Lazarus

1975   The role of activity in anticipating and confronting stressful situations. *Journal of Human Stress* December:4-20.

Gale, A., and J.A. Edwards

1983   The EEG and human behavior. Pp. 99-127 in A. Gale and J.A. Edwards, eds., *Psychological Correlates of Human Behavior*. New York: Academic Press.

Gallwey, W.T.

1981   *The Inner Game of Golf*. New York: Random House.

Garfield, C.

1978   *Peak Performance*. Los Angeles, Calif.: Tarcher Press.

Gasser, T., P. Bacher, and H. Steinberg

1985   Test-retest reliability of spectral parameters of the EEG. *Electroencephalography and Clinical Neurophysiology* 60:312-319.

Gevins, A.S., N.H. Morgan, S.L. Bressler, B.A. Cutillo, R.M. White, J. Illes, D.S. Greer, J.C. Doyle, and G.M. Zeitlin

1987   Human neuroelectric patterns predict performance accuracy. *Science* 235:580-585.

Gevins, A.S., B.A. Cutillo, S.L. Bressler, N.H. Morgan, R.M. White, J. Illes, and D.S. Greer

1989   Event-related covariances during a dimanual visuomotor task. II. Preparation and feedback. *Electroencephalography and Clinical Neurophysiology* 74:147-160.

Gould, D., R. Weinberg, and A. Jackson

1980   Mental preparation strategies, cognitions and strength performance. *Journal of Sport Psychology* 2:329-339.

Graham, F.K.

1979   Distinguishing among orienting, defense and startle reflexes. Pp. 137-167 in H.D. Kimmel, E.H. van Olst, and J.F. Orlebeke, eds., *The Orienting Reflex in Humans*. Hillsdale, N.J.: Erlbaum.

Greenspan, M.J., and D.L. Feltz
  1989 Psychological interventions with athletes in competitive situations: a review. *The Sport Psychologist* 3(3):219-236.
Guttman, M.C., M.L. Pollack, C. Foster, and D. Schmidt
  1984 Training stress in Olympic speed skaters: a psychological perspective. *The Physician and Sports Medicine* 12:45-57.
Hahn, W.W.
  1973 Attention and heart rate: a critical appraisal of the hypothesis of Lacey and Lacey. *Psychological Bulletin* 79:59-70.
Hall, E., and E. Erffmeyer
  1983 The effect of visuo-motor behavior rehearsal with video-taped modeling on free-throw accuracy of intercollegiate female basketball players. *Journal of Sport Psychology* 5:343-346.
Hamilton, S., and W. Fremouw
  1985 Cognitive-behavioral training for college free-throw performance. *Cognitive Therapy and Research* 9:479-483.
Hatfield, B.D., and D.M. Landers
  1987 Psychophysiology in exercise and sport research: an overview. *Exercise and Sport Sciences Reviews* 15:351-387.
Hatfield, B.D., D.M. Landers, and W.J. Ray
  1984 Cognitive processes during self-paced motor performance: an electro-encephalographic profile of skilled marksmen. *Journal of Sport Psychology* 6:42-59.
  1987 Cardiovascular-CNS interactions during a self-paced, intentional attentive state: elite marksmanship performance. *Psychophysiology* 24:542-549.
Hatze, H.
  1976 Biomechanical aspects of a successful motion optimization. Pp. 5-12 in P.V. Komi, ed., *Biomechanics V-B*. Baltimore, Md.: University Park Press.
Hedges, L.V., and I. Olkin
  1985 *Statistical Methods for Meta-Analysis*. Orlando, Fla.: Academic Press.
Heward, W.
  1978 The effects of reinforcement on the offensive efficiency of a barn-storming baseball team. *Behavior Modification* 2(1):25-59.
Heyman, S.R.
  1987 Research and interventions in sport psychology: issues encountered in working with an amateur boxer. *The Sport Psychologist* 1:208-223.
Hird, J.S., D.M. Landers, J.R. Thomas, and J.J. Horan
  1991 Physical practice is superior to mental practice in enhancing cognitive and motor performance. *Journal of Sports Exercise Psychology*. In press.
Horswill, C.A., R.C. Hickner, J.R. Scott, D.L. Costill, and D. Gould
  1990 Weight loss, dietary carbohydrate modifications, and high intensity physical performance. *Medicine and Science in Sports and Exercise* 22:470-476.
Howell, M.L.
  1956 Use of force-time graphs for performance analysis in facilitating motor learning. *Research Quarterly* 27:12-22.
Jennings, J.R., B.E. Lawrence, and P. Kasper
  1978 Changes in alertness and processing capacity in a serial learning task. *Psychophysiology* 17:37-46.
Kahneman, D.
  1973 *Attention and Effort*. Englewood Cliffs, N.J.: Prentice-Hall.
Kendall, G., D. Hrycaiko, G.L. Martin, and T. Kendall
  1990 The effects of imagery rehearsal, relaxation, and self-talk package on basketball game performance. *Journal of Sport and Exercise Psychology* 12:157-166.

Kim, G.B.
    1989 Relative effectiveness of anxiety reduction techniques on levels of competitive anxiety and shooting performance. Pp. 61-74 in *Commemorative Volume Dedicated to Professor Hong-Dae Kim, Young-Nam University.* Dae-Ku, Republic of Korea: Hong-ik Publishing Co.
Kirschenbaum, D., and R. Bale
    1980 Cognitive-behavioral skills in golf: brain power golf. Pp. 275-287 in R. Suinn, ed., *Psychology in Sports: Methods and Applications.* Minneapolis. Minn.: Burgess.
Komaki, J., and F. Barnett
    1977 A behavioral approach to coaching football: improving the play execution of the offensive backfield on a youth football team. *Journal of Applied Behavior Analysis* 10:657-664.
Kubitz, K.A., D.M. Landers, W. Salazar, and S.J. Petruzzello
    1991 A Meta-Analytic Review of the Effects of Acute Exercise on Selected Aspects of Sleep. Unpublished manuscript, Department of Exercise Science and Physical Education, Arizona State University.
Lacey, B.C., and J.I. Lacey
    1964 Cardiac Deceleration and Simple Visual Reaction Time in a Fixed Foreperiod Experiment. Paper presented at the October meeting of the Society for Psychophysiological Research, Washington, D.C.
    1966 Change in Cardiac Response and Reaction Time as a Function of Motivation. Paper presented at the October meeting of the Society for Psychophysiological Research, Denver, Colo.
    1970 Some autonomic-central nervous system interrelationships. Pp. 205-261 in P. Black, ed., *Physiological Correlates of Emotion.* New York: Academic Press.
    1974 Studies of heart rate and other bodily processes in sensorimotor behavior. Pp. 538-564 in P.A. Obrist, A.H. Lack, J. Brener, and L.V. DiCara, eds., *Cardiovascular Psychophysiology.* Chicago: Aldine.
    1980 Sensorimotor behavior and cardiac activity. Pp. 170-179 in I. Martin and P.H. Venables, eds., *Techniques in Psychophysiology.* New York: Wiley.
Lacey, J.I.
    1967 Somatic response patterning and stress: some revisions of activation theory. Pp. 14-37 in M.H. Appley and R. Trumbull, eds., *Psychological Stress: Issues in Research.* New York: Appleton-Century-Crofts.
Lacey, J.I., J. Kagan, B.C. Lacey, and H.A. Moss
    1963 The visceral level: situational determinants and behavioral correlates of autonomic response patterns. Pp. 161-196 in P.H. Knapp, ed., *Expression of the Emotions in Man.* New York: International Universities Press.
Landers, D.M.
    1985 Psychophysiological assessment and biofeedback: applications for athletes in closed skill sports. Pp. 63-105 in J.H. Sandweis and S. Wolf, eds., *Biofeedback and Sports Science.* New York: Plenum Press.
Landers, D.M., M.Q. Wang, and P. Courtet
    1985 Peripheral narrowing among experienced and inexperienced rifle shooters under low- and high-time stress conditions. *Research Quarterly for Exercise and Sport* 56:122-130.
Landers, D.M., M.W. Han, W. Salazar, S.H. Petruzzello, K.A. Kubitz, and T.L. Gannon
    1991a The effects of learning on electroencephalographic and electrocardiographic patterns in novice archers. *International Journal of Sport Psychology.* In press.

Landers, D.M., S.H. Petruzzello, W. Salazar, D.J. Crews, K.A. Kubitz, T.L. Gannon, and M.W. Han
    1991b The influence of electrocortical biofeedback on performance in pre-elite archers. *Medicine and Science in Sports and Exercise* 23:123-129.
Landy, F.J., and R.M. Stern
    1971 Factor analysis of a somatic perception questionnaire. *Journal of Psychosomatic Research* 15:179-181.
Larson, R., and M. Csikszentmihalyi
    1983 The experience sampling method. In H. Reis, ed., *Naturalistic Approaches to Studying Social Interactions.* San Francisco, Calif.: Jossey Bass.
Lawrence, G., D. Druckman, and D.M. Landers
    1990 Mental practice for solderers. Unpublished manuscript, U.S. Army Research Institute, Alexandria, Va.
Lee, A.B., and J. Hewitt
    1987 Using visual imagery in a flotation tank to improve gymnastic performance and reduce physical symptoms. *International Journal of Sport Psychology* 18:223-230.
LeUnes, A., and J.R. Nation
    1982 Saturday's heroes: a psychological portrait of college football players. *Journal of Sport Behavior* 5:139-149.
LeUnes, A., S. Daiss, and J.R. Nation
    1986 Some psychological predictors of continuation in a collegiate football program. *Journal of Applied Research in Coaching and Athletics* 1:1-8.
LeUnes, A., S.A. Hayward, and S. Daiss
    1988 Annotated bibliography on the profile of mood states in sport, 1975-1988. *Journal of Sport Behavior* 11(4):213-240.
Light, K.C.
    1982 Cardiovascular responses to effortful active coping. *Psychophysiology* 18:216-225.
Lobmeyer, D.L., and E.A. Wasserman
    1986 Preliminaries to free throw shooting: superstitious behavior? *Journal of Sport Behavior* 9:70-78.
Loehr, J.
    1989 *Mental Toughness.* Videotape. Available from Grand Slam Communications, 5150 Linton Blvd., Suite 420, Delray Beach, Florida 33484.
Lubin, B.
    1967 *Manual for the Depression Adjective Checklist.* San Diego, Calif.: Educational and Industrial Testing Service.
Mace, R., C. Eastman, and D. Carroll
    1987 The effects of stress-inoculation training on gymnastics performance on the pommelled horse: a case study. *Behavioral Psychotherapy* 15:272-279.
Maddi, S.
    1965 Motivational aspects of creativity. *Journal of Personality* 33:330-347.
Mahoney, M.J., and M. Avener
    1977 Psychology of the elite athlete: an exploratory study. *Cognitive Therapy and Research* 1:135-141.
Maslow, A.
    1971 *The Farther Reaches of Human Nature.* New York: Viking Press.
Massimini, F., and P. Inghilleri
    1987 *L'esperienza Quotidiana.* Milano: Franco Angeli Libri.
Massimini, F., M. Csikszentmihalyi, and M. Carli
    1987 The monitoring of optimal experience: a tool for psychiatric rehabilitation. *Journal of Nervous and Mental Disease* 175:545-549.

Mazziotta, J., and M. Phelps
1984 Positron computed tomography studies of cerebral metabolic responses to complex motor tasks. *Neurology* 34:116.

McCullagh, P., M.R. Weiss, and D. Ross
1989 Modeling considerations in motor skill acquisition and performance: an integrated approach. *Exercise and Sport Science Reviews* 17:475-513.

McCullagh, P., K.J. Evans, K.M. Morrison, and K.M. Petersen
1990a The Use of Videotapes and Imagery to Enhance Skilled Performance. Unpublished manuscript, Department of Kinesiology, University of Colorado, Boulder.

McCullagh, P., A. Meriweather, and D.I. Siegel
1990b The Effectiveness of Sybervision as an Observational Learning Tool for the Tennis Serve. Unpublished manuscript, Department of Kinesiology, University of Colorado, Boulder.

McNair, D.M., M. Lorr, and L.F. Droppleman
1971/ *Profile of Mood States Manual*. San Diego, Calif.: Educational and Industrial
81   Testing Service.

Meyers, A., R. Schleser, and T. Okwumabua
1982 A cognitive behavioral intervention for improving basketball performance. *Research Quarterly for Exercise and Sport* 53(4):344-347.

Miller, B.P., and G.P. Edgington
1984 Psychological mood state distortion in a sporting context. *Journal of Sport Behavior* 7(3):91-94.

Miller, B.P., and A.J. Miller
1985 Psychological correlates of success in elite sportswomen. *International Journal of Sport Psychology* 16:289-295.

Molander, B., and L. Backman
1989 Age differences in heart rate patterns during concentration in a precision sport: implications for attentional functioning. *Journal of Gerontology: Psychological Sciences* 44:80-87.

Morgan, W.P.
1979 Anxiety reduction following acute physical activity. *Psychiatric Annals* 9:141-147.
1980 Test of champions. *Psychology Today* July:92-99.
1981 Psychophysiology of self-awareness during vigorous physical activity. *Research Quarterly for Exercise and Sport* 52:385-427.
1985 Selected psychological factors limiting performance: a mental health model. Pp. 70-80 in D.H. Clarke and H.M. Eckert, eds., *Limits of Human Performance*. Champaign, Ill.: Human Kinetics.

Morgan, W.P., and R.W. Johnson
1978 Personality characteristics of successful and unsuccessful oarsmen. *International Journal of Sport Psychology* 9:119-133.

Morgan, W.P., and M.L. Pollock
1977 Psychologic characterization of the elite distance runner. *Annals of the New York Academy of Sciences* 301:383-403.

Morgan, W.P., D.R. Brown, J.S. Raglin, P.J. O'Connor, and K.A. Ellickson
1987a Psychological monitoring of overtraining and staleness. *British Journal of Sports Medicine* 21:107-114.

Morgan, W.P., P.J. O'Connor, P.B. Sparling, and R.R. Pate
1987b Psychological characterization of the elite female distance runner. *International Journal of Sports Medicine* 8(Supplement):124-131.

Morgan, W.P., D.L. Costill, M.G. Flynn, J.S. Raglin, and P.J. O'Connor
1988 Mood disturbance following increased training in swimmers. *Medicine and Science in Sports and Exercise* 20:408-414.

Morrison, J.E., and S.A. Walker
    1990   Effects of Mental Practice on Tank Gunnery Performance. Technical report no. 873. U.S. Army Research Institute for the Behavioral and Social Sciences, Alexandria, Va.
Mumford, B., and C. Hall
    1985   The effects of internal and external imagery on performing figures in figure skating. *Canadian Journal of Applied Sport Sciences* 10(4):171-177.
Neiss, R.
    1990   Expectancy in motor behavior: a crucial element of the psychobiological states that affect performance. *Human Performance* 2:273-300.
Newell, K.M., J.T. Quinn, Jr., W.A. Sparrow, and C.B. Walter
    1983   Kinematic information feedback for learning a rapid arm movement. *Human Movement Science* 2:255-269.
Newell, K.M., W.A. Sparrow, and J.T. Quinn, Jr.
    1985   Kinetic information feedback for learning isometric skills. *Journal of Human Movement Studies* 11:113-123.
Nisbett, R.E., and T.D. Wilson
    1977   Telling more than we can know: verbal reports on mental processes. *Psychological Review* 84:231-259.
Norcross, J.C., E. Guadagnoli, and J.O. Prochaska
    1984   Factor structure of the profile of mood states (POMS): two partial replications. *Journal of Clinical Psychology* 40:1270-1277.
North, T.C., P. McCullagh, and Z.V. Tran
    1990   Effect of exercise on depression. *Exercise and Sport Sciences Reviews* 18:379-415.
Obrist, P.A.
    1981   *Cardiovascular Psychophysiology: A Perspective.* New York: Plenum.
Obrist, P.A., R.A. Webb, J.R. Sutterer, and J.L. Howard
    1970   Cardiac deceleration and reaction time: an evolution of two hypotheses. *Psychophysiology* 6:695-706.
O'Connor, K.P.
    1981   The intentional paradigm and cognitive psychophysiology. *Psychophysiology* 18:121-128.
O'Connor, P.J., W.P. Morgan, J.S. Raglin, C.M. Barksdale, and N.H. Kalin
    1989   Mood state and salivary cortisol levels following overtraining in female swimmers. *Psychoneuroendocrinology* 14:303-310.
Orwin, R.G.
    1983   A fail-safe N for effect size. *Journal of Educational Statistics* 8:157-159.
Oxendine, J.B.
    1969   Effect of mental and physical practice on the learning of three motor skills. *Research Quarterly* 40(4):744-763.
Pahl, J.
    1990   Positron emission tomography in the study of higher cognitive functions. In A. Schiebel and A. Wechsler, eds., *Neurobiology of Higher Cognitive Function.* New York: Guilford.
Petruzzello, S.J., D.M. Landers, B.D. Hatfield, K.A. Kubitz, and W. Salazar
    1991   A meta-analysis on the anxiety reducing effects of acute and chronic exercise: outcomes and mechanisms. *Sports Medicine* 11:143-182.
Pirozzolo, F.J.
    1991   A developmental neuropsychological model of human performance. *Developmental Neuropsychology* 7:377-391.
Pirozzolo, F.J., and M. Csikszentmihalyi
    1991   Preparation to Perform Under Pressure. Unpublished manuscript, Department of Neurology, Baylor College of Medicine.

Raven, P.B., D. Rohm-Young, and C.G. Blomquist
   1984   Physical fitness and cardiovascular response to lower body negative pressure. *Journal of Applied Physiology* 56:138-144.
Ray, W.J., and H.W. Cole
   1985   EEG alpha activity reflects attentional demands, and beta activity reflects emotional and cognitive processes. *Science* 228:750-752.
Ray, R.L., and H.D. Kimmel
   1979   Utilization of psychophysiological indices in behavioral assessment: some methodological issues. *Journal of Behavioral Assessment* 1:107-122.
Reddon, J.R., R. Marceau, and R.R. Holden
   1985   A confirmatory evaluation of the Profile of Mood States: convergent and discriminant item validity. *Journal of Psychopathology and Behavioral Assessment* 7:243-259.
Richardson, A.
   1967   Mental practice: a review and discussion. Part 1. *Research Quarterly* 38(1):95-107.
Riddick, C.C.
   1984   Comparative psychological profiles of three groups of female collegians: competitive swimmers, recreational swimmers, and inactive swimmers. *Journal of Sport Behavior* 7:160-174.
Robinson, R.
   1990   *The Iron Horse*. New York: Harper and Row.
Roland, P., E. Meyer, T. Shibasaki, Y. Yamamoto, and C. Thompson
   1982   Regional cerebral blood flow changes in cortex and basal ganglia during voluntary movements in normal human volunteers. *Journal of Neurophysiology* 48:467-480.
Roland, P., L. Eriksson, S. Stone-Elander, and L. Widen
   1987   Does mental activity change the oxidative metabolism of the brain? *Journal of Neuroscience* 1:2373-2389.
Rose, D., and R.W. Christina
   1990   Attentional demands of precision pistol-shooting as a function of skill level. *Research Quarterly for Exercise and Sport* 61:111-113.
Rothstein, A.L., and R.K. Arnold
   1976   Bridging the gap: application of research on videotape feedback and bowling. *Motor Skills: Theory Into Practice* 1:35-62.
Ryan, A.J.
   1983   Exercise is medicine. *The Physician and Sports Medicine* 11:10.
Salazar, W., D.M. Landers, S.J. Petruzzello, D.J. Crews, K.A. Kubitz, and M.W. Han
   1990   Hemispheric asymmetry, cardiac response, and performance in elite archers. *Research Quarterly for Exercise and Sport* 61:351-359.
Sandman, C.A., and B.B. Walker
   1985   Cardiovascular relationship to attention and thinking. Pp. 95-122 in V.M. Rental, S.A. Corson, and B.R. Dunn, eds., *Psychophysiological Aspects of Reading and Learning*. New York: Gordon & Breach.
Schmid, W.D.
   1989   Heart rate patterns of archers while shooting. *Fiziologiya Cheloveka* 15:64-68.
Shulhan, D., H. Scher, and J. Furedy
   1986   Phasic cardiac reactivity to psychological stress as a function of aerobic fitness level. *Psychophysiology* 23:562-566.
Silva, J.M., III, B.B. Schultz, R.W. Haslam, and D. Murray
   1981   A psychophysiological assessment of elite wrestlers. *Research Quarterly for Exercise and Sport* 52:348-358.
Silva, J.M., III, B.B. Shultz, R.W. Haslam, T.P. Martin, and D.F. Murray
   1985   Discriminating characteristics of contestants at the United States Olympic wrestling trials. *International Journal of Sport Psychology* 16:79-102.

Singer, R.N., L.A. Flora, and T.L. Abpirezl
1989   The effect of a five-step cognitive learning strategy on the acquisition of a complex motor task. *Journal of Applied Sport Psychology* 1:98-108.

Singer, R.S.
1972   *The Psychomotor Domain: Movement Behavior.* Philadelphia, Pa.: Lea & Febiger.

Smith, R.E.
1980   A cognitive-affective approach to stress management training for athletes. Pp. 54-72 in C.H. Nadeau, W.R. Halliwell, K.M. Newell, and G.C. Roberts, eds., *Psychology of Motor Behavior and Sport—1979.* Champaign, Ill.: Human Kinetics.

Spielberger, C.D., R.L. Gorsuch, and R.E. Lushene
1970   *Manual for the State-Trait Anxiety Inventory.* Palo Alto, Calif.: Consulting Psychologists Press.

Stern, R.M.
1976   Reaction time and heart rate between the GET SET and GO of simulated races. *Psychophysiology* 13:149-154.

Suinn, R.M.
1977   Behavioral methods at the winter games. *Behavioral Therapy* 8:283-284.
1983   Imagery and sports. Pp. 507-534 in A.A. Sheikh, ed., *Imagery: Current Theory, Research, and Application.* New York: Wiley.

Tharion, W.J., S.R. Strowman, and T.M. Rauch
1988   Profile and changes in moods of ultramarathoners. *Journal of Sport and Exercise Psychology* 10:229-235.

van der Molen, M.W., R.J.M. Somsen, and J.F. Orlebeke
1985   The rhythm of the heart beat in information processing. Pp. 1-88 in P.K. Ackles, J.R. Jennings, and M.G.H. Coles, eds., *Advances in Psychophysiology.* Greenwich, Conn.: JAI Press.

Walker, B.B., and C.A. Sandman
1979   Human visual evoked responses are related to heart rate. *Journal of Comparative and Physiological Psychology* 93:717-729.
1982   Visual evoked potentials change as heart rate and carotid pressure change. *Psychophysiology* 19:520-527.

Wang, M.Q., and D.M. Landers
1987   A psychophysiological investigation of attention during archery performance. *Psychophysiology* 23:449.

Weinberg, R.S.
1982   The relationship between mental preparation strategies and motor performance: a review and critique. *Quest* 33(2):195-213.

Weinberg, R., T. Seabourne, and A. Jackson
1981   Effects of visuo-motor behavior rehearsal, relaxation, and imagery on karate performance. *Journal of Sport Psychology* 3:228-238.

Wheeler, R.E., A.J. Tomarken, L.M. Kinney, A.M. Straus, R.C. Doss, and R.J. Davidson
1989   EEG Activation Asymmetries Are Stable Over Time. Paper presented at the annual meeting of the Society for Psychophysiological Research, New Orleans, October.

Whelan, J.P., A.W. Meyers, and J.S. Berman
1989   Cognitive-behavioral interventions for athletic performance enhancement. Paper presented at the annual meeting of the American Psychological Association, New Orleans.

Williams, T., and G. Krahenbuhl
1991   Mood state and running economy in moderately trained male runners. *Medicine and Science in Sports and Exercise* 23(6):727-731.

Wills, B.J.
1966   Mental Practice as a Factor in the Performance of Two Motor Tasks. Unpublished doctoral dissertation, University of Wisconsin, Madison.

Wilson, V.E., N.C. Morley, and E.I. Bird
    1980 Mood profiles of marathon runners, joggers and non-exercisers. *Perceptual and Motor Skills* 50:117-118.
Wurtman, R.
    1982 Nutrients that modify brain function. *Scientific American* 246:42-51.

12

Enhancing Team Performance

The enhancement of one person's performance can be viewed in a variety of ways, as is done in the other chapters of this book. In many situations, however—in sports, the military, the workplace, to name but a few—people do not perform their tasks alone; rather, they do so in conjunction with other people performing parallel, similar, or complementary tasks. The performance of such an aggregate of individual performers is not merely the sum of the individual efforts, but some more complex combination, systems that must be studied on their own. This chapter presents what is known about those aggregates—usually called groups, teams, or crews—and how to affect their performance. (Throughout this chapter, we use the terms group, team, and crew interchangeably.)

RESEARCH ON GROUPS: IN THE LABORATORY AND ON THE JOB

The examination of how teams and groups perform and accomplish their goals and tasks has been studied by a variety of investigators from a number of disciplines. Two of the more prominent traditions of study have been those of experimental social psychology and of human factors.

Social psychology has dealt with groups primarily as theoretical entities. It has sought to elucidate rather general propositions about how groups function from the abstract manipulation of variables, often in experimental laboratory settings. In recent years social psychologists have focused on decision making, and the prototype question has been the study of how groups arrive at a consensus. The major model has been a jury, which is an unorganized group whose members possess similar information and who must arrive at a consensus. The variables most often investigated are group size, rules of procedure, and other structural features.

The field of human factors has dealt primarily with teams or crews, that is, the types of groups found in the workplace. The studies are often addressed to the task of optimizing performance in a particular setting or set of circumstances. The crews and teams under investigation are often studied on the job, and quite commonly, the teams are stratified and functionally differentiated. Such studies often focus on the division of labor among people working in a particular equipment design environment, as, for example, the layout of instruments and controls in an airplane cockpit occupied by several people.

These two traditions tend to parallel an important distinction in group research: the difference between laboratory and field research. Studies in the laboratory, favored by social psychologists, permit researchers to gain a greater amount of control over the factors under investigation. They allow random assignment of people to different experimental conditions and also permit the standardization, minimization, or the measurement of factors not currently under investigation but capable of spuriously affecting outcomes. But because laboratory studies examine "hot-house" variables under usually idealized circumstances, it is often difficult to apply them in any particular case.

Field studies, in contrast, examine groups in their natural environments. While some control of the factors affecting a crew is possible, field studies often must contend with many complex factors. Because randomization of team members is not usually an option, many of the factors are covaried (i.e., related to each other) and often not even identified. Field studies often give good answers about specific questions concerning the composition and work of particular teams, but because of the specific circumstances under which they are conducted, they are difficult to cumulate into general principles for group performance.

It seems clear that the perspective of both traditions—experimental social psychology and human factors—are necessary for addressing the problems faced by those who must design efficient and comprehensive training programs for activities involving group tasks. General principles and applicable specifics are both needed. This chapter attempts such an integration by examining two aspects of the missions of groups or teams: decision making and performance. Both of these aspects can be studied in the laboratory and in the field, but they pose different sets of problems for researchers.

Although the two processes of decision making and performance are intertwined in the functioning of a group, they are often at least conceptually separable. The decision mechanism of a team may be fixed, as in a military unit, but its performance mechanism still needs to be implemented. For example, a football team may have a mechanism for deciding which play to call. The coach or the quarterback decides: if the coach decides, he signals the quarterback, who informs the team in the huddle. The performance, how well the team runs the play, is still problematic. Alternatively, a team or group may be able to coordinate its efforts, but not have a mechanism for selecting and deciding on its strategy and tactics. It is not known what is the best training regimen for a group that is faced with both decisional and performance requirements; there is a strong possibility that the training procedures that are optimal to teach groups to make decisions are the same procedures that are optimal for producing enhanced performance.

With these distinctions of decision making and performance in mind, we now turn to an examination of what is known of the differences between group and individual performances. The object is to ascertain if there are recognized general procedures that can improve the task-oriented performance of work groups. The chapter is divided into three major sections. Following a brief overview of issues of team performance, we review selected studies designed to evaluate the performance of teams in laboratory settings. A third section highlights some problems involved in moving from the experimental laboratory to field situations in which teams perform under pressure: three case studies are presented and the questions for training and research suggested by each of them.

INDIVIDUALS AND TEAMS

The primary functions of many organizations are performed not just by individuals acting alone, but by small teams of two to perhaps a dozen individuals. Members of such task-oriented teams are sometimes highly coordinated (e.g., tank crews, unit staffs) and sometimes largely unorganized (e.g., trouble-shooting groups, research teams), the skill requirements of a group can range from simple perceptual-motor skills to abstract reasoning, and various combinations occur. In short, teams are as diverse as the tasks that confront them and the environments in which they operate. Problems of team performance and the means of solving those problems thus vary considerably, and they are specific to the task and work environment. Nonetheless, it is useful to note some very general issues and problems associated with team performance and team-oriented research, many of which have no precise counterparts in individual performance. The general focus is on interaction processes, organizational structures, and operating procedures that foster and sustain optimal task performance (or fail to do so) and the basis for training designed to maximize such performance.

In principle, a team appears to offer greater resources and processing power than an individual, but teams also involve interpersonal coordination and management problems that do not exist with individuals. Evaluating the tradeoff between these two resembles a cost-benefit analysis, although it is easy to overextend the analogy.

Individual performance can be evaluated according to a variety of standards, depending on the task. For example, performance can be axiomatically correct or optimal (an answer to an arithmetic problem is correct or a mile is run faster than ever before), empirically correct or workable (a piece of a jigsaw puzzle fits or an automobile runs), and so on. At the other end of a spectrum, intuition or the consensus of experts may be the only available standards by which a performance can be judged (the literary worth of a book).

Team performances can be evaluated by similar standards, but in addition, questions of interpersonal management costs and coordination efficiency have to be considered. In other words, baseline against which to judge team performance must necessarily take into account the number of people involved, the time devoted to team effort, and the consumption of other resources relative to the level of performance achieved.

A highly compelling intuition from conventional wisdom, which also arises repeatedly in the research literature, is that small, task-oriented groups are, in general, "good." Such intuitions probably arise from the simple observation that some tasks can *only* be performed by groups (e.g., lifting a large log), unlike some tasks that can be performed either by an individual or a group (solving an arithmetic problem or recalling text). Moreover, when it is feasible to compare groups and individuals *directly*, (e.g., solving a word puzzle with a unique solution), the former is on the average rarely inferior (e.g., see Davis, 1969; McGrath, 1984; Brown, 1988).

Other perspectives are possible, however, and lead to different conclusions. For example, team performance has often been observed to fall short of a reasonable theoretical baseline, relative to the task demands and resources invested (e.g., Steiner, 1972). An example of a baseline is individual performance which assumes that a group will do at least as well as individuals performing the same task. Indeed, such team baseline comparisons are a major tool for evaluating team performance.

Although a shortfall may not be truly universal (i.e., not characteristic of all work environments of interest), team performance decrements have been observed in such a very wide variety of task domains and performance environments that it seems prudent to regard suboptimal team performance as the norm. The critical ingredient in detection has been development of a theoretical baseline relevant to the particular task environment. To some extent, the recognition of various team performance decrements resembles the discovery of decision-making biases in individuals, apparently due to faulty cognitive heuristics (e.g., Tversky and Kahneman, 1974, 1981; Kahneman and Tversky, 1982); these decision biases (e.g., the tendency to overestimate the probability of occurrence of familiar events) have largely been detected as individual performance departures from a reasonable theoretical baseline.

The available research, summarized in detail elsewhere, suggests that team performance is generally suboptimal (see Brown, 1988; Davis, 1969; Hastie, 1986; McGrath, 1984; Steiner, 1972). Before considering the remedies to be sought through the development of better operating procedures, interpersonal process management, and training, we consider briefly some examples of research from various task and performance environments.

TEAM PERFORMANCE

Individual input can vary as a function of a variety of intra-individual variables, but here we are more concerned with extra-individual factors, especially those originating with other members of a team. The interpersonal processing of such input ultimately produces the team action: the aggregation, concatenation, combination, assembly, or other treatment of information (or other kinds of individual contributions) underlies the team output. We consider first individual input issues.

Member Contributions

Audiences and coactors have been observed to influence strongly and systematically the quality and quantity of individual performances before them (see summaries by Geen, 1980, 1989; Zajonc, 1980; Borden, 1980). Even passive audiences can be responsible for arousal in a performer, which in turn generally facilitates performance of well-learned, routine behaviors and inhibits performance of poorly learned responses, including tasks that require processing of substantial information (Zajonc, 1965; Cohen and Davis, 1973). The latter finding does not encourage optimism for performance environments that require problem solving or the processing of information generally—especially those that might be necessary for coordinated team performance in emergencies and high-stress environments typical of the military, law enforcement, and many commercial settings.

If audiences actively respond, or can be interpreted as valuative in character, the audience-coaction effects just noted are generally exacerbated. Obviously, the nature of the task and setting, as well as such background factors as sex and culture of performers, are important in determining performance facilitation or inhibition. In somewhat more complex situations, the presence of others can be comforting, and interestingly enough, can even reduce anxiety and other reactions to stress, especially for subjects who are first-born and only children (e.g., Schachter, 1959; Wrightsman, 1959). Research on intergroup bargaining shows that the presence of constituents during bargaining leads female representatives to become increasingly cooperative through the course of the session (Druckman et al., 1972). Constituents' presence can either impede or facilitate negotiations depending on the culture of the bargaining representatives (Druckman et al., 1976). For example, negotiations over the distribution of resources between American representatives were prolonged while the bargaining between Argentinean representatives were hastened in the presence of an audience.

The literature cited above documents how the mere presence of others can influence the individual member performance where task requirements range from simple perceptual motor skills to abstract reasoning (although studies of the former are more common). Such effects run a time course, and may abate with training and experience. Unfortunately, relatively little research addresses these latter issues, although anecdotes from performers and others support the importance of adaptation through experience.

When several persons act simultaneously, a set of people must in some sense act together. For a wide range of simple tasks, various studies have demonstrated that members do not contribute proportionally to the team effort. First labeled "social loafing" by Latané et al. (1977), the per-member reduction in effort has been observed when team members' efforts are pooled, and the overall magnitude or quantity of output is what is apparent: rope pulling, evaluating proposals, pumping air, shouting, clapping, and the like (see Harkins and Szymanski, 1989, for a concise summary). It seems that more than the lack of member identifiability with input may be involved (e.g., Harkins and Jackson, 1985); social loafing generally appears to be some sort of motivational loss. Increasing member identifiability or providing a standard for the group to evaluate its own performance can erode the social loafing effect; see Kerr (1983), for a discussion of other group motivation loss effects.

Although increases in identifiability and enhancement of evaluation standards would apparently improve upon these motivation losses, exactly how particular techniques would work over a protracted period of time remains unstudied.

Information Processing and Coordination

Most of the tasks in the audience and coaction environments that have been studied were fairly simple, and the appropriate theoretical performance baseline for evaluating team performance was fairly straightforward: team output was essentially a summation or similar aggregation of members' inputs. We now consider more complex interactive tasks that require or especially benefit from interpersonal exchanges of information (solution proposals, decision preferences, critiques, etc.). Such group tasks appear to be increasingly common in industrial settings, public institutions, and military organizations.

Early studies of group performance were generally referred to as group problem solving, whether or not the task was a problem to be solved or some other intellectual task facing the group (Davis, 1969). Most of these studies were concerned with individuals working "together" or "apart," a distinction of some practical importance in that early German educators were interested in the optimal allocation of homework between collective effort and solitary study (see Murphy and Murphy, 1931, for summary remarks). The early general finding was that, in comparison with individuals working alone, groups tended to solve more problems (word puzzles, arithmetic problems, and other tasks that emphasized abstract reasoning) and at a faster rate (e.g., Shaw, 1932). By the mid-1950s, however, a number of simple empirical demonstrations (e.g., Taylor, 1954; Marquart, 1955) made it clear that group efforts were not routinely superior to individual efforts: given the resources committed per unit time, they were in fact demonstrably inefficient in terms of an appropriate baseline (e.g., Taylor, 1954; Lorge and Solomon, 1955; Marquart, 1955). For example, imagine a population composed of solvers and nonsolvers for a problem that has a correct answer (e.g., a word puzzle). A randomly composed team contains a solver with probability p, and a nonsolver with probability $(1 - p)$. Suppose that interaction is neither helpful nor deleterious (i.e., interaction does nothing), that members behave independently of each other, and that a team solves the puzzle if it contains at least one solver. The probability of a group solving it is then, $1 - (1 - p)^r$ (where r is group size). It is this value (and analogous "predictions" for other tasks and environments), that ad hoc freely interacting teams do not exceed and generally fall well below (see summaries by Hastie, 1986; Davis, 1969). Some data suggest that even experienced groups organized for task performance fall below the

above, best-member baseline (e.g., Davis et al., 1971), but so little research has addressed groups organized and trained to the task that little
can be said about actually engineering group efficiency in the various
contexts in which teams must perform.

Not all suboptimal performance can be attributed to lowered input at
the level of the individual member, and Steiner (1972), among others,
has outlined the nature of the losses due to faulty interpersonal processes required for pooling or otherwise combining information and responses into a group product (see recent summaries by McGrath, 1984;
Brown, 1988). Efforts to engineer improvements in group performance
have typically emphasized procedural mechanisms that both promote
discussion and efficient structuring of effort and enhance personal productivity (see summary by Hackman and Morris, 1975).

Brainstorming (Osborn, 1957) has been among the most popular of
the widely publicized devices to further group productivity—especially
teams engaged in tasks requiring "creative" problem solving. Brainstorming, which is essentially a set of guidelines for managing discussion, has proved highly popular with organizations as a procedural corrective and as a solution and idea-stimulating technique, despite critical
research evaluations from shortly after its introduction. Early empirical
evaluations found that, relative to a "best-member" baseline, brainstorming
did not successfully enhance performance; rather, isolated individuals
were relatively more productive (quality and quantity of ideas, solutions, etc.) (Taylor et al., 1958; Dunnette et al., 1963). However, brainstorming has survived and continues to be a popular means for organizations of various kinds to use to attempt to enhance performance of their
task-oriented teams. Recent empirical studies have confirmed earlier
research showing that brainstorming techniques, despite their continuing
popularity, do not alter the suboptimal performance of problem-solving
groups (Diehl and Stroebe, 1987; 1990; see also meta-analyses by Mullen
and Johnson, 1991). After exploring a variety of procedural manipulations, Diehl and Stroebe attribute the productivity loss to "blocking"—
an inability of a member to produce ideas while others are talking, a
kind of distraction notion.

It is easy to understand why organizations pursue techniques for the
enhancement of suboptimal performance. It is less easy to understand
the continued popularity of brainstorming, which has been shown to
have no demonstrable value.

Consensus Decision Making: Choice Shifts

Many teams exist essentially to reach a consensus on a choice among
alternatives (events, things, ideas) or a judgment about an amount of

something. The team output is either a recommendation to another decision-making authority (e.g., a staff analysis or a personnel committee recommendation) or its consensus choice is itself decisive (e.g., a village council vote or a court verdict). The emphasis may be less on the interpersonal processing of information than on achieving agreement about the correct or optimal decision.

Conclusions about suboptimal performance (discussed above) are also applicable in team decision making, but it is worth briefly considering the implications of another research literature: team decisions under risk or uncertainty.

Conventional wisdom traditionally regarded decision making groups to be prudent, or, at least, cautious in the sense that a typical team decision was not likely to be extreme. Considerable surprise met the discovery that a set of group decisions tended to be more "risky" on the average than the same or comparable individual decisions (Stoner, 1961; Wallach et al., 1962). Subsequent research found that team decisions were often either a "risky shift" or a "cautious shift" (see summaries by Dion et al., 1970; Davis et al., 1991).[1] The ensuing efforts to identify the basis of the counterintuitive "choice shift" phenomena focused on the nature of risk and social values, rather than the interpersonal consensus process. However, such shifts have been observed in tasks devoid of social content, let alone containing much social value. It can be shown that such simple and widespread consensus rules, e.g., plurality or majority wins, are sufficient to produce group-level shifts in decision distributions, given skewness at the individual, input level (see Davis et al., 1991).

Choice shifts can be a logical consequence of aggregating according to common team decision rules, and while there is no necessary remedy, it is clear that many problems come from adopting a single decision or recommendation for the record. The minority views—that may later be valuable—are lost, a reduction in information that could later prove to be serious, i.e., any tendency in the frequency distributions of individuals will be exaggerated in the distribution for groups.

The more general nature of choice shifts—increased extremity of decision in either direction—only increased their practical implications; team work does not protect against "extremism" and may even increase it. In particular, the tendency of ex-group members also to be more extreme (group polarization) in the direction of their team's decision, although less extreme than the group of which they had been a part, also hold implications for practice (see reviews by Myers and Lamm, 1976). However, as noted above, almost all research on this phenomenon addressed ad hoc groups whose members lacked mutual experience, operating procedures, or training that might serve as a corrective.

Major concerns of team consensus decision making, especially in organizational contexts, have been the balancing of biases and expertise as well as the interests of various constituencies, concerns that have no counterpart in individual performance. A good example of enhancement techniques applied to team decision making comes from group judgmental forecasting, although the following discussion could in principle apply to other team tasks as well (see Davis et al., 1991, for a more general summary). The forecasting of future events—weather, market share, economic conditions, enemy troop deployments, population change, and the like—can sometimes be accomplished moderately well with statistical models, given sufficient current knowledge. However, in the face of substantial ignorance but serious need, experts sometimes must make intuitive forecast judgments, often with a minimal empirical basis, and teams of forecasters may also extrapolate from current to future conditions. It is desirable not only for individuals to be as accurate as possible, but also for the team members to combine their preferences in such a way that the consensus forecast is as accurate as possible.

Among the several methods that have been proposed for engineering team performance, we consider two that have enjoyed some enduring popularity: the Delphi technique and the nominal group technique. We do not consider strictly mathematical or statistical means for aggregating forecasts (or other decisions), although such conceptual notions produce the theoretical baselines essential for evaluating actual behavioral or quasibehavioral forecasts. Although much of this research has focused on ad hoc groups under laboratory conditions, Janis (1972, 1982) has analyzed a number of actual cases in which group decisions were sometimes successful and sometimes unsuccessful according to subsequent events. These case studies agree with laboratory experiments in particular respects, namely that faulty interpersonal processes (e.g., misdirected conformity pressures, cohesiveness) are largely responsible for suboptimal team decisions, despite the clear possibility of optimal actions.

In light of this well-known effect, both the Delphi and nominal group techniques constrain interaction with the aim of eliminating or moderating faulty interaction processes. Delphi (Dalkey, 1969, 1970) exercises elicit participants' judgments or opinions privately, summarizes these results while maintaining the anonymity of their source, and circulates the results to all team participants. Iterations of this procedure continue until individual positions stabilize (see Linstone and Turoff, 1975, for variations). This technique has enjoyed considerable popularity, especially in judgmental forecasting contexts. The nominal group technique also begins with the private elicitation of individual opinion, but members then meet for face-to-face exchanges of information; contributions are recorded and summarized by an outsider; members revise own opinions in private; and contributions are combined mathematically to yield a team decision (see, e.g., Delbecq et al., 1975).

Despite the popularity of such techniques for enhancing team performance involving consensus decisions, surprisingly little valuative research has been carried out to determine their effectiveness. However, the evidence to date on team performance accuracy enhancement is not encouraging (e.g., Fischer, 1981; Rohrbaugh, 1979; Gough, 1975). McGrath (1984:75) concludes that "neither one does any better than the freely interacting groups, whose 'deficient' processes these techniques were designed to improve."

In summary, the attempts to enhance team performance by imposing procedural remedies for nonoptimal interpersonal processes on the path to consensus have met with negligible success. However, long-term training of teams has rarely been studied, and even ad hoc laboratory groups have not received the research and development attention that serious attempts to engineer enhancement techniques should receive. Although performance on many different tasks that commonly confront teams consistently falls below reasonable theoretical baselines, in principle performance increments could be established through better interpersonal procedures, including training over protracted periods of time.

Teams, of necessity, will continue to perform a variety of tasks within organizations of all kinds. Unfortunately, the research and development programs committed to team performance enhancement are infrequent. An intuitively attractive explanation for the modest investment in the engineering of optimal procedures and interpersonal processes, as well as the training of individual team members, is that conventional wisdom and common sense, on the face of it, seem to provide such reasonable guidance. Unfortunately, however, the research evidence to date contradicts much of that apparent wisdom.

TEAM PERFORMANCE: FROM LABORATORY TO FIELD

The review of what we know about group performance is more striking for what is missing than for what is known. Although the issues can be discussed in the abstract, a brief description of three actual training and performance regimens can help to illustrate some unaddressed issues and point to ways in which the knowledge base could be expanded to productively address questions that are central to improving the performances of real groups in their work situations. The first part of this section presents three examples—two military and one industrial setting: the Special Forces, the Army's Ranger training, and control rooms in nuclear power plants. The next parts consider the training and research questions raised by these examples.

Three Field Examples

Special Forces

The Special Forces branch of the Army uses a squad as its basic operating unit; the typical squad consists of 12 soldiers. Within each squad, two members are trained in each of six specialties, for example, medic, weapons, combat engineering. The squads are trained to work together as a unit, either functioning independently or in collaboration with other squads as part of a larger operation. As an example of the first case, a squad with minimal or no support facilities might be assigned as military advisers to the armed forces of an allied country. Special Forces squads differ in their particular missions: they may have a squad-wide special mission or capability, such as underwater specialists or airborne units. There are further gradations within mission specialties: some of the airborne squads are HALO—high altitude low opening—units.

HALO is a specific type of parachuting operation which differs from the mass low-altitude operations of the regular infantry airborne units. A HALO squad is expected to jump from a high-flying, and, hence, relatively quiet plane, free fall for some distance, and then open its parachutes at a low altitude. Practice is needed not only in the individual skills, but also in coordinating the squad members' ability to land close to each other at the target.

A HALO squad has two distinct training needs: each of its members must be trained in his subspecialty, such as weapons, and the squad as a whole must practice in HALO team operations. In theory, these two training aspects, one splitting the squad into at least six subgroups and the other assembling the squad for joint training, could be scheduled so that the squad rotated between periods when all members were together with periods when all members were at their specialty training. In practice, however, this cannot be done because the individual specialties have different lengths of training, different needs for updating and recertification, and attend training at different sites. Thus, there are several important issues raised by the special forces training needs.

First, what is the optimal balance between individual training and squad training? When does a medic forgo more medical training in order to practice HALO skills? Conversely, when is a HALO squad coordinated enough to allow its members to disperse for specialty training? How can the plan be adjusted for the different training needs of the different specialties?

Second, what is to be done when a squad is not complete? For instance, a squad may have to be deployed when some of its members are absent for individual training. What are the best solutions to having incomplete squads: secondary training in other subspecialties for each member to serve as back-up for absent members or the assignment of specialists who are new to the squad to fill in for the missing soldiers?

Third, should squads be kept together throughout their term of service to induce better team coordination and performance or should component members be rotated through several squads to facilitate interchangeability and minimize the disruption of substitute members?

Ranger Training

The Army has a special program of Ranger training for selected soldiers. Troops from all of the Army's units are eligible for the Ranger program on the basis of superior performance in their basic and general training and nomination from their supervising officers. Nominees are subjected to a rigorous series of selection procedures. If accepted into the Ranger program, the soldiers undergo several weeks of extensive training in a variety of habitats, such as mountains, swamps, deserts, and the like. The training procedures are physically gruelling and are characterized by extreme deprivation of sleep and food and extraordinary physical demands. Upon successful completion of the Ranger course, a soldier is given a Ranger patch and other identifying insignia. Although some Rangers are assigned to serve in all-Ranger battalions, most are rotated back to their original units in which they serve as ordinary soldiers, but are identified as role models by their Ranger accomplishments.

There is probably no question that the Rangers are a superior group of soldiers. But there is a major issue raised by the training and assignment procedures, that of formal and informal leadership within the unit. A squad with a noncommissioned officer (NCO) in charge and a Ranger among its members has two leaders, one explicit and one implicit. It is not known to what extent there is a possibility for conflict or discrepant messages from these two sources. What happens if the NCO in charge changes? Does the Ranger assume a bigger leadership role? Does the presence of a Ranger facilitate or hinder the ability of the new NCO to assume leadership?

Nuclear Reactor Control Rooms

Nuclear reactors, even within the same plant, differ from each other in fundamental design, by changes made because of different dates of manufacture, and by different solutions to basic engineering questions made by different manufacturers. Because of this variety, at most plants there is a simulated control room for each reactor. The simulated control rooms duplicate the instrumentation of their particular reactors, and, through computer models, interact with the instrumentation to produce the effects on the gauges and information displays that would be shown in the actual control room of the modeled reactor.

The simulation control rooms are used for initial training of operators as well as for retraining, certification, and general assessment of operational skills. They are extremely complex: some of the later model reactors may have more than 10,000 individual displays and a similar number of input controls. Personnel differ for each reactor, but a typical control room is staffed by a group of four people—two operators, a foreman, and a shift supervisor.

At a training session a reactor crew will be placed in the simulation control room with a reactor simulation in progress. Trainers situated behind one-way glass simulate a malfunction of the reactor through appropriate manipulation of the simulation computer. The control room crew are monitored on their ability to recognize that a malfunction is occurring, to work through the requisite diagnostics, and to take the necessary corrective actions, shutting down the reactor if needed. Many of the procedures are algorithmic in nature: when a certain dial shows an abnormal reading, for example, the shift supervisor may locate a manual that has step-by-step rules for isolating the underlying fault. The foreman then reads each step as the two operators carry out the foreman's commands, reporting back information and outcomes as requested. The procedures are not rigid: the team must make a series of operational decisions as well come to agreement on the nature of the problem, its seriousness, and the steps needed to rectify the situation. Each member of the team has a different function, but the members are interdependent with respect to the larger problem. The shift supervisor's choice of diagnostic algorithm depends on information from the operators; the foreman's instructions to the operators depend on the shift supervisor's choice of diagnostic procedure manuals; the operators' choice of dial readings to report and of switches to set depend on the foreman's instructions. The control of a reactor involves periods of quiescence punctuated with anomalous events that may or may not represent serious malfunctions or emergencies. Successful operation of a reactor depends on the control room's crew to work its way to a correct set of decisions about what is wrong, if anything, and what needs to be done.

Observation of a control room simulation reveals some issues that are generic to team training, decision making, and performance. First, not all group decision making involves the type of consensus setting usually studied in free discussion groups such as juries. In a control room, the group's decision is arrived at only after a set of sequential decisions are made by individuals, so that a consensual agreement at the end of the process, based on the "facts" then in hand, may be flawed by errors or biases introduced along the way. How does one train crews to monitor and provide quality control along the way?

Second, because the four members of the control room staff are interdependent, the result is a "weak-link model," that is, the team performance will not be able to rise above that of the weakest member. Thus, two questions are clear: Is the crew aware of the performance weaknesses of its members? If aware, can the members compensate, monitor, or double-check that performance? In at least one simulation that was observed by the committee, the substandard performance of a shift supervisor, though detrimental to the crew's decisions, was not recognized by the crew because they had never worked with any other shift supervisor; they had no basis for knowing a good job by a shift supervisor.

Third, the trainers in control of the computers that simulate the reactor are able to manipulate representations of each electromechanical component of the reactor. Simulations of problems invariably involve programming a malfunction of a piece of hardware and observing the crew's reaction. Studies of actual control room mistakes, however, usually reveal that in large part, it is human reaction to electromechanical events or malfunctions that are at the heart of an "accident." Yet human mistakes are rarely built into the simulations, so training is rarely designed to overcome them. What would happen if a foreman asked an operator to read dial A305, for instance, and the operator reported a reading from dial A306? How would this affect the foreman's application of the diagnostic algorithm? What is the sensitivity of the group decision process to such human error? Such issues are not limited to reactor control rooms but arise in most command-and-control structures.

Challenges to Training

These illustrations suggest a series of questions of both immediate concern to the organizations involved—the Special Forces, the Rangers, and nuclear power plant control rooms—and to many other military and industrial settings.

Should work groups be trained together as a unit or should members be trained separately and assembled into units? The advantages of maintaining groups through both training and performance are coordination and the elimination of the duplicative effort of retraining. However, separate training with subsequent assembly of a group minimizes disruption when a team member needs to be replaced and gives practice in adapting to changed groups.

In groups in which members have different tasks, skills, or functions, what is the optimal division of training for the members in terms of primary and secondary tasks? If a team member spends all of the training time acquiring greater facility on his or her primary task, the member does not get trained in a second specialty and cannot take on the task of a team member who is unavailable when the team must perform. Yet too much time spent acquiring secondary skills may distract from learning or maintaining the primary ones.

How should the time of team members be allocated between their training in individual specialties and team training when both types of training are necessary? The length of time for the specialty requiring the longest training defines the minimum amount of time for the entire team to train or practice together.

How should those responsible for making time and training allocation decisions be trained? At what operational level should staffing decisions be made? If a group loses the services of a member, someone must decide whether the group can still function, which of the members can fill in the missing specialty, when replacement members are required, and many other staffing questions. It is yet to be determined what training is required for the circumstances to be accurately evaluated and for well-reasoned decisions to be made.

How should groups whose members have different tasks and specialties to preserve combine information from the diverse members? Equally important, how are members to be trained to evaluate the performances of other specialists, that is, to recognize deficiencies in other parts of the team? When a group has some divergent opinions or strategies for accomplishing its mission, how are the divergent viewpoints and minority information to be retained and utilized? Finally, when group tasks are for situations that cannot be created in training, such as warfare or nuclear disaster, how can the use of simulation in training contribute to real-life effectiveness?

These questions are not a complete set of what would be developed from systematic observation of the Special Forces, Rangers, or nuclear power plant control rooms, and not all of these questions are new or unresearched. It would be difficult, however, to give specific answers to questions in the contexts of particular situations on the basis of existing research on groups. It should also be noted that the research answers to the questions depend on the products desired. Some of the answers to questions posed by Ranger training depend on specifying the priorities of the different goals of the training: for example, is Ranger training foremost a specialty skill or is it primarily a vehicle for building self-sufficiency and self-esteem? If research is designed to answer Ranger training questions, it may serve the useful function of forcing a further specification of the desired outcome and purpose of the training.

Challenges to Research

Most of the questions from the three work examples are not covered by existing research. In the social psychological work, the experimental groups are most often not comparable to the ones that exist in the military and in industry. First, most working groups are faced with problems that are mixed in nature. They are neither pure decision making nor pure performance problems. The group's task is usually a variety of activities, involving some decision or consensus, some performance, some information gathering, and moving back and forth between these activities in the performance of their mission. The group's task could be broken down into smaller, typologically purer, subunits, in an effort to make research applicable to each component of the complex task, but then linking the subunits back together would immediately reinstate the problems the disassembly was designed to eliminate. Few, if any, social psychological studies use the complex problems that are present in any practical situation. It is difficult to predict how simple tasks combine in a group's attack on complex problems without research directed to that very issue.

Second, groups in social psychological research tend to be homogeneous. Although the early literature on group dynamics (cf., Festinger and Thibaut, 1951) examined some aspects of stratification, differences in rank, authority, prestige, and knowledge are generally missing variables in the research groups. For example, in an early line of work, Torrence (1954) studied B-26 combat crews in decision making situations. He compared existing crews consisting of an officer pilot, an officer navigator, and an enlisted gunner with crews consisting of the same personnel but who had never worked together. Torrence was able to show that rank, status, and previous experience influenced how the crews came to agreement. For example, when given problems with objective solutions, the gunners had difficulty getting their correct answers accepted by the officers, and the pilots were able to impose their incorrect answers on the other crew members. The distortions from optimal performance were greater in the permanent than in the temporary crews. Important as are these considerations for real-life team and group activities, investigation of factors such as these is now virtually nonexistent.

Third, most group studies are single-session experiments, or, at most, several-session experiments. These temporary groups, together for a short period of time, are hardly comparable to the extended, long-term interactions of actual groups in the workplace. The reasons for this lack are understandable: the financial and logistic difficulties of conducting longitudinal research with experimental groups are so formidable as to preclude it from the consideration of most investigators.

If the community studying the social psychology of groups is not doing the research needed to answer the questions raised by the observations illustrated above, does the field of applied psychology and human factors do so? Our answer is a qualified "no." Foushee's (1984) examination of small groups in the cockpits of airplanes is an excellent example of solutions to particular problems. Foushee's method was to intensively review hours of video tapes of groups in cockpits; it will undoubtedly provide improvements in procedures and benefit both crews and airlines using that cockpit configuration. Yet it is difficult to imagine how to generalize these findings to other tasks for which the specific items of job performance are very different and the size and nature of the group does not resemble those in the cockpits.

The tradeoffs between abstract, basic group research, generalizable in principle but of little help in specific situations, and applied, mission-oriented research, of use in a specified situation but not generalizable to other situations, has long been recognized (see, e.g., Mahoney and Druckman, 1975). One of the early explications of group research in social psychology—Festinger's (1953) description of laboratory research in social psychology—articulated the issues clearly. Unfortunately, little progress has been made in the almost four decades since these problems were presented. The problem is that neither stream of research by itself gives satisfactory solutions to the problems raised by some of the complex training needs of the military or of industry. If both approaches could focus on the same problem and combine their results, much could be gained.

There are several ways such an amalgam could be obtained. One way would be an attempt to generalize from a series of applied studies in particular settings. There is useful information in such reviews, but the usual problems of interpreting results when so much is going on at the same time make application of the generalizations difficult. Typically, such results work fairly well when applied to situations similar to those from which the data were gathered; they are not as applicable to somewhat different or to novel situations.

A better way would be to conduct parallel studies in field and laboratory settings. One could examine the abstract proposition in laboratory studies and simultaneously explore ecological validity of the propositions by testing them in naturalistic, field settings. Examples of this type of coordinated research are rare. One example is the study of some relationships between employee satisfaction and job performance during periods of change in a work task. A field study at an appliance plant, conducted by Schachter et al. (1961), was paralleled by a laboratory test of the same hypotheses by Latané and Arrowood (1963). Another example is the research conducted by Hopmann and his colleagues on negotiation processes; results from analyses of simulated negotiation groups were compared with results obtained from content analyses of the transcripts of the actual negotiations (see Druckman and Hopmann, 1989, for a review). These studies provide a useful model for guiding future research on group processes.

Clearly, studies in the field, but with experimental controls—true field experiments—could answer many of the questions posed by the training needs of, for example, the Special Forces. If the studies could be done longitudinally, so much the better. Most of the current funding practices and incentive structures work against the chances that studies of this type will be undertaken. Human factors investigators must concentrate on the particular group being studied, at the expense of designing studies that speak to general issues. Social psychologists explore theoretical propositions in studies of temporally limited, ad hoc groups. There are few organizations or funding agencies that have supported the study of experimentally manipulated groups, over time, in natural settings, despite the general utility of such investigations.

If formal research does not seem to be of immediate help in solving the problems raised by the training and performances of real groups, are there informal research procedures that might be of help? Quite often, in the military or in industry, training procedures or task requirements are changed. Such modifications made in the training and adaptations of on-going groups contain information that might be useful for constructing generalizations about what works in group training. Lacking control groups, these natural quasi-experiments are not a substitute for rigorous research on the same issues, but they could provide important information about the performance effects of changes in training regimens. Unfortunately, even this information is lost: few procedural changes are ever made with a rigorous evaluation component built in, so that actual effects of the changes on performance can be determined.

CONCLUSIONS

Many problems and issues in team performance are potentially answerable by research, but research on group structure and function, once a mainstay in social psychology, is now not a major focus of the work. Moreover, most of these studies are of unstratified groups, making them less relevant for real-world problems involving stratified groups and command structures.

Research on group problem solving indicates that teams perform at suboptimal levels. While a number of techniques (e.g., the Delphi technique, nominal group technique) have been used to try to improve the group process and outcomes, only a few of these interventions have been evaluated systematically, and the available evidence does not provide clear support for the techniques.

The research on group processes has focused in recent years on decision making with an emphasis on jury-like studies. Some of this is directly relevant to group training, but it leaves unaddressed many of the group performance questions.

Case studies of actual groups have contributed a number of questions about optimum training procedures as well as hypotheses to be explored by systematic research, but the findings have proven difficult to generalize.

Some of the difficulties of experimentation on group performance are logistic. It is difficult to find a suitable number of comparable groups that remain stable over time to compare the effects of experimental differences on their training and performance. Large numbers of comparable groups do exist in the Army and other military services, and they provide the possible experimental subjects and conditions for effective study of team training, decision making, and performance. Since the military recruits young people who are comparable to the entering U.S. labor force, the results of such group studies may also have applicability to industrial and commercial settings.

NOTE

1. The difference between a "risky" and "cautious" shift refers to the choice made by experimental subjects on the lowest acceptable probability for the risky play in question to be attempted. The probabilities range from "1 in 10 that the play would succeed" (risky) to "9 in 10 that it would succeed" (cautious).

REFERENCES

Borden, R.J.
    1980 Audience influence. In P. Paulus, ed., *Psychology of Group Influence*. Hillsdale, N.J.: Erlbaum.
Brown, R.
    1988 *Group Processes: Dynamics Within and Between Groups*. Oxford, England: Basil Blackwell.
Cohen, J.L., and J.H. Davis
    1973 Effects of audience status, evaluation and time of action on performance with hidden word problems. *Journal of Personality and Social Psychology* 37:822-832.
Dalkey, N.C.
    1969 Analyses from a group opinion study. *Futures* 1:541-551.

1970 Use of self-ratings to improve group estimates. *Technological Forecasting and Social Change* 1(3):283-291.

Davis, J.H.
1969 Individual-group problem solving, subject preferences, and problem type. *Journal of Personality and Social Psychology* 13:362-374.

Davis, J.H., P.A. Bates, and S.M. Nealey
1971 Long-term groups and complex problem solving. *Organizational Behavior and Human Performance* 6:28-35.

Davis, J.H., T. Kameda, and M. Stasson
1991 Group risk taking: selected topics. In J.F. Yates, ed., *Risk Taking Behavior.* New York: John Wiley & Sons.

Delbecq, A.L., A.H. Van de Ven, and D.H. Gustafson
1975 *Group Techniques for Program Planning: A Guide to Nominal Group and Delphi Processes.* Glenview, Ill.: Scott, Foresman.

Diehl, M., and W. Stroebe
1987 Productivity loss in brainstorming groups: toward the solution of a riddle. *Journal of Personality and Social Psychology* 53:497-509.
1990 Productivity Loss in Idea-Generating Groups: Tracking Down the Blocking-Effect. Paper presented at the biennial meeting of the European Association of Experimental Social Psychology, Budapest, Hungary.

Dion, D.L., R.S. Baron, and N. Miller
1970 Why do groups make riskier decisions than individuals? In L. Berkowitz, ed., *Advances in Experimental Social Psychology.* New York: Academic Press.

Druckman, D., and P.T. Hopmann
1989 Behavioral aspects of negotiations on mutual security. In P.E. Tetlock et al., eds., *Behavior, Society, and Nuclear War.* New York: Oxford University Press.

Druckman, D., D. Solomon, and K. Zechmeister
1972 Effects of representational role obligations on the process of children's distribution of resources. *Sociometry* 35:387-410.

Druckman, D., A.A. Benton, F. Ali, and J.S. Bagur
1976 Cultural differences in bargaining behavior: India, Argentina, and the United States. *Journal of Conflict Resolution* 20:413-452.

Dunnette, M.D., J. Campbell, and K. Jaastad
1963 The effect of group participation on brainstorming effectiveness for two industrial samples. *Journal of Applied Psychology* 47:30-37.

Festinger, L.
1953 Laboratory experiments. In L. Festinger and D. Katz, eds., *Research Methods in the Behavioral Sciences.* New York: The Dryden Press.

Festinger, L., and J. Thibaut
1951 Interpersonal communication in small groups. *Journal of Abnormal and Social Psychology* 46:92-99.

Fischer, G.
1981 When oracles fail—a comparison of four procedures for aggregating subjective probability forecasts. *Organization Behavior and Human Performance* 28:96-110, 133-145.

Foushee, H.C.
1984 Dyads and triads at 35,000 feet: factors affecting group process and aircrew performance. *American Psychologist* 39:885-893.

Geen, R.G.
1980 The effects of being observed on performance. In P.B. Paulus, ed., *Psychology of Group Influence.* Hillsdale, N.J.: Lawrence Erlbaum Associates.
1989 Alternative conceptions of social facilitation. In P.B. Paulus, ed., *Group Influence*, 2nd ed. Hillsdale, N.J.: Lawrence Erlbaum Associates.

Gough, R.
1975 The effect of group format on aggregate subjective probability distributions. In D. Wendt and C.J. Vlek, eds., *Utility, Probability, and Human Decision-Making.* Dordrecht, The Netherlands: Reidel.

Hackman, J.R., and C.G. Morris
1975 Group tasks, group interaction process, and group performance effectiveness: a review and proposed integration. In L. Berkowitz, ed., *Advances in Experimental Social Psychology,* Vol. 8. New York: Academic Press.

Harkins, S.G., and J.M. Jackson
1985 The role of evaluation in eliminating social loafing. *Personality and Social Psychology Bulletin* 11:457-465.

Harkins, S.G., and K. Szymanski
1989 Social loafing and group evaluation. *Journal of Personality and Social Psychology* 56:934-941.

Hastie, R.
1986 Review essay: experimental evidence on group accuracy. In B. Grofman and G. Guillermo, eds., *Information Pooling and Group Decision-Making.* Greenwich, Conn.: JAI Press.

Janis, I.L.
1972 *Victims of Groupthink.* Boston, Mass.: Houghton Mifflin.
1982 *Groupthink: Psychological Studies of Policy Decisions and Fiascos.* Boston, Mass.: Houghton Mifflin.

Kahneman, D., P. Slovic, and A. Tversky, eds.
1982 *Judgment Under Uncertainty: Heuristics and Biases.* New York: Cambridge University Press.

Kerr, N.
1983 Motivation losses in small groups: a social dilemma analysis. *Journal of Personality and Social Psychology* 45:819-828.

Latané, B., and A.J. Arrowood
1963 Emotional arousal and task performance. *Journal of Applied Psychology* 47:324-327.

Latané, B., K. Williams, and S. Harkins
1977 Many hands make light the work: the causes and consequences of social loafing. *Journal of Personality and Social Psychology* 37:822-832.

Linstone, H.A., and M. Turoff
1975 *The Delphi Method: Techniques and Applications.* Reading, Mass.: Addison-Wesley.

Lorge, I., and H. Solomon
1955 Two models of group behavior in the solution of Eureka-type problems. *Psychometrika* 20:139-148.

Mahoney, R., and D. Druckman
1975 Simulation, experimentation, and context: dimensions of design and inference. *Simulation and Games* 6:235-270.

Marquart, D.I.
1955 Group problem-solving. *Journal of Social Psychology* 41:103-113.

McGrath, J.E.
1984 *Groups: Interaction and Performance.* Englewood Cliffs, N.J.: Prentice-Hall.

Mullen, B., and C. Johnson
1991 Productivity loss in brainstorming groups: a meta-analytic integration. *Basic and Applied Social Psychology.* In press.

Murphy, G., and L. Murphy
1931 *Experimental Social Psychology.* New York: Harper.

Myers, D.B., and H. Lamm
  1976 The group polarization phenomenon. *Psychological Bulletin* 83:602-627.
Osborn, A.F.
  1957 *Applied Imagination.* New York: Scribners.
Rohrbaugh, J.
  1979 Improving the quality of group judgment: social judgment analysis and the Delphi technique. *Organizational Behavior and Human Performance* 24:73-92.
Schachter, S.
  1959 *The Psychology of Affiliation.* Stanford, Calif.: Stanford University Press.
Schachter, S., B. Willerman, L. Festinger, and R. Hyman
  1961 Emotional disruption and industrial productivity. *Journal of Applied Psychology* 45:201-213.
Shaw, M.E.
  1932 Comparison of individuals and small groups in the rational solution of complex problems. *American Journal of Psychology* 44:491-504.
Steiner, I.D.
  1972 *Group Process and Productivity.* New York: Academic Press.
Stoner, J.A.F.
  1961 A comparison of individuals and group decisions involving risk taking. *Journal of Abnormal and Social Psychology* 65:77-86.
Taylor, D.W.
  1954 Problem solving by groups. In *Proceedings XIV, International Congress of Psychology.* Amsterdam, The Netherlands: North Holland Publishing.
Taylor, D.W., P.C. Berry, and C.H. Block
  1958 Does group participation when using brain storming facilitate or inhibit creative thinking. *Administrative Science Quarterly* 3:23-47.
Torrence, E.P.
  1954 Some consequences of power differences on decision-making in permanent and temporary three-man groups. *Research Studies of the State College of Washington* 22:130-140.
Tversky, A., and D. Kahneman
  1974 Judgment under uncertainty: heuristics and biases. *Science* 185:1124-1131.
  1981 The framing of decisions and the psychology of choice. *Science* 211:453-458.
Wallach, M.A., N. Kogan, and D.J. Bem
  1962 Group influence on individual risk taking. *Journal of Abnormal and Social Psychology* 65:75-86.
Wrightsman, L.S.
  1959 The Effects of Small-Group Membership on Level of Concern. Unpublished doctoral dissertation, University of Minnesota.
Zajonc, R.B.
  1965 Social facilitation. *Science* 149:269-274.
  1980 Compresence. In P.B. Paulus, ed., *Psychology of Group Influence.* Hillsdale, N.J.: Lawrence Erlbaum Associates.

APPENDICES

A

Committee Activities

In order to cover the disparate topics of our charge, the committee undertook a wide range of activities—including commissioned papers, site visits to relevant field settings, and briefings by experts—in addition to full committee meetings and reviews of the available literature.

The committee met four times during 1989-1990, three of them at National Research Council facilities in Washington, D.C., and Irvine, California, and once at the Training Doctrine Command (TRADOC) headquarters at Fort Monroe in Norfolk, Virginia. Those meetings included presentations by Army experts to acquaint us with both specific Army interest in particular topics and Army experience and practice:

Dr. Herbert Barber, Army War College
Dr. Gordon H. Barland, Fort McClellan
General John Crosby, TRADOC
Colonel Louis Csoka, West Point
Dr. Schlomo Dover, Army Research Institute
Dr. Michael Drillings, Army Research Institute
Dr. William Fedor, Office of the Secretary of Defense
Dr. Robert Frank, Center for Army Leadership
Dr. Stephen Goldberg, TRADOC
Dr. Jack Hiller, Army Research Institute
Dr. Owen Jacobs, Army Research Institute
Dr. Edgar Johnson, Army Research Institute
Colonel Keith Knightingale, Fort Benning
Dr. George Lawrence, Army Research Institute
Dr. Judith Orasanu, Army Research Institute
Lt. Col. Keith Skiles, Fort Leavenworth

Most of the rest of the committee's work was carried out through subcommittees on specific topics. Our subcommittee organization tracks almost directly to the chapter organization of this report, and members wrote the initial draft chapters. In one case the work of one subcommittee (hiding and detecting deception) resulted in two chapters.

Long-Term Retention   Robert W. Christina and Robert A. Bjork constituted this subcommittee. It carried out site visits to Fort Bragg, North Carolina (September 1989), to the Sillin Nuclear Training Center in Connecticut (January 1990), and to Vic Braden's Tennis Academy in Trabuco Canyon, California (July 1990).

Modeling Expertise   Michelene T.H. Chi and Robert A. Bjork constituted this subcommittee. It also visited Fort Bragg, North Carolina (September 1989), and Vic Braden's Tennis Academy in Trabuco Canyon, California (July 1990).

Developing Careers   Daniel Druckman and Lyman W. Porter constituted this subcommittee. In addition to a site visit to Fort Bragg (September 1989), the members also received briefings on career development by Dr. Owen Jacobs of the Army Research Institute and Dr. Herb Barber of the Army War College. The subcommittee also designed a questionnaire administered to students at the Army War College and surveyed the Army's self-assessment programs.

Two papers were commissioned for this subcommittee: "The Myers-Briggs Type Indicators and Enhancing Human Performance," by Paul Thayer, Department of Psychology, North Carolina State University; "Army Officer Career Development: Opportunity for Assessment, Planning, and Professional Growth," by Manuel London, Harriman School for Management and Policy, State University of New York, Stony Brook.

Subliminal Self-Help   Eric Eich and Ray Hyman constituted this subcommittee. It surveyed the market of available subliminal tape packages.

Meditation   Gerald C. Davison and Francis J. Pirozzolo constituted this subcommittee. It was briefed by David Shannahoff-Khalsa, of the Khalsa Foundation for Medical Science, and Schlomo Dover of the Army Research Institute. Mr. Shannahoff-Khalsa also prepared a commissioned paper for the subcommittee, "A Commentary on the Jasper Brener and Samuel R. Connally Report: Meditation, Rationales, Experimental Effects and Methodological Issues."

Managing Pain   Gerald C. Davison and Laura Darke, a consultant to the committee, constituted this subcommittee. Dr. Darke of the University of California, Los Angeles, also prepared a paper, "Psychological Factors in the Management of Pain."

Hiding and Detecting Deception Daniel Druckman and Ray Hyman constituted this subcommittee. The subcommittee made a site visit to Fort Belvoir, Virginia (January 1990), to meet with Army experts on deception and received briefings from General Stanley Hyman and his staff. William Fedor of the Office of the Secretary of Defense and Gordon Barland from Fort McClellan also briefed the subcommittee.

Motor Techniques Richard Thompson and Eric Eich constituted this subcommittee. It focused exclusively on reviews of the literature, particularly on vascular theories of emotion.

Optimizing Performance Under Pressure Daniel Landers and Francis J. Pirozzolo constituted this subcommittee. It made site visits to the West Point Academy (October 1989) and to the U.S. Olympic Committee (October 1989) and carried out an experiment on the effects of mental practice on soldering performance at the Redstone Arsenal, Alabama (September 1989). The subcommittee was also briefed by Colonel Louis Csoka, Denny Forbes, and Colonel James Anderson, all from West Point.

Enhancing Team Performance James H. Davis and Jerome E. Singer constituted this subcommittee. It made site visits to Fort Bragg, North Carolina (September 1989), and to the Sillin Nuclear Training Center in Connecticut (January 1990). It also benefited from a site visit made to Fort Benning, Georgia (March 1986), by Jerome E. Singer during the committee's first phase.

B

Biographical Sketches

ROBERT A. BJORK is professor of psychology at the University of California, Los Angeles. He received a B.A. degree in mathematics from the University of Minnesota and a Ph.D. degree in psychology from Stanford University. He has been a visiting scientist at Bell Laboratories, the University of California, San Diego, and the Rockefeller University. His research interests center on human information processing, particularly human memory, and on the practical application of that research to instruction and the optimization of performance. He is the author of numerous publications and has presented lectures and seminars to many groups, including corporate executives, college alumni, educators, lawyers, and physicians, in this country and in Europe. He served as editor of *Memory and Cognition* from 1981 to 1985 and has been on the editorial boards of several other journals. He is a fellow of the American Psychological Association and of the Society of Experimental Psychologists and is a member of the Psychonomics Society and the Cognitive Science Society.

MICHELENE T.H. CHI is professor of psychology and a senior scientist at the Learning Research and Development Center at the University of Pittsburgh. She received a B.S. degree in mathematics and a Ph.D. degree in psychology, both from Carnegie-Mellon University. Her research foci are understanding changes in knowledge structure as one learns a new domain, and how such restructuring effects the way the acquired knowledge is used. Her work also entails the development of rigorous analyses of talk-aloud protocols as a methodological tool for uncovering knowledge structures of complex domains. She serves on the editorial boards of *Journal of the Learning Sciences*, *Cognitive Development*, and *Human Development*. She has received the Spencer Fellowship from the National Academy of Education and the Boyd McCandless Young Scientist Award from the American Psychological Association. She is a fellow of the American Psychological Association and has an invitation to be a fellow at the Center for the Advanced Study in the Behavioral Sciences. She has published widely, including a recent edited volume on *The Nature of Expertise*.

ROBERT W. CHRISTINA is professor and chair of the Department of Physical Therapy and Exercise Science at the State University of New York at Buffalo. Previously, he was at the Pennsylvania State University and the State University of New York, College at Brockport. He earned a B.S. degree at Ithaca College, and M.A. and Ph.D. degrees at the University of Maryland. His research focuses on understanding the processes by which humans control and learn motor skills and on determining the most effective conditions for acquiring, remembering, and performing movement skills. He is the author of numerous scientific and professional publications and currently serves on the editorial boards of the *Research Quarterly for Exercise and Sport* and *Human Performance*. He has presented lectures and seminars to the Professional Golfers Associations of America and to many of the national sport governing bodies of the U.S. Olympic Committee, including the U.S. Ski Coaches Association, U.S. equestrian team, U.S.A. Wrestling, U.S. Diving Association, U.S. Rowing Association, and the U.S. shooting team. He coauthored *Coaching Young Athletes* and *Coaches Guide to Teaching Sport Skills*. He is past president of the North American Society of the Psychology of Sport and Physical Activity and current president of the American Academy of Physical Education.

JAMES H. DAVIS is professor of psychology at the University of Illinois. He previously was at Miami University and Yale University. He received a B.S. degree from the University of Illinois in psychology and a Ph.D. degree in social psychology from Michigan State University. His research interests center around judgment and decision making by small groups and individuals. He is a fellow of the American Psychological Association and a member of the Psychonomics Society, the American Association for the Advancement of Science, and the Japanese Psychological Association, among others. He was a Lansdowne Fellow at the University of Victoria in 1984 and a fellow at the Center for Advanced Study in the Behavioral Sciences in 1987-1988. He is a member of the editorial boards of a number of journals, including *Orga-

nizational Behavior and Human Decision Processes and *Behavioral Decision Making.* He has presented addresses in both the United States and abroad (England, Germany, China, and Japan) and published numerous articles.

GERALD C. DAVISON is professor of psychology at the University of Southern California and previously was also director of clinical training and department chair. He received an A.B. degree from Harvard University and a Ph.D. degree from Stanford University. His current research is concerned with cognitive assessment, stress, and hypertension. He has published on cognitive behavior therapy and experimental personality research and is coauthor of three books. He is a fellow of the American Psychological Association and the American Psychological Society and has served on the executive committee of the APA's Division of Clinical Psychology, on the Board of Scientific Affairs, and on the Committee on Scientific Awards. He is also past president of the Association for the Advancement of Behavior Therapy. He has served on the editorial board of several journals, including the *Journal of Consulting and Clinical Psychology, Behavior Therapy, Cognitive Therapy and Research,* and the *Journal of Psychotherapy Integration.*

DANIEL DRUCKMAN is study director of the Committee on Techniques for the Enhancement of Human Performance, study codirector of the Committee on the Human Dimensions of Global Change, and senior staff officer for the Committee on International Conflict and Cooperation at the National Research Council. He is also an adjunct professor of conflict management at George Mason University and has been a visiting research scholar at the International Institute of Applied Systems Analysis in Vienna, Austria. He was previously the mathtech scientist at Mathematica, Inc., and senior scientist and program manager at Booz, Allen, and Hamilton. He has also been a consultant to the U.S. Foreign Service Institute, the U.S. Arms Control and Disarmament Agency, and the U.S. delegation to the Vienna talks on force reductions. He received a Ph.D. degree in social psychology from Northwestern University and was a winner of the American Institutes for Research's best-in-field award for his dissertation. He is a member of the Society of Experimental Social Psychology and the International Studies Association. His primary research interests are in the areas of conflict resolution and negotiations, nonverbal communication, group processes, and modeling methodologies, including simulation. He has published five books and numerous articles and chapters on these topics. He currently serves on the editorial boards of the *Journal of Conflict Resolution* and *Negotiation Journal.*

ERIC EICH is associate professor of psychology at the University of British Columbia. He earned a B.A. degree from the University of Maryland and a Ph.D. degree in cognitive psychology from the University of Toronto. His research is chiefly concerned with matters relating to human memory and amnesia, with special emphasis on the state-dependent effects of drugs, emotions, and environments on learning and remembering. Support for this research has been provided by a University Research Fellowship, awarded by the Natural Sciences and Engineering Research Council of Canada, a Killam Memorial Research Fellowship, and by grants from various American or Canadian agencies. He is a member of the American Psychological Society and currently serves on the editorial board of *Memory and Cognition*.

RAY HYMAN is professor of psychology at the University of Oregon. He received a Ph.D. degree from the Johns Hopkins University. Previously, he taught at Harvard University, and he has also been a consultant to the General Electric Company, a Fulbright-Hays research scholar (University of Bologna), a National Science Foundation faculty fellow, and a visiting professor of psychology at Stanford University. He serves on the editorial board of *The Skeptical Inquirer* and is an associate editor of the *Zetetic Scholar*. His numerous publications include several books, encyclopedia chapters, and technical articles in such journals as *Proceedings of the IEEE* and the *Journal of Parapsychology* and articles on topics related to parapsychology that have appeared in both parapsychological and other journals.

DANIEL M. LANDERS is a regents' professor of exercise science and physical education at Arizona State University. After receiving graduate degrees from the University of Illinois, he was on the faculty at the University of Illinois, Champaign-Urbana, the University of Washington, and the Pennsylvania State University. His recent research has dealt with psychophysiological theory and methodology applied to sport and exercise, with a focus on understanding how athletes control arousal and focus concentration so as to maximize performance. He is a fellow in the American Psychological Association; the American College of Sports Medicine; the Research Consortium of the American Alliance of Health, Physical Education, Recreation and Dance; and the American Academy of Physical Education. He is former president of the North American Society for the Psychology of Sport and Physical Activity and the Division of Exercise and Sport Psychology of the American Psychological Association and a member of the Society for Psychophysiological Research and the American Psychological Society. His advisory work has included membership on education and training committees for national sport governing bodies as well as membership on the visual performance and enhancement and sport psychology committees of the U.S. Olympic Committee. He was the cofounder and editor of the *Journal of Sport and Exercise Psychology* and has also edited or authored seven books and many journal articles.

FRANCIS J. PIROZZOLO is chief of the neuropsychology service and associate professor in the Department of Neurology at Baylor College of Medicine. He received a B.A. degree from Wilmington College in psychology, an M.A. degree from the University of Chicago, and a Ph.D. degree from the University of Rochester in neuropsychology and learning. His professional interests fall into two categories: one is neuropsychology, in which his research and clinical activities focus on assessment and treatment of age-related neurodegenerative disorders, such as Alzheimer's and Parkinson's diseases; the second is human performance, in which his research and clinical practice centers around understanding the biochemical basis of behavior in sports with elite athletes. He is the editor-in-chief of *Developmental Neuropsychology*; is on the boards of several journals, including *Brain and Cognition*, *Neurology of Aging*, and the *International Journal of Clinical Neuropsychology*; and is a contributing editor for *Sports Strategy and Performance Report*. He is a member of the National Research Council of Italy's task force on memory disorders in the aged and an advisory council member of the Sports Psychology Institute. In addition to writing several books, he has published in a variety of journals such as *Neurology*, *Brain and Language*, and *Science*. He received the Phillip Rennick Award for excellence in neuropsychological research from the International Neuropsychological Society in 1977.

LYMAN W. PORTER is professor of management and psychology in the Graduate School of Management at the University of California, Irvine. He was formerly dean of the Graduate School of Management there and on the faculty of the University of California, Berkeley. His major fields of interest are organizational psychology and management. He received a B.A. degree from Northwestern University and a Ph.D. degree in psychology from Yale University. He is past president of the Academy of Management and in 1983 received that organization's award for scholarly contributions to management. He also served as president of the Division of Industrial-Organizational Psychology of the American Psychological Association. He is the author and coauthor of six books and many articles in these fields.

JEROME E. SINGER is professor and chair of the Department of Medical Psychology at the Uniformed Services University of the Health Sciences. He received a B.A. degree in social anthropology from the University of Michigan and a Ph.D. degree in psychology from the University of Minnesota. He has taught at the Pennsylvania State University and the State University of New York at Stony Brook. He has been a visiting scholar at the University of New York at Stony Brook and at the Educational Testing Service, a guest researcher at the University of Stockholm, a staff associate at the Social Science Research Council, and study director at the National Research Council. He has been the recipient of the American Association for the Advancement of Science's sociopsychological prize and the outstanding contributor award of the Division of Health Psychology of the American Psychological Association. He is founding editor of the *Journal of Basic and Applied Social Psychology* and coeditor of two monograph series, *Advances in Environmental Psychology* and *Handbook of Psychology and Health.*

RICHARD F. THOMPSON is the Keck professor of psychology and biological sciences and director of the Neurosciences Program at the University of Southern California. His previous positions include Bing professor of human biology and professor of psychology at Stanford University; professor of psychobiology in the School of Biological Sciences at the University of California, Irvine; professor of psychology at Harvard University; and professor of medical psychology and psychiatry at the University of Oregon Medical School. He received a B.A. degree from Reed College and a Ph.D. in psychobiology from the University of Wisconsin. His research is in the broad field of psychobiology, with a focus on the neurobiological substrates of learning and memory. He is a member of the National Academy of Sciences, the American Academy of Arts and Sciences, and the Society of Experimental Psychologists; councillor of the Society for Neurosciences; chair of the Psychonomics Society; and president of Division 6 of the American Psychological Association. He has received the Howard Crosby Warren medal of the Society of Experimental Psychologists, the distinguished scientific contribution award of the American Psychological Association, and a research scientist career award from the National Institute of Mental Health.

Index